WRITERS FOR THE NATION

WRITERS FOR THE NATION
American Literary Modernism

C. Barry Chabot

The University of Alabama Press
Tuscaloosa and London

Copyright © 1997
The University of Alabama Press
Tuscaloosa, Alabama 34587–0380
All rights reserved
Manufactured in the United States of America

∞

The paper on which this book is printed meets the minimum
requirements of American National Standard for Information
Science–Permanence of Paper for Printed Library Materials,
ANSI Z39.48-1984.

Library of Congress Cataloging-in-Publication Data

Chabot, C. Barrry, 1944–
    Writers for the nation : American literary modernism / C. Barry
Chabot.
        p.   cm.
    Includes bibliographical references and index.
    ISBN 0-8173-0877-6 (alk. paper)
    1. American literature—20th century—History and criticism.
2. Modernism (Literature)—United States.   3. Politics and
literature—United States—History—20th century.   4. Literature and
society—United States—History—20th century.   5. United States—
Intellectual life—20th century.   6. Brooks, Van Wyck, 1886–1963.
I. Title.
PS228.M63C48   1997   96–45920
810.9′112–dc21

British Library Cataloguing-in-Publication Data available

For my parents

CONTENTS

ACKNOWLEDGMENTS

I BEGAN WORKING on what became this book longer ago than I now care to remember. Over the years many friends and colleagues have helped me find my way—by reading and commenting on portions of the manuscript, by recommending books and articles for me to read, and by talking with me about the argument I was trying to construct. When we were colleagues at the National Humanities Institute, Robert Knoll told me that I must read Willa Cather; I'm grateful to him for many years of pleasure. My current colleague Edgar Tidwell introduced me to Sterling A. Brown's poetry and has generously shared with me his definitive knowledge of Brown's long and varied career. Jim Finnegan, Chris Knight, Steve Matanle, Kirt Moyer, Bill Pratt, Jim Sosnoski, and Matt Wilhelm all read the manuscript at various stages and tried, with mixed success, to save me from errors of fact and judgment I was determined to make. I have tried to indicate my extensive debts to other scholars in the notes and bibliography.

Although it was partially conceived prior to my arrival at Miami University, *Writers for the Nation* has largely been written during my tenure here. I am grateful for the support and patience my colleagues and the institution have so generously provided. Former dean Stephen Day and my departmental colleagues allowed me to put administrative duties aside at a crucial stage, when the manuscript largely took its current shape. I've learned enough over the years about conditions in higher education to recognize my good fortune in being able to live and work in a community that approximates my earliest fantasies about an academic life.

Finally, I need and want to thank my family. My wife, Susan, has not yet read this book and might never do so. She accepts on faith my protestations about needing to work, and there is no way that this or any acknowledgment can adequately express my gratitude to her. Our sons, Jeff and Justin, have grown into their own lives while I've worked on this book and have helped me keep it in proper perspective.

Writers for the Nation is dedicated to my parents. My late father introduced me early to the pleasures of reading, and my mother continues to instruct me in the demands of common sense.

Portions of chapters 3 and 5 were previously published in *Southern Quarterly* and *Georgia Review,* respectively. I thank the editors for permission to include them here.

I also wish to thank the following for permission to use material under copyright:

"Ma Rainey," "Sporting Beasley," "Slim in Hell," "Maumee Ruth," and "When de Saints Go Ma'ching Home," from *Southern Road* by Sterling A. Brown. Copyright 1932 by Harcourt, Brace, & Co. Copyright renewed 1960 by Sterling Brown. Included in *The Collected Poems of Sterling A. Brown,* selected by Michael S. Harper. Copyright © 1980 by Sterling A. Brown. Reprinted by permission of HarperCollins Publishers, Inc.

"Glory, Glory," "Harlem Happiness," and "Negro Improvement League," in *The Collected Poems of Sterling A. Brown,* edited by Michael S. Harper. Copyright © 1980 by Sterling A. Brown. Reprinted by permission of HarperCollins Publishers, Inc.

Excerpt from *The Cocktail Party,* copyright 1950 by T. S. Eliot and renewed 1978 by Esme Valerie Eliot, reprinted by permission of Harcourt Brace & Company, and by Faber & Faber, Ltd.

Excerpts from "Preludes," "Portrait of a Lady," "Gerontion," and "The Waste Land," in *Collected Poems 1909–1962* by T. S. Eliot, copyright 1936 by Harcourt Brace & Company, copyright © 1964, 1963 by T. S. Eliot, reprinted by permission of Harcourt Brace & Company, and by Faber & Faber, Ltd.

Excerpts from Jessie Redmon Fauset's *Plum Bun: A Novel without a Moral,* first published in 1928 by Frederick A. Stokes Company, New York. First published as a Beacon Press paperback in 1990.

From *Collected Poems* by Langston Hughes. Copyright © 1994 by the Estate of Langston Hughes. Reprinted by permission of Alfred A. Knopf, Inc., and by Aitken and Stone, Ltd.

From *Collected Poems* by Wallace Stevens. Copyright 1954 by Wallace Stevens. Reprinted by permission of Alfred A. Knopf, Inc., and by Faber and Faber, Ltd.

From *Opus Posthumous* by Wallace Stevens. Copyright © 1957

by Elsie Stevens and Holly Stevens. Reprinted by permission of Alfred A. Knopf, Inc., and by Faber and Faber, Ltd.

Permission granted by Louisiana State University Press from *The Fathers* (Revised Edition), by Allen Tate with an Introduction by Thomas Daniel Young. Copyright © 1938, 1977 by Allen Tate. Introduction copyright © 1977 by Louisiana State University Press.

Excerpt from "Ode to the Confederate Dead" from *Collected Poems, 1919–1976* by Allen Tate. Copyright © 1977 by Allen Tate. Reprinted by permission of Farrar, Straus, & Giroux, Inc.

WRITERS FOR THE NATION

INTRODUCTION

"What isolated particles we all are!"

Brooks, *Brooks-Mumford Letters* 26

I

THIS IS A study of American literary modernism in the years between the world wars. It begins with a chapter built around the career of Van Wyck Brooks, who for a time in the teens provided many of his contemporaries with terms for articulating their aversions and aspirations. Chapters 2, 3, and 5 are devoted to Willa Cather, to T. S. Eliot and Allen Tate, and to Wallace Stevens, respectively. In the fourth chapter I consider the literary dimensions of the emergence of Harlem as a material symbol of an unprecedented prosperity and self-confidence among African Americans. The sixth and final chapter is devoted to the collective ambitions of the thirties, especially those of several writers who experienced the drama of that decade in their youth and whose subsequent novels, published during and after World War II, chart a decisive cooling of millennial aspirations. This is in some respects an odd assortment of writers; it includes some, such as Eliot and Stevens, who are widely considered to be central to American literary modernism, as well as others, such as Brooks and Cather, who are rarely included in any such census. These figures themselves would have thought it odd to be considered together. When in 1946 John Hall Wheelock invited Van Wyck Brooks to a dinner party that Allen Tate would also attend, Brooks initially declined: "I can't go then. . . . Allen Tate is my enemy. He hates my point of view. I . . . hate *his* point of view" (R. Nelson 267). Although there is doubtless something excessive, even melodramatic, about Brooks's response to Wheelock's invitation, it nevertheless illustrates the differences among these writers

1

and the seriousness with which they took themselves and their intellectual positions.

I trust that these differences are respected in the chapters that follow. I nonetheless want to claim that these writers and their contemporaries share a common project that we can now see resulted in the emergence of American literary modernism as a distinctive and unusually strong body of literature. That project took form around a shared dismay about the character of American social and cultural life in the early years of this century. In *New York Intellect,* Thomas Bender observes that Van Wyck Brooks and his contemporaries more often understood themselves as a generation than as a class, but that they were nonetheless drawn primarily from the middle class. "The Young Intellectuals," he writes, "were the first generation to come of age within a bourgeois culture that had consolidated itself politically, financially, and culturally" (229).[1] These writers came to maturity in the years immediately after the muckrakers and American literary naturalists had expressed alarm about the lives increasingly allotted to the less fortunate classes. Although the Young Intellectuals were typically among the beneficiaries of the new social order, they followed the naturalists in drawing up a lengthy and varied list of grievances against the quality of life it made available— it was exploitative, it was too industrial, it was changing too quickly, its culture had become refined to the point of irrelevance; but, whatever the particulars, such complaints eventually and centrally concluded that the nation no longer afforded its citizens with terms for living companionable lives. American literary modernism, in other words, involves the recognition that even the seemingly fortunate are victimized by current economic and social life. As I understand it, American literary modernism was primarily animated by efforts to repair this deficiency, to imagine conditions that would either restore to the national life the possibility that all citizens could enjoy access to functioning and supportive communities, or, failing restoration, at least provide something by way of a substitute. On these terms, the emergence of American literary modernism was not only roughly contemporaneous with the progressivism of a Herbert Croly or Walter Lippmann but was also animated by similar convictions about the nation's needs. It is not an accident, in other words, that the *New Republic, The Masses,* and *Seven Arts* all began publication in New York City within a few years of one another. In a brief memoir about *Seven Arts,* James Oppenheim, its founding editor, explains that he had been "inanely jealous of the gang of fellows who had shot the *New Republic* into existence, a 'journal of opinion,' mind you, when the real thing would be a journal of art," since he believed that "that lost soul among nations, America, could be regenerated by art, and that the artist was always a Jean-Christophe with the power to do the job" (156). American literary modernists were not always able to muster or to sustain such confidence in their ability to accomplish this collective mission, but they were united by their sense of its urgency, as by the seriousness with which they pursued their self-appointed charge.

American literary modernists also differed as to the specific strategies they favored for meeting their nation's apparent needs. My selection of writers for inclusion in this study has been guided largely by the desire to represent this strategic variety, and I have found it helpful to conceive of these strategies primarily along two axes: first, whether the imagined alternatives to a lamentable present were to be found in the past or in the future, and second, whether they involved primarily personal or more thoroughly social changes. In the second chapter, for instance, Willa Cather represents an alternative that is simultaneously personal and oriented toward the past. After working for many years in industrial Pittsburgh and then New York, Cather came to the conclusion that the era of her childhood in Nebraska, and other frontier communities even more remote in time and place, had uniquely provided conditions for satisfying lives. She had little conviction that such conditions could be restored and was prepared to draw comfort from contemplating memories and reconstructions of such lost social moments. The subjects of the third chapter, T. S. Eliot and Allen Tate, were both, like Cather, notoriously oriented toward the past, but both were more sanguine than she about the possibilities for restoring or preserving what they took to be preferable ways of life. Both also recognized that such acts of preservation required the cultivation of social institutions compatible with those forms of life; accordingly, both for a time resigned themselves to engaging in a period of social agitation. In their different ways, then, Eliot and Tate represent a strategy that is similar to Cather's in being oriented to the past, and different in being broadly social in nature. In the fifth chapter, another poet, Wallace Stevens, represents a strategy that is both personal, because it is dependent upon the resources of the individual imagination, and oriented toward the future, toward an integration that the poet's imagination must continuously provide. The emergence of Harlem in the years just after World War I, as we shall see in the fourth chapter, lent credence to the belief that a new day was already at hand for African Americans. The rhetoric of the New Negro era oscillates between celebrating the changes that had occurred as already inaugurating that new day and taking them as promissory notes due in the very near future. These expectations were in time frustrated, but for a brief cultural moment it was imaginable that in enclaves like Harlem the benefits of full citizenship were at last becoming available to African Americans. Finally, in the thirties a group of writers emerged that imagined an alternative that, like Stevens's, was oriented toward a possible future, and yet that recognized, as did Eliot and Tate, that their aspirations were dependent upon the transformation of the nation's extant institutions. The chapters that follow, in other words, sketch something like a typology of the literary and cultural strategies developed within American literary modernism.

This typology is in several respects unusual. Cather, for instance, is rarely considered a modernist, even though in recent years her fiction is again being read with renewed appreciation. I obviously hope that the discussion of her work in the second chapter will contribute to the broad reassessment already under way of her place in our literature. Its ability to demonstrate Cather's affinity with canonical American literary modernists is among the special advantages of the typology proposed in the following chapters. Perhaps the more striking claim, however, involves the inclusion in the fifth chapter of writers from the thirties, writers who are more commonly thought to represent a decisive and deliberate break from American literary modernism and a reversion to an earlier, seemingly less sophisticated, literary program. When American literary modernism as a whole is understood primarily as a response to the felt needs of the nation, and when it is recognized that those needs consistently included the provision of a sense of community, then the novelty of the proletarian fiction of the thirties can be understood as deriving primarily from the solution it proposes. The community it envisions for a troubled nation is thoroughly egalitarian, and it is willing to engage directly in the political process in order to bring such a community into existence. Whereas Eliot and the Agrarians recognized the institutional and thus political dimensions of their own rather different visions, they characteristically stopped short of involving themselves directly in the political process. Although it largely lay dormant for some years, this radical and more directly political variant of American literary modernism was present from the first, where it can be found during the teens in the pages of *The Masses* and even in Van Wyck Brooks's *America's Coming-of-Age*. If in the teens there was an emerging consensus about the need to restore some sense of community to the nation, few American writers and intellectuals were then prepared to adopt such seemingly radical solutions, believing that the process of reform already evident in the progressive movement would eventually prove sufficient. When conditions dramatically worsened in the thirties, it became easier for many to imagine that only equally dramatic changes in the social fabric could suffice.

What must seem most odd about the conception of American literary modernism proposed here is my claim that it was preoccupied by the need to restore some sense of community to the nation. Modernism is usually thought to be at best indifferent to social life, to be preoccupied by narrowly aesthetic concerns. At its worst, the examples of Ezra Pound and, to a lesser degree, T. S. Eliot are taken to demonstrate that modernism possessed an inherent affinity for fascism. In the following chapters I hope to demonstrate the inadequacy of both these familiar conceptions of modernism. American literary modernists *were* concerned about the state of our literature and *were* dedicated to its renewal. However, they typically understood that state as symptomatic of the state of society as a whole, and recognized that their success in reviving the former required doing as much for the latter. The genteel poems that these writers abhorred had equally genteel readers, and the modernists were as interested in changing the mental habits of the latter as they were in altering the diction and form of the former. If Pound, Eliot, and others assumed that their project involved restoring to literature a degree of the vigor it possessed at other times and places, they also assumed that it needed to be complemented by the wholesale restoration of traditional social institutions. Since they are exemplary moderns, their example makes claims that modernism per se is inherently conservative, even fascistic, initially plausible. I would ar-

gue, however, that their conservatism derives from their tendency
to assume that only the traditional institutions that in another era
had seemingly made available the sense of community were capable
of doing so in their own. They would no doubt have agreed with
the Blum brothers in Willa Cather's *A Lost Lady,* who believed that
"a fortunate and privileged class was an axiomatic fact in the social
order" (14). Not all American literary modernists shared this questionable assumption. Van Wyck Brooks, the writers associated with
The Masses, and many others in the thirties believed that socialism
or other altogether new forms of social life could provide people
with that crucial sense. The latter were not prepared to accept economic and social privilege as essential features of stable societies;
they believed, instead, that it must be possible to distribute social
benefits equitably among all members of a community. Certainly
the New Negro writers did not accept the social and economic places
historically allotted by this nation to African Americans. American
literary modernists, in other words, commonly recognized that any
sense of community had been eroded among their contemporaries
and were united in their efforts to make it again widely available.
They differed in their judgments as to the means through which
this could most effectively be accomplished, and thus they advocated various remedies. Some of these remedies were clearly compatible with fascism; just as clearly, others were not. Thus American
literary modernism as a whole possessed no inherent political bias,
conservative or otherwise. What it did possess was a strong conviction that history had at some point (a point these writers would
identify differently) deprived them and their contemporaries of a
sense of community, as well as a commitment to rectifying that
regrettable absence. They proposed a variety of remedies, each with
its peculiar political inflection. One of my purposes in the following
chapters is to contest the equation of cultural modernism with reactionary political programs by illustrating the full range of political agendas available within American literary modernism.

II

Since the conception of American literary modernism operative
here differs in substantial ways from most others now available, it
might be useful to suggest briefly how and why I have come to it.

I have rarely been satisfied by any of the available definitions of modernism, none of which seems to do justice to the full range of practices that intuitively seem to have some claim to being termed modernist.[2] The sheer number and variety of proposed definitions suggest that others share my discomfort. I have come to believe that most extant definitions fail for either of two reasons: either they attempt to derive an expansive definition from the practices of one or another exemplary figure, or they attempt to be responsive to the international character of developments in many arts during the early years of this century. Let me briefly indicate the shortcomings of each approach.

Marjorie Perloff has nicely captured the difficulties critics have encountered in trying to define modernism by attending to the work of exemplary figures. In "Pound/Stevens: Whose Era?," the first chapter in her *The Dance of Intellect*, she summarizes the differences between critics such as Hugh Kenner in *The Pound Era*, who would make Pound's practices definitive of modernism, and others, such as Harold Bloom in *Wallace Stevens: The Poems of Our Climate*, who would do the same for Stevens. She observes that the advocates of each tend to employ distinctive vocabularies drawn primarily from these poets themselves: "For such key words in Stevens criticism as *imagination, consciousness, being* and *self,* Poundians would substitute terms like *precision, particularity, image, technique, structure, invention.* Again, such value tags as *Keatsian, Wordsworthian,* or *Emersonian,* ubiquitous in Stevens criticism, find their counterparts in the Pound annals in such adjectives as *Confucian, Homeric,* or *Provencal* on the one hand; in *experimental, avant-garde,* and, especially, *new* on the other" (13). Perloff also observes that Stevens's advocates seem more concerned with *what* is said, Pound's with *how* it is said (22); the first seem to privilege the lyric, the latter collage (15–16). And finally, the former typically conceive of modernism as a continuation of romanticism, the latter as a break with it (21). Neither set of terms or values is particularly receptive to the other; as a result, the advocates of each must in part make their case by reading the other out of modernism. In *The Dance of the Intellect* and elsewhere, Perloff leaves no doubt about her own preference for Pound. Having chosen to identify modernism with Pound, she cannot accommodate Stevens within it. One must admire Perloff's consistency, but surely there is something amiss here. She has produced a tidy conception of modernism, but purchased it by ruling out a writer many others take to be central to the character and accomplishment of the age. One suspects, too, that others must be similarly dismissed—Eliot, Frost, Marianne Moore, and so on—until modernism seems a term with very little descriptive reach.

I have begun with Perloff's essay because it usefully puts the issue in such sharp terms; I am less concerned about her own final advocacy of a modernism modeled on Pound—a preference for Stevens would have been equally troubling—than about the similar consequences of any attempt to extrapolate a description of modernism as a whole from the example of a single writer. I suspect that Americanists might be unusually sensitive to this problem, since the models, especially in prose, seem so often to be European. When Joyce, Kafka, or Mann is used as the definitive center of modernist fiction, his American counterparts often seem to be timid laggards. Hemingway, for instance, might have done something to the sentence (though something quite different from Joyce) and might have initiated a vogue for seemingly hard-boiled prose, but his stylistic experiments seem like small beer in comparison with Joyce's. Should he too be read out of the modernist canon? For all his elegance, Fitzgerald seems even less venturesome than Hemingway, more Henry James's dissolute younger brother than the champion for a new age. I sometimes suspect that Faulkner holds a disproportionately large place in many studies of American literary modernism because his conspicuous prose and narrative structures at least lend credence to claims that Americans participated in significant ways in the making of this literature. I am not suggesting that one of the latter might present a more opportune initial model of modernism; instead, I am suggesting that it is inevitably a mistake to take the pronouncements and practices of any single writer, no matter how seminal he or she might seem, as definitive of the phenomenon as a whole.

If some proposed definitions of modernism finally seem inadequate because they derive too exclusively from the example of single figures, others attempt to account for too much. People interested in this literature cannot help but be impressed by two things: first, the degree of reciprocal influence among artists working in different media; and second, its international character. Pound wrote *Gaudier-Brzeska, a Memoir* to celebrate the example of his friend, a sculptor recently killed in World War I; Gertrude Stein was a patron and apologist for the new painters in Paris; Wallace Stevens's prose, commonplace books, and letters are filled with numerous references to painters; even Van Wyck Brooks apprenticed himself to J. B. Yeats in Greenwich Village during the early teens, attending dinners with Yeats and younger American painters at Petitpas's. The first postimpressionism exhibit in London (1910) and later the Armory Show in New York (1913) were obviously important cultural moments, and by their own testimony literary figures were inspired by these exhibits to undertake similar experiments of their own. Many critics, observing the obvious influences taking place among the arts, have sought to define modernism in ways responsive to this crucial fact of its genesis and thus as a movement common across the various arts.[3] The results are rarely encouraging, and typically suffer from the interaction between two liabilities. First, when a writer is inspired by a painting to attempt something similar in poetry or fiction, he or she is nonetheless forced to work with words instead of colors and lines; as a result, the most the writer can hope to accomplish is an analogous effect. When writers or critics focus on such analogies, they necessarily minimize the constraints imposed upon any cultural artifact by its medium and obscure its place in the tradition of its form. When all is said and done, one does not *paint* in words; one *writes*, and it makes a difference that one necessarily does so with words, words that are familiar or strange, words joined together in ways that readers will readily recognize or need to puzzle out, words that adhere to generic expectations or violate such expectations in telling ways. Second, the effort to articulate relations among these analogies inevitably drives critics out of the vocabularies customary in the several arts and toward more abstract terms that are seemingly better able to accommodate developments across the arts. Attention is drawn to such similarities at a considerable (and I would argue, excessive) cost of specificity. If modernism at times seems to have been unusually responsive to abstract and philosophical issues, that impression is as often the product of scholars' efforts to construct continuities among the arts as from the perspicacity of these writers themselves.

Finally, it is instructive to observe that as a discourse seemingly able to accommodate such analogies among the arts emerges, it simultaneously becomes less responsive to the broader but more

mundane social ambitions and implications of any art. I do not believe that such unresponsiveness is often an operative intention of
such work; it is more likely that a critic's contextual interests simply
become exhausted in the effort to relate developments occurring
across the arts. Be that as it may, such scholarship contributes to the
impression that the crucial relations for any art are those with its
sister arts, thereby minimizing whatever social tasks artists might
hope their work will accomplish. Thus "art for art's sake" ironically but necessarily becomes reinscribed as the implicit agenda of
modernism as a whole, even though many modernists were attempting to discard precisely an aestheticism they thought to be habitual
among an earlier generation.[4]

The excitement generated by the Armory Show not only illustrates the way literary modernists sought to learn from contemporaries working in the other arts, it also suggests the new international character of artistic production during the early years of this
century. This international character of modernism is by now a critical commonplace; "Modernism, in short, is synonymous with internationalism," concludes Alfred Alvarez (9–10). Marinetti traveled
to Paris, London, and Moscow to deliver his futurist manifestos;
Frost and Eliot traveled to England with poems in their suitcases,
seeking and finding publication of their first books, thanks partially to the good offices of Pound, who was already in residence
there; and after the war, seemingly everyone wrote for a time in
the cafés of Paris. The arts were seemingly becoming thoroughly
cosmopolitan. It was not simply that writers (painters, etc.) from
many national traditions read, met, and learned from one another,
but also that they felt free to draw upon the resources of one another's traditions for fulfilling their own purposes. As we shall see
in the fourth chapter, the activities of Yeats and Lady Gregory in
rehabilitating the literary image of the Irish were important examples to Sterling Brown and others associated with the Harlem or
New Negro Renaissance. I do not want to dispute the importance
of such influences, which surely altered and hastened developments
throughout the arts. American literature would be different and
poorer if Pound had stayed at Wabash College or if Gertrude Stein
had not taken up residence in Paris and made her home a shrine to
everything that was culturally up-to-date. In addition to putting
their awareness of international literary developments to use in their

own work, both served crucial roles as vendors for these developments to their contemporaries.

At the same time, it seems to me important to acknowledge that
these diverse cultural influences were being assimilated into established national traditions and distinctive cultural situations. These
circumstances disposed writers to be particularly receptive to some
influences and disinterested in others; they also altered the significance of any gesture that a writer adapted from another national
tradition. The Armory Show and early ventures to Europe, for instance, initially exposed young American writers to the excitement
of dadaism. Its irreverence and energy won converts, and for a time
in the early twenties it seemed possible that dada might become as
estimable within American literary circles as it had already become
in France and elsewhere in Europe. The young Malcolm Cowley and
Matthew Josephson embraced dadaism, believing that it could in-
ject vigor into an American literary scene they alternatively characterized as sedate and ponderous. In "The Great American Billposter," Josephson celebrated the vitality of advertising copy, finding
"forms and word constructions which are at times breath-taking, if
anything, and in all cases far more arresting and provocative than
99 per cent of the stuff that passes for poetry in our specialized
magazines" (309). The dadaists of course expected and courted expressions of outrage by custodians of the genteel tradition, and they
were not disappointed. The criticisms of Edmund Wilson and Waldo
Frank, on the other hand, were another and entirely more serious
matter. Wilson and Frank shared the dadaists' disdain for the official
culture, but they were willing to oppose it only in the service of
something better, not by joining the dadaists in celebrating the energy and products of the commercial sphere. Writing in the February 1922 issue of *Vanity Fair,* Wilson observes that in the aftermath
of World War I many young French writers seem fixated by their
image of a distant and vital America. He concludes by addressing
these dadaists directly:

> The electric signs in Times Square make the Dadaists look timid;
> it is the masterpiece of Dadaism, produced naturally by our race
> and without premeditation which makes your own horrors self-
> conscious and which makes them offend our taste doubly be-
> cause we know that they first offended yours. Our monstrosities
> are at least created by people who know no better. But yours are

like risqué stories; told by well-bred girls to show off their sophistication; they sadden even the ribald; they make even the barbarian
wince! (100)

Frank was equally dismissive of the prospects for dadaism in the
United States. He freely conceded that dadaism might have fulfilled
a necessary cultural function in Europe, but went on to declare that
it "did nothing more ridiculous than the installation of the Dada
mood in American letters. Europe called for Dada by antithesis:
America for analogous reasons calls for the antithesis of Dada. For
America *is* Dada. . . . A healthy reaction to our world [i.e., to the
American scene] must, of course, be the contrary of Dada: it must
be ordered and serious and thorough" ("Seriousness and Dada"
129–30). Wilson and Frank situate American dadaism within its
specific social and cultural contexts. Impulses that seem useful or at
least explicable within some contexts seem less so in others. Both
finally believe that writers who are weighed down by national literary traditions must follow a different course than their American
counterparts, who lack such traditions.[5]
   Finally, many of the overtly international enthusiasms that swept
across Europe in the first decades of the twentieth century were
themselves tinged by nationalism. After citing several curious and
seemingly contradictory letters by Blaise Cendrars in *The Futurist
Moment,* Marjorie Perloff declares that it is now "almost impossible
to understand this particular mixture of radicalism and patriotism,
of a worldly, international outlook and a violently nationalist faith"
(6). She later observes that the debates about the relative merits of
cubism and futurism on the one hand, and of vorticism and futurism on the other, were motivated in part by the "aggressive nationalism of the *avant guerre*" (171). As we shall see in the first chapter,
cultural nationalism also played a critical role in determining the
agenda set out by Van Wyck Brooks and others associated in the
mid-teens with *Seven Arts.* It is my impression that critics have typically become mesmerized by the manifest and obviously influential
international character of literary modernism. As a result, they often
assume that a literary gesture bears the same significance, even when
it is being assimilated into quite distinct cultural situations; likewise,
they usually either minimize or altogether miss the degree to which

some literary movements of the time articulated the needs and as-pirations of nations.

In order to sidestep such difficulties, I have chosen in the follow-ing pages to concentrate exclusively upon American literary mod-ernism. I want to understand how these writers situated themselves vis-à-vis the nation as a whole, what cultural work they sought to accomplish, and the measure of success they achieved. I do not deny that these writers were influenced productively by work in other ar-tistic and national traditions. I believe, however, that these writers were engaged just as deeply in a broad conversation about the char-acter and quality of the national life, and that their work was shaped as much by their participation in this conversation as by artistic de-velopments occurring elsewhere. In recent years, Ann Douglas, James Knapp, Walter Benn Michaels, Lisa Steinman, and Cecilia Tichi have all demonstrated that various American literary modern-ists were more responsive to the several discourses that were alter-ing the shape of American life than critics have previously acknowl-edged; by concentrating on the communal concerns and ambitions common among these writers, I hope that *Writers for the Nation* can contribute to this line of inquiry.

The following chapters are meant to be representative of the cul-tural concerns and strategies of American literary modernism. An exhaustive mapping of even this limited portion of modernism would require a considerably longer book. Each chapter illustrates a particular cultural strategy pursued by one or more American liter-ary modernists. Although these strategies share a common concern and some techniques, they are in the end mutually exclusive, each articulating a particular possible strategy for restoring or estab-lishing a sense of community to American life. The chapters collec-tively represent the cultural debate that American literary modern-ism staged about how this national problem could best be resolved. I assume that sympathetic readers will be able to recognize how other writers might be located within the typology provided in the following chapters. I assume, too, that some readers will recognize ways in which the ambitions and accomplishments of some mod-ernists working in other national traditions could be at least par-tially described in similar terms. Although I have chosen to concen-trate upon American literary modernism, I do not claim that the resultant descriptions apply exclusively to the American scene. Indeed, one would expect a measure of similarity among contemporaries working in different national traditions, especially in light of their extensive pattern of interaction.

Finally, the chapter titles stress the limitations of each variant of American literary modernism. It should be understood that these limitations involve the larger programs for social and cultural renewal articulated by these variants and are not assessments of their literary accomplishments. On the contrary, I trust that my admiration for this body of work will be clear. At the same time, it seems to me important to stress that these writers were unable to imagine and implement genuine solutions to the social and cultural difficulties that so concerned them. No one else has either, so in large measure the problems they addressed remain our problems, often now exacerbated with the passage of time. We should honor them now as much for the courage and intellectual seriousness they displayed in assuming such broadly social responsibilities as for the power of the literature they thereby produced. In the end, I would argue that that power derives precisely from the intensity and perceptiveness of their engagement with matters of the greatest cultural urgency.

1

VAN WYCK BROOKS AND THE VARIETIES OF AMERICAN LITERARY MODERNISM

It is our faith and the faith of many that we are living in the first days of a renascent period, a time which means for America the coming of that national self-consciousness which is the beginning of greatness. In all such epochs the arts cease to be private matters; they become not only the expression of the national life but a means to its enhancement. . . . In short, the *Seven Arts* is not a magazine for artists, but an expression of artists for the community.[1]

IN THE SUMMER of 1920 Van Wyck Brooks apparently wrote T. S. Eliot from New York, asking if the latter would be interested in writing reviews for *The Freeman,* the journal Brooks had recently helped to found. At the time Brooks wrote, Eliot was just emerging as a literary figure of some consequence. The previous February, Eliot's *Poems* had been issued in New York by Knopf; the first collection of his occasional prose, *The Sacred Wood,* would be published in London by Methuen later in the year. Despite these signs of his later prominence, in 1920 Eliot was still earning his keep in London at Lloyd's Bank. He politely declined Brooks's offer, explaining that his job left him little opportunity to write and that he was often overcommitted. Although Eliot was unfamiliar with *The Freeman,* he did acknowledge that he had been aware of Brooks for many years, since their days as undergraduates at Harvard: "I remember you very much better than you think, when I was a Freshman at Harvard and you were a prominent man of letters there" (*Letters* 397).[2] There is, of course, something precious about an undergraduate reputation, even at Harvard, as a "prominent man of letters," and it is hard to determine whether, in responding to Brooks's inquiry, Eliot was aware of the potential irony and deprecation available in his ostensive praise. Be that as it may, by 1920 the careers of these two young, intensely ambitious literary figures were already on quite different arcs, and this was almost the last moment when the slightly younger Eliot in writing Brooks could conceivably have used this phrase, so central to the ambitions of them both, without obvious condescension.

In November 1922, Eliot's *The Waste Land* was published in *The Dial;* the following month, its editors announced that he was the recipient of the second Dial Award. The editors especially praised Eliot's cosmopolitan vision. "There are in his poems," they wrote, "certain characters, certain scenes, and even certain attitudes of mind, which one recognizes as particularly American; yet there is nowhere in his work that 'localism' which at once takes so much of American writing out of the field of comparison with European letters and (it is often beneficial to their reputations) requires for American writers a special standard of judgement" (686). Brooks would receive the same award the following year, suggesting that, at least for a brief time during the early twenties, the critic Brooks was considered as influential in the making of contemporary literature as the poets who typically received the award in this era, poets who included Marianne Moore, Ezra Pound, and William Carlos Williams as well as Eliot. However, the editors' announcement of Brooks's award, published in the January 1924 issue, was decidedly less enthusiastic than their earlier notice about Eliot's. In fact, the journal devotes about as much space to Yeats's recent Nobel Prize as to Brooks's accomplishments, and it concedes that one can recognize the latter without accepting "the whole body of his doctrine" (96). Since Brooks was identified precisely with the "localism" the editors had chastised when presenting the award to Eliot, the terms in which these awards were announced suggest that *The Dial* at least already considered Eliot the more consequential figure.

We usually and for good reasons continue to associate American literary modernism more with Eliot than with Brooks. In doing so, however, we eclipse an earlier but decisive moment when it seemed to be emerging under the tutelage of Brooks and others who shared his convictions. This is the moment that saw the founding of new journals such as the *New Republic, The Masses,* and *Seven Arts.* It occurred in Chicago and New York, not in Paris or London. It vested immense cultural authority and responsibility in the figure of the artist. It was critical of both the consolidating industrial order and genteel culture. It also shared in the confidence of the progressives that these obstacles to a fuller national life could be overcome. It was aware of cultural activities elsewhere and at times drew upon them, but finally was preoccupied with the renewal of social and cultural life in the United States. In particular, it wished to rectify the individualism it assumed to be characteristic of American life by propagating a set of values or concerns that could weld a disparate people into a vital community. It was, in brief, preoccupied by things American—the nation's past, its social life, its culture, and especially its unfulfilled promise. In this chapter I wish first to reconstruct this preliminary moment in the emergence of American literary modernism by focusing on the representative contributions of Van Wyck Brooks. In his writings of the teens we can locate a specific crystallization of issues that provided many of his initial readers with their sense of cultural purpose. An appreciation of this early moment in the emergence of American literary modernism will provide a useful background for the fuller treatment of later moments in subsequent chapters.

This configuration did not survive World War I. In later years, Brooks himself would come to believe that the war had decisively altered the course of American literature. The cultural energies concentrated in lower Manhattan during the early teens had been dispersed, as some joined the war effort and others drifted elsewhere in search of livelihoods. More critically, he believed that the war sapped young intellectuals and writers of their energy and especially of their optimism. Those who came of age after the war seemed to lack the confidence that had seemed so definitive of the prewar years. If the young were no more reconciled to the constraints of life in the United States, they were less inclined to imagine utopian alternatives, and many instead sought shelter in Paris or London, where they thought the literary life might still be possible amidst the wreckage of older ways of life. By the time American literary modernism began to fulfill some of the promise that Brooks and others had seen in it, it was typically less confident about the prospects for cultural renewal and considerably more diverse. It typically retained, however, the earlier aspiration to identify and call into being a community of interest that would shield at least some from the loneliness and strain of lives apart. This community would rarely be the nation as a whole, as it had been for Brooks and others in the years before World War I; but it would be invoked to render a similar service.

In subsequent chapters I shall trace the shapes of several representative later variants of American literary modernism. These variants are typically animated by one or more of the concerns originally articulated by Brooks and others in the teens, often adapted and shaped to meet the somewhat altered cultural situation in the United States during the twenties and thirties. Brooks was generally disappointed by the course of American literary modernism, and in later life he became one of its most outspoken critics. His hostility makes it difficult to appreciate the degree to which this literature continued to be animated in part by his own earlier formulations. In later sections of this chapter I shall briefly suggest the continuity between Brooks and representative American literary modernists. This survey will serve several purposes. It will introduce issues and writers to be studied at greater length in subsequent chapters; it will suggest their derivation from an earlier and more optimistic moment; and it will restore an appreciation of the formative role that Brooks and other cultural nationalists played in setting the varied agendas to be fulfilled by American literary modernism.

I

Brooks was raised in the relative comfort of a middle-class home in Plainfield, New Jersey. By the time he matriculated at Harvard College in 1904, he was already determined to become a writer. As he explains in his *Autobiography*, "while I did not know what I wanted to write, I knew that write I must and even the kind of writing that I was fit for; and for my purpose Harvard was the greenest of pastures" (101). The chapter in Brooks's autobiography devoted to his years at Harvard describes with obvious fondness the intensely literary society he discovered there among other students and faculty. Although Brooks and his friend John Hall Wheelock privately published *Verses by Two Undergraduates* in his second year at Harvard, from the beginning his literary ambitions seem largely to have been outside what we now take to be the usual genres. Brooks comments upon what he takes to be the subsequent narrowing of literary aspirations in a 1945 letter to Lewis Mumford: "Then, curiously enough, *writing*, in this age, in this country, means simply fiction and poetry (and sometimes the drama), and writing here is a cult too while it excludes from the field all the Renans and Carlyles and Emersons of our day. Very strange, these traits of the time which I *hope* I shall be able to mark when I reach this period in my history [i.e., in *The Confident Years*]" (289–90). Brooks was especially sensitive to these apparent exclusions no doubt because by the forties it was obviously clear that he had made the unusual choice to model his own literary career more on the examples of Carlyle, Ruskin, and Pater rather than on those of the novelists or poets who now more commonly serve this purpose for aspiring writers. For Brooks, writing cultural history and commentary was a form of literary activity every bit as important and honorable as writing fiction or poetry.

During the years between his graduation from Harvard in 1907 and the publication of *America's Coming-of-Age* in 1915, Brooks earned his keep variously—working for a time as journalist in England, in various publishing enterprises in New York, teaching at Stanford and later in an adult education program back in England. His first book, *The Wine of the Puritans* (1908), was written and initially published during his first extended stay in England. It is in the form of a dialogue about their native land between two Americans who are presumably rambling about in the hills overlooking Naples. Although it introduces many of the issues that would preoccupy Brooks in the coming years, *The Wine of the Puritans* is frankly a weak book. It develops through a series of discrete observations about America and American life. Brooks seemingly felt that the use of an imaginary dialogue relieved him from the obligation to develop a sustained argument; at the same time, he is unable to invest either of his speakers with a distinctive personality, so that in the end the volume feels as insubstantial as it criticizes American life for being. By the early teens, when, during another stay in England, he wrote *America's Coming-of-Age*, he was more in command of his point of view and able to write what became a manifesto for his generation.

In *The Wine of the Puritans*, Brooks uses the image of ruined wine to suggest what has gone wrong in American culture: " 'You put the old wine into new bottles,' I suggested, 'and when the explosion results, one may say, the aroma passes into the air and the wine spills on the floor. The aroma, or the ideal, turns into transcendentalism, and the wine, or the real, becomes commercialism. In any case, one doesn't preserve a great deal of well-tempered wine'" (6). The analysis in *America's Coming-of-Age* is much the same, but in the latter book Brooks uses the terms "highbrow" and "lowbrow" to characterize what he takes to be the strange split within American culture that he traces back to the Puritans.[3] Faced with the necessity of making their lives in the wilderness of New England, the earliest settlers were pressed by circumstance to give unusual attention to practical matters. Their preoccupation with such matters, according to Brooks, in time changed, devolving initially into "catchpenny opportunism, . . . becoming a philosophy in Franklin, passing through the American humorists, and resulting in the atmosphere of contemporary business life" (84). If conditions might excuse the earliest settlers for their devotion to securing livelihoods, that excuse is less available to each successive generation; what began as a regrettable necessity became in time an unreflexive national habit, an unfortunate part of our native tradition. Simultaneously, the Puritans' emphasis upon an immediate and personal bond with the divine kept them from developing social and political bonds of any consequence. Their religiosity, according to Brooks, was largely a personal matter, and finally had as little to do with the quality and character of their social lives as with their struggle to survive in the wilderness. This highbrow side of American culture underwent a devolution comparable to that experienced by its counterpart, passing through transcendentalism and eventually producing "the final unreality of most contemporary American culture" (84). Brooks argues that between them these two strands of the Puritan heritage continue to dictate the character of American life. They coexist, but highbrow piety and noble sentiments have never been allowed to interfere with lowbrow exertions, and the latter activities, no matter how sordid, do not seem to qualify the former.

For the most part, *America's Coming-of-Age* is a sketch of American cultural history in these terms. I am not particularly concerned about its adequacy; certainly Brooks himself, who in later years would rewrite this history in the five large volumes of *Makers and Finders*, came to hold very different opinions about the value of the native tradition. In the teens, however, Brooks is exercised by the frankly material bias of so much in American life, and especially by the indirect costs that bias exacts upon individual lives. These costs show up not only in strife among competitors in the market-place, but also in an inevitable narrowing of an individual's interests. "You cannot have personality, you cannot have the expressions of personality so long as the end of society is an impersonal end like the accumulation of money" (95). According to Brooks, highbrow culture did nothing to blunt or soften, much less to redirect, this emphasis upon winning a material advantage. "The immense, vague cloud-canopy of idealism which hung over the American people during the nineteenth century was never permitted, in fact, to in-terfere with the practical conduct of life" (99). In a society ruled by these imperatives, the rare individual who aspires to other ends finds little encouragement and rarely manages to accomplish anything of lasting significance; more often, he "not only suffers acutely and be-comes abnormal, he actually cannot accomplish anything healthily fine at all" (95).

Brooks's animus in *America's Coming-of-Age,* in other words, is due to his sense that his culture thwarts and stunts individual lives. He would prefer that highbrow and lowbrow be joined into some middle realm and that an organic community thereby come into existence. In its economic and social forms, that community, Brooks states, would necessarily be socialistic. Socialism would provide people with material security and a sense of collective purpose; it would free them to develop as individuals, and thus would accom-plish more to foster the development of distinctive personalities than current social arrangements. As his title suggests, Brooks sees reason to be encouraged that such sweeping changes are possible. He points, first of all, to the inspiration available in the example of Whitman, whom he credits with having "precipitated the American character. All those things which had been separate, self-sufficient, incoordinate—action, theory, idealism, business—he cast into a cru-cible; and they emerged, harmonious and molten, in a fresh demo-cratic ideal, which is based upon the whole personality" (131). Al-though Whitman might finally have been too indiscriminate and complacent, Brooks believes that he was the first person to provide "the nation a certain focal center in the consciousness of its own character" (131), that "with him originated the most contagious, the most liberating, the most unifying of native impulses" (135).

More immediately, Brooks is encouraged by his sense that others among his contemporaries share his vision for another and better nation. He cites his friend and mentor J. B. Yeats by way of confirming this sense—"The fiddles are tuning as it were all over America" (148)—but otherwise provides little evidence that confirms this impression. In the end, Brooks's optimism in *America's Coming-of-Age* itself seems primarily a legacy from the national tradition he would now in other respects refashion. If the first settlers were able to establish new settlements in the wilds of a strange land, surely he and his contemporaries could now provide the nation first with a sense of collective purpose, and then with institutional forms that would foster it. Although Brooks already saw himself primarily as a writer and not as a political figure or social commentator, his literary purpose in *America's Coming-of-Age* included contributing toward the collective task of reimagining the nature of social life in his native country.

America's Coming-of-Age was one of several similar commentaries published in the years before the United States entered World War I. These books share an impatience with the character of contemporary conditions in the United States and a conviction that they might be improved. Even Ezra Pound, already embarked upon a life abroad, felt able in "Patria Mia" (1913) to declare his "belief in the imminence of an American Risorgimento" that would "have its effect not only in the arts, but in life, in politics, and in economics" (111).[4] Although Pound believes that American editors typically seem exclusively devoted to the styles of 1870, in the apparently increasing numbers of expatriates he thinks he hears "the creaking of a scattered discontent" that could eventually build into a broad cultural awakening (133). "Patria Mia" contains even less sustained argument than *America's Coming-of-Age;* Herbert Croly's *The Promise of American Life* (1909), on the other hand, offers a fuller analysis of the cultural history that Brooks sketches so quickly. Like Brooks, Croly traces the deficiencies of American social and cultural life early in the twentieth century to the era of the pioneers. He too believes that the individualistic ethos of that era has become dysfunctional in a modern, increasingly urban and corporate America. Croly's emphasis is more immediately social and political than Brooks's. Unlike many progressives, who seemingly felt that the labor unions, trusts, and other large organizations of the era were inherently undemocratic, Croly concedes their inevitability and potential utility. He simply wants them to acknowledge that they exist at the sufferance of the public at large and, accordingly, that they must in the end serve its good, not simply the private interests of owners or union members. In other words, Croly seemed to believe that these large corporate entities, formed to advance particular interests, might eventually foster circumstances enabling citizens to identify their own interests with those of the entire nation.

The Promise of American Life is an exercise in social analysis and advocacy; although Croly had previously served as an editor for *The Architectural Record, Promise* devotes relatively little attention to the place of the arts in the life of the nation. It thus might seem to have little in common with *America's Coming-of-Age*. I wish to call attention to three similarities that suggest their common participation in a discourse that was influential in shaping the aspirations of many otherwise dissimilar contemporaries. First, both identify an excessive and inappropriate individualism as the underlying cause of national difficulties. As they understand it, American individualism might legitimate a preoccupation with securing one's economic advantage, but it otherwise leaves people without guidance and feeling unfulfilled.[5] Second, both would correct this individualism by providing their contemporaries with a sense of national purpose within which their private interests could be absorbed, redirected, and finally satisfied. Both understand the adoption of national interests as a condition for individual fulfillment. "It is . . . essential," writes Croly, "to recognize that the individual American will never obtain a sufficiently complete chance of self-expression, until the American nation has earnestly undertaken and measurably achieved the realization of its collective purpose" (409). Croly would institutionalize this sense of national purpose in a strengthened federal government; Brooks is characteristically less specific about the institutional implications of his position, but he implies something similar in his passing references to the necessity of socialism. Finally, for all their awareness of the difficulties facing the nation, both Brooks and Croly are confident that these difficulties can be addressed, that the nation can come of age and its promise can be fulfilled. The reasons for their optimism might differ, but Brooks in particular took this basically positive attitude to be definitive of their cultural moment.

Both *The Promise of America* and *America's Coming-of-Age* eventually led to other opportunities for their authors. Croly became the founding editor of the *New Republic,* which began publication in late 1914, and Brooks in 1916 was invited to join the editorial board of *Seven Arts,* a monthly that now seems thoroughly representative of its time and place.[6] In the "Announcement to Authors" I have already quoted as an epigraph for this chapter, the *Seven Arts* editors make clear their conviction that the United States was entering a period of unusual cultural promise. In such a period, they continue, "the arts cease to be private matters; they become not only the expression of the national life but a means to its enhancement." Since we have commonly come to assume that the arts are indeed private matters, and that they evolve independently from if not in opposition to other aspects of the national life, it is important to appreciate that *Seven Arts* set itself a quite different agenda. It would be a literary periodical addressed to the community at large, not just to other writers; and it would contribute in bringing the nation to self-consciousness and so to greatness. Like another characteristic periodical of the time, *The Masses,* the literary and broadly social dimensions of *Seven Arts'* charge were inseparable, and both were unmistakably nationalistic.

Brooks's imprint is everywhere in *Seven Arts.* The editors and contributors invoke Whitman continually as a cultural prophet, as Brooks had done in *America's Coming-of-Age.* Brooks might have written the following sentences from Waldo Frank's "Emerging Greatness," which appeared in the first issue: "Our artists have been of two extremes: those who gained an almost unbelievable purity of expression by the very violence of their self-isolation, and those who, plunging into the American maelstrom, were submerged in it, lost their vision altogether, and gave forth a gross chronicle and a blind cult of the American Fact" (73). The first issue of *Seven Arts* also contains an essay by Romain Rolland, writing from a France already at war, rejoicing "at the founding of a magazine in which the American Spirit may seek and achieve consciousness of its nature and its role" (47). Rolland goes on to charge American writers with responsibility for articulating the aspirations of the nation's ethnically diverse people: "You must harmonize all of the dreams and liberties and thoughts brought to your shores by all your peoples. You must make of your culture a symphony that shall in a true way express your own brotherhood of individuals, of races, of cultures banded together. You must make real the dream of an integrated and entire humanity" (50).[7] Rolland's conception of the task awaiting American writers is consistent with Brooks's own cultural nationalism, but the former implies that success would not only be serving a national need, but would also be providing Europe with possible terms for an eventual peace. *Seven Arts* consistently placed such aspirations for American culture in an international context. In *America's Coming-of-Age,* Brooks had expressed his admiration for Mazzini and other influential cultural nationalists of the nineteenth century. *Seven Arts* published a series of articles on "Young Japan," "Young Spain," "Young India," and "Youngest Ireland," as well as Brooks's own "Young America," suggesting that the cultural revival under way in the United States was part of an international ferment in which young writers were reviving their national literary traditions.

Only twelve monthly issues of *Seven Arts* appeared, between November 1916 and October 1917. In these twelve issues, however, the editors managed to publish work by Robert Frost, Amy Lowell, Sherwood Anderson, Theodore Dreiser, D. H. Lawrence, Vachel Lindsay, John Dos Passos, and Eugene O'Neill. The editors of *The Masses,* Max Eastman and Floyd Dell, were both published in *Seven Arts.* It also published social commentary, especially on whether the United States should enter the war, by Randolph Bourne, John Dewey, H. L. Mencken, and Bertrand Russell. The editors' opposition to American participation in World War I finally cost *Seven Arts* the support of its patron;[8] the October 1917 issue contains an initial plea "To the Friends of *The Seven Arts,*" a plea that begins with the following reiteration of editorial purpose:

> In short, the task we set ourselves was that of understanding, interpreting and expressing that *latent America,* that *potential America* which we believed lay hidden under our commercial-industrial national organization: that America of youth and aspiration: that America which desires a rich life, a finer fellowship, a flowering of mature and seasoned personalities. From this viewpoint, we looked upon art as a sharing of life, a communism of experience and vision, a spiritual root of nationalism and internationalism.
> Across this current, like a sudden dam, came the war. (n. pag.)

In 1918, Brooks extensively revised and published his own contributions to *Seven Arts*, giving them the title *Letters and Leadership*, suggestive of the formative role he assumes literary figures should play in the national life. In most respects these forceful essays repeat and amplify points already made in *America's Coming-of-Age*. He continues, for instance, to rail against the false and shallow individualism that "is only an inherited bad habit, a bad habit that is perpetuated by the want of objectives in the truly vacuous world with which it finds itself confronted" (58). What is new and invigorating in *Letters and Leadership* is Brooks's ability to identify in the contemporary scene additional reasons for his confidence that the cultural life of the nation can indeed be renewed. Perhaps his editorial labors on behalf of *Seven Arts* had made him appreciate how many others shared his hopes for a possible future; more likely, the change is primarily due to the influence of his friendship with Randolph Bourne.[9] When the two met in 1915, Bourne was already, like Brooks, an outspoken cultural nationalist. In "Our Cultural Humility," an essay published in 1914 by *Atlantic Monthly*, Bourne had roundly castigated the American habit of prostrating oneself before European cultural accomplishments. "The only remedy for this deplorable situation," he wrote, "is the cultivation of a new American nationalism" (506). In his introduction to a posthumous collection of Bourne's essays entitled *History of a Literary Radical*, Brooks writes that his friend's work was propelled by the desire "for a new fellowship in the youth of America as the principle of a great and revolutionary departure in our life, a league of youth, one might call it, consciously framed with the purpose of creating, out of the blind chaos of American society, a fine, free, articulate cultural order" (xi–xii). The essays Brooks contributed to *Seven Arts* follow Bourne in vesting the task of cultural renewal in the young. In the piece entitled "Young America," he writes that this new generation desires "to live creatively, to live completely, to live in behalf of some great corporate purpose" (*Letters and Leadership* 60). In the final chapter, "Toward the Future," he acknowledges that until now the United States has lacked a unified student class that might provide leadership, but also expresses his conviction that "there are . . . many signs that such a class is rapidly coming into existence" (124). The pages of *Seven Arts, The Masses,* and similar periodicals of the time were the surest indications that this class was emerging.

Although some in his generation had already fallen victim to despair and others were lost "in a confused and feeble anarchism" (127), Brooks is confident that his own generation could and would lead the nation toward the future, when "we shall become a luminous people, dwelling in light and sharing our light" (129). The luminous quality of Brooks's prose when he evokes this possible future is perhaps an index of his own yearning to live in what Bourne, in "Trans-National America," called the "Beloved Community" (264).

Brooks's confidence and cultural nationalism in *America's Coming-of-Age* and *Letters and Leadership* are notes that now seem to have been characteristic of the teens. It might be useful to define Brooks's particular version of these qualities by means of a comparison. *The Soil: A Magazine of Art* was almost exactly contemporaneous with *Seven Arts*. The first issue appeared in December 1916; the fifth and final issue is dated July 1917. The masthead of *The Soil* lists Enrique Cross as its literary editor and R. J. Coady as the art editor, but the latter was clearly its presiding spirit. Robert Coady was a minor figure in New York art circles; during its brief life, the editorial address of *The Soil* was the same as an art gallery run by Coady.[10] Although *The Soil* published work by Gertrude Stein and Wallace Stevens, it paid more attention to popular culture and the visual arts than to the emerging literature of the time.[11]

Coady announced an agenda for *The Soil* in "American Art," which ran in the first two issues. The first installment consists of three brief paragraphs of exposition, the first separated from the second and third by a long catalogue illustrating the sweep and vitality Coady finds in American art:

> There is an American Art. Young, robust, energetic, naive, immature, daring and big spirited. Active in every conceivable field.
>   The Panama Canal, the Sky-scraper and Colonial Architecture. The East River, the Battery and the "Fish Theatre." The Tug Boat and the Steam-shovel. The Steam Lighter. The Steel Plants, the Washing Plants and the Electrical Shops. . . . Christy Mathewson, Ty Cobb. Robert and Alfred Taylor, Prunnetta Henderson, Greatorex. Football. (3)

Coady's catalogue largely consists of similar items drawn from industry and popular culture. When it acknowledges accomplishments that are artistic in more traditional terms, it typically refuses to grant them any special status. Thus Coady includes *Others* and *Poetry* in his catalogue as examples of an emerging American art, but in a series equating them with *Boxing Record* and *Police Gazette;* he includes Whitman and Gertrude Stein, but also Howells, Artemus Ward, and Krazy Kat.

The first installment of "American Art" is largely affirmative in tone; the final paragraph observes that "isms have crowded it out of 'the art world,'" but Coady concludes by expressing confidence that American art will continue to flourish: "It has grown out of the soil and through the race and will continue to grow. It will grow and mature and add a new unit to Art" (4). In the second installment, it becomes clearer that Coady's insistence upon the unique character of American art is based upon his prior conviction that American society is unique. Art, for Coady, is an expression of a people; and since the United States has citizens drawn from many cultural traditions, its art will somehow express its composite character: "We are developing a new culture here. Its elements are gathering from all over the earth. We are making adjustments and getting results— physical, intellectual, aesthetic. Traditions are being merged, blood is being mixed. Something new, something big is happening here" (54). He urges the makers of this new art to learn from practices at other times and places, but in the end they must be able to adapt these lessons to the special circumstances of American life. In a sense, Coady's argument resembles Bourne's complaint about American cultural humility, but it seems to include resistance to dadaism and postimpressionism as well as to more traditional norms. Coady certainly admired much European art; his gallery apparently introduced Juan Gris and Diego Rivera to American viewers, and *The Soil* published plates illustrating work by Van Gogh, Cézanne, and Picasso, among others. In short, Coady was neither ignorant about international art nor indifferent to its merits. He simply worried that American artists might slavishly attempt to follow its example, thereby neglecting the special cultural opportunities open to them. He believed, finally, that the United States needed an indigenous art that would express the composite aspirations of an increasingly composite people: "We will be a hyphenated nation until we have an art" (56). This concluding sentence seems to belie Coady's apparent confidence that art was already thriving in the United States, if not in the usual places and forms. It suggests that Coady hoped that American contributions to "the art world" would eventually display an energy and inventiveness comparable to contemporary activities in industry and other cultural spheres.

Coady's optimism and cultural nationalism are comparable to Brooks's, but they have distinctly different sources. Brooks nowhere expresses anything like Coady's enthusiasm for machinery and other products of corporate America, or especially for popular culture. Both admire Walt Whitman, but I suspect that the reservations Brooks expresses about Whitman in *America's Coming-of-Age* could appropriately be elaborated to include Coady. Brooks admires Whitman's democratic ethos and declares that the "real significance of Walt Whitman is that he, for the first time, gave us the sense of something organic in American life" (128). At a time when culture in this country seemed to signify a studied remoteness from everyday life, Whitman's joyous immersion in that life was especially tonic. At the same time, Brooks worries that Whitman is insufficiently critical, too complacent, too willing to affirm every expression of American life (135). Coady is equally eager to celebrate the life he finds around him. His confidence about the prospects for American art seems finally rooted in his satisfaction with the status quo. His American art is already intimate with the rhythms of American life. Coady seems to desire more of the same. Brooks, on the other hand, is not nearly so catholic as Coady in what he is willing to term art. When Brooks writes about American art, he writes in the tradition of Matthew Arnold; he decries what he takes to be the irrelevance of this art to the activities of daily life. He calls for an art that will provide commentary upon everyday life and will ultimately serve as an agent in its reform. He is not averse to having his contemporaries learn from the examples of writers in other national traditions; he is more concerned that they eventually produce an American culture that is at least the equal of that already available in other national traditions.

Since he seems satisfied with the terms of American life, Coady can find reasons for optimism everywhere and can itemize them in a catalogue that could in principle be expanded infinitely. Coady does not mention any institutional or political changes needed to ease the emergence of his American art. Brooks's optimism in these years, by way of contrast, stems from signs that the status quo is possibly being transformed into something that promises to be more worthy of being celebrated. These signs for Brooks include the possibility that the national economy will evolve into a form of socialism. He yearns for a nation that just might be coming of age. The reasons for Brooks's confidence during these years in the prospects for cultural renewal in the United States are now harder for us to identify; and, in retrospect, that confidence seems to have been misplaced. At least, the United States would prove unwilling to embrace socialism and our literature would evolve in directions that Brooks himself regretted.

However, many years later, when he came to write about this era in the final volume of *Makers and Finders*, Brooks gave it the title *The Confident Years*, thereby reiterating what he took to be a definitive characteristic of American culture in the years prior to this nation's entry into World War I. The comparison of Brooks with Robert Coady demonstrates that this confidence had various sources and bespoke divergent ends. Despite these differences, when writing about these years in his *Autobiography*, William Carlos Williams links *Seven Arts* and *The Soil* and declares that each "was an unconscious collaborator in fostering the new spirit" (147). In these years, of course, Williams was himself working out the terms for what would become an equally confident vision for an indigenous American art. The "new spirit" Williams evokes in his *Autobiography* was a vague cultural ambition more than a movement with specific aims: the production of an indigenous American culture seemed to many, including the editors of *Seven Arts* and *The Soil*, at once crucial and possible. *America's Coming-of-Age* and *Letters and Leadership* articulate an especially forceful version of this ambition, making Brooks, for a time, a prominent participant in the larger cultural conversation about the quality of the national life.

II

By the time Brooks published *Letters and Leadership* in 1918, *Seven Arts* was already a casualty of World War I. An essay he published that same year in *The Dial* would largely set the direction for his own future work. "On Creating a Usable Past" is exclusively concerned with the situation of American writers, who are—so Brooks believes—uniquely deprived of a literary tradition that might inform their work. We have already seen that early in his career Brooks stressed the limitations of earlier American writers. In this essay, however, he argues that the deprivations experienced by contemporary writers are the product of a "vendetta between the two generations" (220). Elder scholars reserve their praise for earlier writers who participated in the exploitative values of the society as a whole, thereby effectively depriving young writers with different ideals of any sense that earlier writers might have shared their exasperation with the terms of American life. The contemporary American writer, as a result, "not only has the most meager of birthrights but is cheated out of that" (221). This apparent lack of precedents has the regrettable consequence of forcing young writers back upon their own resources, and too many lose their way, producing little of value.

By way of remedy, Brooks proposes that his generation break the seal placed by elder scholars upon the American literary tradition and discover one that is more immediately useful. By way of demonstrating that other conceptions of this tradition are already in circulation, he calls his readers' attention to the views of the English, French, and Russians, all of whom value American writers who are usually slighted by the academic keepers of our tradition. He proposes that this review of the American literary tradition not search for neglected masterpieces; he urges instead that it trace the fate of the creative impulse—noting where it emerges, what shapes it takes, what obstacles it encounters. This proposed review of American literature would of necessity be broadly cultural, since it would seek an understanding of the relationships among a writer, the writer's works, immediate readership, and the surrounding culture. Brooks believes that such histories would produce at least two benefits for contemporary writers:

> Knowing that others have desired the things we desire and have encountered the same obstacles, and that in some degree time has begun to face those obstacles down and make the way straight for us, would not the creative forces of this country lose a little of the hectic individualism that keeps them from uniting against their common enemies? And would this not bring about, for the first time, that sense of brotherhood in effort and in inspiration which is the best promise of a national culture? (226)

As these concluding sentences demonstrate, in "On Creating a Usable Past" Brooks was particularly concerned about the situation of contemporary writers. He agrees with the scholars that these writers often go wrong; however, he takes no pleasure from this observation, and attributes their shortcomings to their isolation both from one another and from a usable past. In the long term, this situation will not improve until American social life as a whole is overhauled, so that no citizens are forced to shift for themselves and so that all can participate fully in the national culture. In the meantime, Brooks would provide contemporary writers at least with the brotherhood potentially available within the national literary tradition, with the recognition that others have shared their aspirations and aversions. Although knowledge of other literary traditions could obviously be useful to contemporary American writers, the native tradition possesses a special pertinence, since it specifically exemplifies the successes and failures of one's predecessors in addressing themselves to the unique social formations of the United States.

Brooks devoted the better portion of his remaining career to producing just such an understanding of the American literary tradition. His initial efforts emphasize the finally debilitating tensions that existed between some writers and the culture at large. In *The Ordeal of Mark Twain* (1920), he presented an image of a writer whose work in the end was compromised by a too intimate commerce with the existing culture. In *The Pilgrimage of Henry James* (1925), he presented an image of a writer whose work in the end was compromised by a too scrupulous refusal of all commerce with that culture. In these initial efforts to create a usable past, Brooks understands the special difficulties faced by the American writer in terms consistent with those he had advanced in *America's Coming-of-Age*. The example of James is particularly telling and would subsequently inform his assessment of later expatriates. Brooks understands and largely shares James's aversion to so much in American life. At the same time, he finds James's later novels especially weak, and attributes their weaknesses to the expatriate's loss of contact with the life of the nation. Brooks's study of James becomes a cautionary tale illustrating the fate awaiting writers who fastidiously deny themselves all sustaining contact with their native traditions and societies, no matter how debilitating that contact might initially seem to be.

By the time Brooks came to write *The Flowering of New England* (1936) and the later volumes in his *Makers and Finders* series, he thought better of his predecessors, who no longer seemed inevitably stunted by their immediate cultural circumstances. Perhaps Brooks himself had partially been victimized by the scholars he chastises in "On Creating a Usable Past"; certainly the literary culture he describes at Harvard in his *Autobiography* placed little value upon American writing. Be that as it may, in later years Brooks would freely admit to having criticized the American literary tradition before taking the trouble to read it carefully. In his *Autobiography,* for instance, he concedes, "I had scarcely read 'Our Poets' of whom I was to write, in *America's Coming-of-Age,* so cavalierly" (115). Whatever its shortcomings, *Makers and Finders* is obviously the product of a remarkable immersion in the cultural life of the United States during the nineteenth century. Brooks subsequently describes his intentions for this series in *The Writer in America,* using terms that are consistent with "On Creating a Usable Past": "It seemed to me that, collectively speaking, our writers formed a guild, that they had even worked for a common end,—an elevating end and deeply human—and that living writers, aware of this, could never quite feel as they had felt before, that they were working alone and working in the dark" (46). Brooks believed this awareness could be valuable to all American writers, but perhaps especially to those whose own origins here were more recent and who had had less opportunity to be schooled in the literary tradition of their new nation. Brooks was at pains to make the series inclusive, believing that the inclusion of less-celebrated writers provided living connections among the better-known, who might otherwise seem to have been isolated figures. He wants to demonstrate that American writers have been sustained both by their interactions with one another and by their engagement with the culture at large. The "guild" that Brooks imagines for American writers is a later image for the "brotherhood" that he calls for in the concluding sentence of "On Creating a Usable Past." If American writers in the twentieth century seem afflicted with an especially intense sense of isolation, in the five volumes of *Makers and Finders* Brooks would demonstrate how much they shared with their predecessors, thereby providing them with what he took to be a viable substitute community. In the process, he perhaps minimized the degree to which these predecessors were at odds with the culture at large; as a result, his readers must be excused if they could not always recognize their own estrangement in Brooks's history, and thus not consistently see its relevance to their own situations.

If Brooks's labors on *Makers and Finders* from the thirties through the early fifties were in part an attempt to minister to the needs of contemporary writers, during these years he was increasingly out of sympathy with major tendencies in our literature. Raymond Nelson suggests that this estrangement began considerably earlier, and that "by the beginning of 1923 Brooks was no longer firmly in charge of the literary situation" (162). In an August 1923 column in *The Freeman* Brooks was already regretting that "a strange, brittle cerebral aristocratism has succeeded the robust democratism" that seemed so pervasive in the culture prior to the war ("Reviewer's Notebook" 527). Although he had begun his own career as a writer in England, he later had little sympathy for those who judged that the literary life could best be cultivated as an expatriate.[12] Although the book that initially secured his reputation, *America's Coming-of-Age,* was severely critical of the character of American cultural life, he became increasingly impatient with similar indictments by others, especially when he sensed that they were unprepared to concede it any merits. Although he espoused socialism, he seems from the beginning to have had little sympathy for Marxism, and he became distrustful of the motives and tactics of the more radical writers during the thirties. Although he considered himself primarily a critic, his models were Carlyle and Ruskin, and he had little appreciation for the new criticism that was emerging in these years. "I scarcely wished any longer to be called a critic when the word assumed these connotations," he sadly concludes in his *Autobiography* (378). He became especially exercised by what he took to be an excessive emphasis on technical matters, whether this emphasis occurred among writers or critics. In several speeches he made and subsequently published in the late thirties and early forties, he would seemingly be as dismissive of contemporary writers as he once had been of nineteenth-century American culture.[13] In 1941, writing in *Partisan Review,* a journal that was in many respects reviving the legacy of *Seven Arts,* Dwight Macdonald attacked Brooks, claiming in effect that he had become the very sort of philistine that he had earlier attacked himself. In a subsequent issue, *Partisan* published responses to Macdonald's piece by numerous literary figures. None had a good word to say for Brooks. Although he would continue to publish for another two decades, Brooks's influence on American literature had effectively come to an end. He had become irrelevant, even quaint; it was no longer either necessary or productive for others to argue with him, since it could be and was assumed from the outset that he had little useful to contribute to an understanding of our cultural life. In retrospect, we can see that he was a spokesperson for a particular cultural moment, when the constellation of issues that animated his own work enabled him to speak for and to his contemporaries. He remained faithful to that constellation in later years, but it no longer reflected the conditions of his audience, which had come apart.[14] If American literary modernism as it emerged after World War I did not fully embody Brooks's hopes, it continued, as we shall see, to be animated by its own varied conceptions of the "guild" or "brotherhood in effort and in inspiration" that Brooks himself had hoped to call into existence.

III

We have already seen that in 1920 Brooks thought well enough of T. S. Eliot to invite him to write reviews for *The Freeman,* and that Eliot had earlier expressed admiration for Brooks's *The Wine of the Puritans.* At the time, Brooks was a prophet for Young America and the writers who would bring it into being. Although Brooks was correct in his predictions about the emerging power of American writers, his pleasure at this emergence was compromised by his sense that the more powerful and influential voices among them were charting a course very different from the one he had anticipated. He had called upon the writers of his generation to challenge the nation's preoccupation with commercial success and material gain, which he considered the unfortunate legacy of Puritanism. However, he had expected this challenge to be in the American grain—that is, to be finally progressive and optimistic in tone—and he anticipated that it would issue in a general social and cultural renewal. Brooks recalled this initial confidence in *On Literature To-day* (1941):

Thirty years ago, when I began to write, the future was an exciting and hopeful vista. Everyone believed in evolution, as a natural social process. We took the end for granted. Mankind was marching forward, and the only questions were of ways and means. I do not need to say how far the first world-war destroyed this happy vista. The young and sensitive minds who grew up in its shadow were utterly disillusioned by what they saw. They felt they had been betrayed, and, as evil triumphed, they came to feel that nothing else was real. (19)

Brooks in turn was distressed when these writers often seemed thoroughly dismissive of the prospects for human betterment or more interested in achieving an exclusively aesthetic renewal.

In later years, Eliot came to represent for Brooks this betrayal of an early promise. The cumulative force of Brooks's overt hostility is too great to be accounted for exclusively in intellectual terms. As Eliot increasingly claimed the prophetic role for his generation that had once seemed to be vested in Brooks, the latter might simply have become envious; but Raymond Nelson also demonstrates that Eliot's public career involved choices that had at one time tempted Brooks: "As Brooks choked back his juvenile Anglophilia, Eliot became a British subject. As Brooks steeled himself to resist his hunger for Europe, Eliot became the most celebrated of expatriates. As Brooks wrenched himself away from Catholicism, Eliot announced his Anglo-Catholic orthodoxy" (239). When Brooks excoriated Eliot, in other words, he was reiterating the series of personal choices that marked his own difficult conversion to cultural nationalism.

Brooks and Eliot are exponents of competing versions of American literary modernism. We should not allow the obvious emotional and intellectual differences between them to obscure the degree to which they nonetheless continued to share a common discursive field. These similarities can perhaps best be seen by comparing their influential statements about the writer's need for a sense of tradition. Brooks's "On Creating a Usable Past" was initially published in the April 1918 issue of *The Dial;* Eliot's "Tradition and the Individual Talent" initially appeared in London the following year, in the September and December numbers of *The Egoist.* Despite this curious proximity, I see no evidence that Eliot's piece is a response to Brooks; it seems, instead, that each was responding in his own way to a broader cultural need. In "On Creating a Usable Past," Brooks defines the need exclusively in American terms, and his response is immediately pragmatic—if American writers are harmed by the apparent lack of an indigenous literary tradition, let us by all means provide them with one. Eliot initially implies that he is troubled by the British denigration of tradition, but his essay quickly becomes more general and philosophical, so that he could claim with some justice that his analysis is germane to the needs of all writers. Both Brooks and Eliot regret the effects that this absence or disregard of a tradition produces, and both understand these effects in similar terms. Brooks begins by lamenting the anarchy that seems characteristic of contemporary American writing, Eliot by lamenting that "traditional" has become a term of censure, so that young writers are encouraged to strive for novelty. It is difficult to imagine the stately Eliot writing the following sentence, but he would surely share Brooks's dismay at the fate of the American writer who has been led to disregard the literary tradition: "Seeing nothing in the past but the oblivion of all things that have meaning to the creative mood, he decides to paddle his own course, even if it leads to shipwreck" (222).

Brooks and Eliot, in other words, share an assessment of contemporary writing as being marked and weakened by excessive individualism; both invoke tradition by way of redress. Eliot's description of the writer's need to sacrifice himself or herself on behalf of the tradition is well known; I shall have more to say about it in the third chapter. There is nothing comparable in "On Creating a Usable Past." In *Letters and Leadership,* however, there is a passage that suggests Brooks's essential agreement with Eliot about the desirability of an individual becoming absorbed by shared values and goals. After cataloging any number of American cultural deficiencies, Brooks writes: "Of all this individualism is at once the cause and the result. For it has prevented the formation of a collective spiritual life in the absence of which the individual, *having nothing greater than himself to subordinate himself to,* is either driven into the blind alley of his appetites or rides some hobby horse of his own invention until it falls to pieces from sheer craziness" (19; my emphasis). "On Creating a Usable Past" is concerned precisely with the need to establish, in the form of an American literary tradition, something to which writers could subordinate themselves, thereby minimizing the aimless anarchism that Brooks thought now too characteristic of their efforts.

In the late teens, then, Eliot and Brooks were largely in accord about the condition of contemporary letters, and both believed that that condition might be improved if their contemporaries were able to subordinate themselves to a tradition. Although Eliot would be some years in coming to this recognition, both finally understood the tradition they invoked as a figure for a community of belief that enabled its members to define themselves as participants in some continuing collective endeavor, what Brooks termed a "brotherhood in effort and in aspiration." They differ, as do most competing versions of American literary modernism, primarily in their conceptions of that brotherhood. Eliot's initially might seem the more inclusive, since he insists that a writer must possess a sense of the entire Western literary tradition, whereas Brooks's only urges that the American writer be provided with an indigenous tradition. By the time he comes to appreciate the larger social dimensions of his call for tradition, however, Eliot was concerned to protect its orthodoxy, as in his unfortunate remarks in *After Strange Gods*. One way of understanding Eliot's expatriation and eventual change of citizenship is to notice that England seemed to promise him membership in an older and less ethnically adulterated social community. Brooks, by way of contrast, seemed to believe that American life and literature would be enriched by the contributions of recent immigrants, whose own cultural traditions had little in common with indigenous Puritanism. For Eliot, finally, the entire process of submission to authority and tradition seems a joyless release from the torments of personality; for Brooks, on the other hand, that submission promises the release of personality from its isolation into conditions that allow it greater opportunities for fulfillment.

Brooks was so dismayed by what he took to be Eliot's betrayal of the American tradition that he could never concede the degree to which their assessments of the cultural situation in the late teens had overlapped. Brooks consistently took Eliot's decision to live in England as a repudiation of the American tradition; in *The Confident Years* and elsewhere he argues that it illustrates Eliot's failure to heed his own imperative, spelled out in "Tradition and the Individual Talent," that the writer command a knowledge of his or her national literary traditions (596–99). In recent years interest in Eliot's debt to his native tradition has renewed, and we can now see that it is both more pervasive and deeper than either Brooks or Eliot would have acknowledged (Sigg). I wish to make a slightly different point: Eliot's expatriation itself curiously identifies him as an American literary modernist. It was motivated by his perception that American life lacked a shared sense of community and thus left each person too dependent on his or her own resources. He would have agreed with Brooks's observation in *Letters and Leadership* that the United States "is rapidly breeding a race of Hamlets the like of which has hardly been seen before" (55). Despite his protestations to the contrary, Prufrock is such a Hamlet. Eliot's eventual allegiance to British social and cultural traditions represents his own solution to a problem he shared with other American writers in the early decades of this century. It is obviously an extreme solution, one suggesting that, unlike Brooks, he had little confidence that American society could be altered enough to provide its members with anything comparable. However, the different means that Eliot chose should not finally cause us, as it did Brooks, to lose sight of the fact that he and Brooks were in search of similar ends.

IV

Expatriation was not the only alternative tried as the cultural nationalism so characteristic of the teens waned. Other American literary modernists gave their loyalties instead to particular regions of the nation. In most cases such regionalism was either a diminished version of cultural nationalism or an alternative to it; it implicitly claimed that the culture of a particular time or place was the promised America, and that it must be remembered and defended against the deprecations of other, less hospitable, ways of life. If at other moments American literary modernism delivers an indictment against the provincialism of life in Sherwood Anderson's Winesburg or Sinclair Lewis's Gopher Prairie (Hilfer), regionalism represents a return to such towns and the discovery within them of some saving grace. This return, like Nick Carraway's in *The Great Gatsby,* usually follows a disillusionment in the greater world, and the sting of that disappointment enables writers to think better of provincial life. Willa Cather, for example, wrote *O Pioneers!* and the other prairie novels after living for two decades in the East, and Allen Tate became a convert to Agrarianism while pursuing a literary career in New York. The regionalism that emerged among American literary modernists, in other words, is typically a self-conscious choice and not the spontaneous expression of satisfaction about one's native region. It represents a deliberate choice among alternatives, usually one involving diminished expectations. And it is typically shadowed by the memory of some defeat experienced on the larger stage and by worry that a comparable fate awaits the little society in which one has temporarily found refuge.

Brooks remained a cultural nationalist to the last and was never a regionalist in the manner of Cather, the Southern Agrarians, or Faulkner. During the twenties and thirties, however, he came to appreciate the reasons for the emergence of regional loyalties among other writers. He devotes a chapter to this phenomenon in *Opinions of Oliver Allston,* in which he lightly fictionalizes his own opinions as those of Allston, his alter ego. "Born in a suburb, he had no deep local attachments" (258), Brooks writes about himself in the person of Allston. Nonetheless, he "rejoiced in the rise of the regional feeling" (260). Brooks's appreciation of such feeling seems to have two intellectual sources. First, it appears to be a transposition of Randolph Bourne's hopes for a transnational America. In "Trans-National America," Bourne observes that recent immigrants were retaining their cultural loyalties even as they became economically assimilated. He urges readers to consider this not as a failure of the melting pot but an opportunity for the United States to become "a federation of cultures," "the first international nation" (256, 258). Instead of melting these various cultures down into some common denominator, Bourne writes that we should appreciate that each has a unique contribution to make toward the creation of a new, varied, and vibrant social order (Hollinger). Brooks seemingly adapts this logic some years later in his discussion of regionalism. Regional loyalties would assure the diversity and vitality of the national culture. Brooks also seemingly drew upon Lewis Mumford in his appreciation of regionalism. After reading Mumford's *The Culture of Cities* (1938), Brooks wrote to congratulate his friend, singling out his emphasis on regional planning for special praise: "I'm a little overwhelmed at moments by the total impression and can't go into details. . . . But in all your remarks on regionalism, on small communities, local interests, and a hundred and one other matters, you have certainly caught the secrets of the younger people" (150). Mumford was something of a social engineer, and *The Culture of Cities* is less concerned with regional affections than with rational social planning that would take regional considerations into account. In a similar pragmatic spirit, Brooks in *Opinions of Oliver Allston* argues that "the size and the chaos of the country necessitate" regionalism (261), since individuals are better able to identify with specific ways of life than with something so large and necessarily so abstract as the nation as a whole.

In later chapters I shall explore two quite distinct versions of this regionalism. A portion of the third chapter is devoted to the Agrarian phase of Allen Tate's career. The Southern Agrarians represent the pure type of regionalism within American literary modernism. The Agrarians believed that the cultural continuity of their region was endangered by the increasing encroachments of modern business practices. They were as opposed to these practices as Brooks and the other cultural nationalists had been in the teens, and they similarly assumed that literary figures might play a critical role in formulating and advocating an alternative. If the Agrarians did not from the first believe that traditional southern life had been particularly conducive to high culture, it at least seemed preferable to the prospects imaginable within a thoroughly industrial social order. Whereas Brooks had earlier been hopeful about the nation's coming of age because he could imagine that its maturity would include the provision of shared values, the Agrarians saw that maturity as boding only the further erosion of a distinctive and already threatened southern way of life. Although the Agrarians' conception of a viable community was similar to Eliot's, they did not follow him to England, because they could imagine that the life of their region still afforded them with everything he seemingly could only find abroad.

Willa Cather's prairie novels are as decisively marked by time as by place. *O Pioneers!*, *My Ántonia*, and *A Lost Lady* are all set on the plains in the era of her own childhood. The landscapes and people are described with obvious affection. Cather's two historical novels, *Death Comes for the Archbishop* and *Shadows on the Rock*, are set in remoter times and places, but otherwise they are similarly evocative in their depictions of specific landscapes and frontier communities. The lives that Cather depicts in these novels obviously involve the hardships that were an inescapable part of life in such settlements.

At the same time, Cather's immigrant settlers often bring to their new lives a strong attachment to traditional learning and culture. Cather's respect for this European heritage is perhaps clearest in the later historical novels, in the depictions of Archbishop Latour and the French settlement at Quebec, but it is already evident in her depiction of the Bohemian community in *O Pioneers!* and in the pathetic dignity of Ántonia's father in *My Ántonia.* The Nebraska of the 1880s might have been unable to nurture comparable cultural aspirations once it gave rise to them, causing Cather and several of her protagonists to flee at the earliest opportunity; but she would revert to it later in her strongest and most characteristic fiction, at a time when she had experienced more of modern life and was able to think better of it. Unlike Brooks, on the one hand, Cather had no confidence that the future held the promise of a better era; unlike the Agrarians, on the other, she had no faith that the future could be averted. Instead, she believed that America had already come of age, and regretted what it had become. The Nebraska of her childhood would hold the same place in her imagination that New England in the nineteenth century would eventually hold in Brooks's: It was a representation of what social life might be and thus an oblique commentary on what it in fact had become.

V

Of all the figures to be discussed in subsequent chapters, Brooks initially seems to have the least affinity with Wallace Stevens. The poet is scarcely mentioned in any of Brooks's major assessments of his contemporaries— *Opinions of Oliver Allston, The Writer in America, The Confident Years,* or *An Autobiography.* Although Stevens might have been spared Brooks's contumely because he never ventured abroad, choosing instead to live and work quietly in New York and then Hartford, the comparable lateness of his prominence was probably a more decisive factor. By the time Stevens began to rival Eliot for preeminence among modern American poets in the late fifties, Brooks had largely turned to other matters and was no longer scolding writers who seemed to stray.

Stevens and Brooks had much in common. The somewhat older poet preceded Brooks by several years at Harvard, where they would both become associated with the *Advocate.* Upon leaving Cambridge, both initially planned to earn their keep as journalists in New York. Stevens in fact worked there as a reporter for the *New York Tribune* for a time before turning instead to law school in the fall of 1902. On a visit to New York some months before his graduation in 1907, Brooks sought the advice of Paul Elmer More and William Dean Howells on how he might most effectively establish himself as a writer there; they were not particularly encouraging, and he eventually settled upon the equally romantic expedient of beginning his career as a Fleet Street journalist in London. By the mid-teens, Stevens and Brooks were both living in New York and participating in its various literary circles. While Brooks was editing and writing for *Seven Arts*, Stevens was serving as a lawyer for New England Equitable Insurance Company and publishing his early poems in several little magazines, including *Others*. Dedicated to publishing experimental work by younger writers, *Others* typically avoided the political issues that were also integral to the agendas of *The Masses* and *Seven Arts*. In addition to works by Sherwood Anderson, Amy Lowell, and Carl Sandburg, who also appeared in *Seven Arts*, between 1915 and its final issue in 1919 *Others* published works by Eliot, Ezra Pound, Marianne Moore, William Carlos Williams, and Mina Loy, as well as by Stevens.

In many respects the poems Stevens published during the teens in *Others, Poetry,* and elsewhere seem to participate in the tone that Brooks and *Seven Arts* took to be symptomatic of a revival in American letters. They issue a challenge to the genteel tradition and the pieties of the established order; they are inventive, energetic, and irreverent. They are also seemingly devoid of any political intention, and are not in any obvious way concerned about the character of the national life. Stevens might thus seem to dwell completely outside the discursive concerns that preoccupied Brooks throughout his career. In these years Stevens wrote little prose; but the prose he wrote later, often in response to specific invitations, demonstrates that he shared many assumptions with Brooks. The following sentences from "The Noble Rider and the Sound of Words," initially delivered as a public lecture at Princeton in 1941, for instance, might have come from Brooks's *America's Coming-of-Age:* "I think that [the poet's] function is to make his imagination theirs and that he fulfills himself only as he sees his imagination become the light in the minds of others. His role, in short, is to help people to live their lives" (*Necessary Angel* 29). Stevens in turn might well have written the following passage from Brooks's *Letters and Leadership:* "When we have 'feelings and desires,' [writes Brooks, quoting William Morris] when, rather, we have poets to formulate them, to create for us emblems of a greater life, magnetic ideals grounded in our own field of reality, then our social problems, effectively handled by the very minds that fumble now because they cannot distinguish between ideals and methods, will begin to solve themselves" (116).

In calling attention to the similarities between these passages, I do not mean to imply that Stevens was in any way influenced by Brooks. I do claim that they participated in the same discursive field. This field vests writers with remarkable cultural powers, suggesting that they are destined to set the terms in which their contemporaries will understand and live their lives. This discourse is also typically confident that writers can in fact make good on this promise, thereby granting works informed by this vision a definite buoyancy and optimism. In the teens Brooks and the other Young Intellectuals drew upon this discourse in their characterizations of the cultural renascence they thought was already under way; in their writings, it became entangled with an equally confident socialism, and both finally informed a specific vision of national destiny. When Stevens later invokes this discourse, it is usually unaccompanied by any specific political program. He is more concerned to define the writer's function per se, although he occasionally allows that the need for writers to discharge their function has become more extreme in the aftermath of World War I. Finally, Stevens typically places so much stress upon the individual poet's powers to provide terms for living that readers can overlook the fact that these powers are presumably exercised on behalf of society as a whole. We cannot now know what Brooks might have thought about Stevens's poetry, nor would such knowledge be of more than anecdotal interest. We can be confident, however, that he would have recognized Stevens's project as a variant of his own, though one seemingly divorced from the immediate political context that so concerned him.

VI

Throughout most of his career, Brooks was a member of the Socialist Party. In his *Autobiography,* he recalls that he "caught [his] first glimpse of the socialist movement at Harvard when Jack London, still in his twenties, lectured at the Union" (160). He reports that such political convictions were commonplace in New York during the teens: "Every writer I came to know called himself a radical, committed to some programme for changing and improving the world; . . . moreover, they had, or wished to have, a feeling of common cause, the sense of a community of writers building a new culture" (271–72). Raymond Nelson reports that Brooks eventually joined the Socialist Party of New York in early 1916, shortly after the publication of *America's Coming-of-Age* (80). The casualness with which Brooks declared his socialist convictions is now surely one of the more remarkable features of that volume: "It will remain of the least importance to patch up politics . . . unless, in some way, personality can be made to release itself on a middle plane between vaporous idealism and self-interested practicality; unless, in short, self-fulfillment as an ideal can be substituted for self-assertion as an ideal. On the economic plane that implies socialism; on every other plane it implies something which a majority of Americans in our day certainly do not possess—an object in living" (95–96). Neither here nor elsewhere in the volume does Brooks pause to define or describe socialism; nor is he in the least defensive about his political claims. Some might wonder about a socialism that finds its ideal in self-fulfillment and suspect that it would be only too compatible with the American tradition of individualism.[15] For Brooks, however, socialism represents the political dimension of a possible future that would heal the breach between highbrow and lowbrow, thereby creating an organic community dedicated to the fulfillment of its members. Brooks's socialism was an integral part of his influential early criticism; it demonstrates, whatever its political shortcomings, that his cultural criticism was from the beginning concerned about the entire range of American life and not only the fate of writers and others possessing definite cultural pretensions. It also suggests how deeply his own work participated in the ferment that produced *The Masses* and other symptoms of cultural renewal in the years just prior to World War I.

Brooks retained his political convictions throughout the twenties, when they were decidedly less fashionable. As we have seen, his antipathy to Eliot derives in part from his suspicion about the latter's professed political allegiances. Although the revival of interest among writers in various leftist political programs during the thirties seemingly held the possibility that Brooks would again become part of the cultural mainstream, it finally did little to halt his own increasing alienation within the literary community. His political convictions now seemed as much quaint as radical. During these years, at a time when he was working on *The Flowering of New England,* both Brooks and his wife ran unsuccessfully for public office in Connecticut on the Socialist ticket. The letter in which he announces his own candidacy to Lewis Mumford begins by relating the information that he had just addressed a large audience in New York, at a dinner honoring Norman Thomas (*Brooks-Mumford Letters* 141). Like many others in these years, he also joined the League of American Writers, and in November 1938 he addressed a league meeting held in New Haven. In that address, Brooks expressed his misgivings about communism and urged his audience to heed instead a native Yankee tradition. "If we wish collectivism, we do not have to go to Russia," he declared, thereby reiterating in a new way his consistent plea that the national tradition be respected ("Personal Statement" 41). Like many others, Brooks eventually resigned from the league when the membership refused to denounce the Soviet Union in the months leading up to World War II. In his letter of resignation, he continued to espouse socialism, but likewise retained his conviction that "this country can only be socialized *in the American grain*" (qtd. in R. Nelson 230)—that is, in a way compatible with the American tradition.

In the sixth chapter we shall consider other writers who for a time in the thirties believed that only a form of socialism could adequately redress the economic and cultural ills that had befallen the nation. I believe that these writers can best be understood as developing belatedly a variant of American literary modernism that had been available from the first. A future socialist society represents another version of the community within which citizens might live with dignity and satisfaction. Most writers who came to this conviction assumed that such a society would represent a decisive break from past forms of social life, whereas Brooks believed that it would be the fulfillment of our national promise. We shall later see that Brooks was not alone in his conviction. By the standards of the thirties, Brooks's investment in socialism throughout his career might seem tepid and sentimental. For a time, especially during the early thirties, being a socialist was considered by others on the Left as little different from being a registered Republican. Brooks placed so much emphasis upon the promise of individual fulfillment implicit in socialism that its collective dimension rarely emerged with any clarity in his various publications. At a time when many of his contemporaries were preoccupied by the need to imagine solutions to the immediate social crisis, Brooks was immersing himself in the New England of the previous century; *The Flowering of New England* probably contains his closest approximation to a society that afforded its members the greatest chance for decent lives and personal fulfillment. Certainly, Brooks had little of the political fervor so characteristic of a Mike Gold or James T. Farrell, and he seems to have participated very little in the sectarian disputes that were so characteristic of the Left in these years.

In the end, as we know, Brooks's political hopes, like those of his more militant contemporaries, were disappointed. That disappointment, as I shall try to show in the final chapter, has proven to be even more consequential to subsequent American literature than the initial, bright hopes. In the forties and fifties, writers often took the collapse of the millennial aspirations common in the thirties as proof that all such aspirations are inherently misplaced. American literary modernism did not expire after World War II, but this intensely political variant of it certainly did, and its demise served in part to redirect energies toward other variants. Some chastened American intellectuals were now prepared to lend credence to Eliot's sense of human depravity; others would find new virtues in Stevens's less overtly political faith in the capacities of the imagination, the final, abstract source of the hope Brooks had seen on all sides during the halycon days before World War I.

2

WILLA CATHER AND THE LIMITS OF MEMORY

> If I can only hold to the memory
> I can bear any future. But I must find out
> The truth about the past, for the sake of the memory.
>
> Eliot, *Cocktail Party* 47

WILLA CATHER IS a transitional figure. Although she lived until 1947, and although she published her strongest and most characteristic fiction in the teens and twenties, when the ferment of American literary modernism was most intense, she has rarely been accorded a place in our literature comparable to those won by Eliot, Hemingway, Stevens, and Faulkner. Her biographer James Woodress believes that her continuing prominence "as one of the most significant American novelists" is assured (xiii); but Phyllis Rose is understandably less sanguine, and feels it necessary to mount a case in her behalf. The sheer accessibility of her fiction might seem to tell against her; her readers need not struggle with conspicuous difficulties when reading Cather's fiction, and they rarely encounter evidence of Cather's struggles in composing it. When making a gift of Cather's final novel to a friend, Wallace Stevens found it necessary to insist upon her artistry: "Miss Cather is rather a specialty. You may not like the book; moreover, you may think she is more or less formless. Nevertheless, we have nothing better than she is. She takes so much pains to conceal her sophistication that it is easy to miss her quality" (*Letters* 381).

Sexual politics has doubtless played a role in relegating Cather to a lesser place in American literature than the more overtly adventurous men and women who were writing in the first decades of the century. At the same time, I would insist that the accidents of birth

and the fact that she was somewhat older than Eliot and other celebrated literary modernists are at least equally important to any assessment of the reasons for her partial eclipse. Her early ambitions
and tastes were formed earlier, in the 1880s and 1890s, and her early
poetry and fiction tinkle with the sentiments and diction that Eliot
and others would almost from the first work so hard to replace. This
is from the revised version of her poem "Aftermath," as it appeared
in *April Twilights:*

> Can'st thou conjure a vanished morn of spring,
>   Or bid the ashes of the sunset glow
> Again to redness? Are we strong to wring
>   From trodden grapes the juice drunk long ago?
> . . . .
>   Thou art more lost to me than they who dwell
> In Egypt's sepulchres, long ago fled;
>   And would I touch—Ah me! I might as well
> Covet the gold of Helen's vanished head,
>   or kiss back Cleopatra from the dead! (39)

The archaic diction, classical allusions, and cultivated sense of futility in these early lines scarcely suggest the direct force of Cather's
mature fiction. She would learn that she could indeed conjure in her
writing "a vanished morn of spring," but to accomplish such resto-
rations she would need to set aside the mannerisms of such verse
and to fashion other literary tools.

In many respects Cather's anomalous status among American literary modernists is comparable to that of Robert Frost, her near
contemporary. Both produced their earliest works in the 1890s
but then underwent long and difficult apprenticeships before their
stronger and more characteristic work found an appreciative audience in the teens. Frost was forty before a small London publisher
issued *North of Boston,* his first volume, in 1914; Cather was thirty
when her only volume of poetry was published in 1903, and herself
nearing forty when her first novel, *Alexander's Bridge,* appeared in
1912. Both came to be identified by the reading public with their
native regions, and in both cases this identification seemed to place
them nearer the earlier local colorists than to the militantly international aspirations of others who were beginning their literary careers in the teens. Neither was overtly experimental, and the work of

both was thus comparably accessible. This accessibility itself seemed to separate them from seemingly more demanding writers of the time. They can seem complacent, especially at a time when American literary modernism seems synonymous with difficulty and when writers and critics are making a fetish of the experimental. Frost was more effective managing his literary career than he was managing his series of New England farms; and as a result, critics have long had to contend with his prominence in their accounts of American literary modernism. He has consistently had his admirers, but it was perhaps not until the publication of Richard Poirier's *Robert Frost: The Work of Knowing* in 1977 that Frost has been recognized as not only an older contemporary of Eliot and Pound but also as their equal in the making of American literary modernism.

Willa Cather awaits her Poirier. Several appreciative and insightful studies of her work have been published in recent years, but it must be said that none has proven able to rescue her from her earlier popularity. She seems to be so decisively fixed on the margins of American literary modernism that I doubt that any study devoted exclusively to her work could now win sufficient readers and her a more central place. In this chapter I would like to join Phyllis Rose in arguing that Cather belongs in the company of other, acknowledged makers of American literary modernism. I shall concentrate on her strongest and most representative fiction. In *Willa Cather: The Emerging Voice,* Sharon O'Brien has admirably documented the long and uncertain process through which Cather acquired first her literary ambitions and then the confidence to write in what we now recognize as her characteristic manner. I want to insist that this manner represents a variant of American literary modernism.

I

Cather would subsequently consider *O Pioneers!* her first novel. In "My First Novels (There Were Two)," she suggests that she had used "interesting material" and a "conventional pattern" (91) when composing *Alexander's Bridge,* much as she had earlier used worn "poetic" diction and themes in her poetry. When writing *O Pioneers!* the following year, by way of contrast, she risked drawing upon memories of her earlier years in Nebraska, material that might interest few, and she felt able to cast it in the loose, episodic structure that would become characteristic of her later fiction. She did not disown *Alexander's Bridge* completely, as she did several earlier stories she refused to republish, but she did relegate it to the third volume of the Autograph and Library collected editions of her work published between 1937 and 1941. *O Pioneers!*, the first of Cather's extended fictions to evoke her Nebraska years, would be the first volume in these editions, as if it were the effective beginning of her literary career.

The landscape has a special prominence in *O Pioneers!, My Ántonia,* and even *A Lost Lady.* "The great fact," declares the narrator of *O Pioneers!*, "was the land itself, which seemed to overwhelm the little beginnings of human society that struggled in its sombre wastes" (13). When Jim Burden in *My Ántonia* recalls his first impressions of his new home, he reports being overwhelmed by its size and its difference from his (and Cather's) native Virginia: "There seemed to be nothing to see; no fences, no creeks or trees, no hills or fields. If there was a road, I could not make it out in the faint starlight. There was nothing but land: not a country at all, but the material out of which countries are made. . . . Between that earth and that sky I felt erased, blotted out" (7–8). Both *O Pioneers!* and *My Ántonia* are in part about the struggle to transform this initially unpromising land into a country. The first section of *O Pioneers!*, "The Wild Land," depicts the Bergson family early in this process; Mr. Bergson dies and his sons want to relinquish their homestead for more promising land, but Alexandra convinces them again and again to persevere in their efforts. The second section, "Neighbouring Fields," is set sixteen years later, at a time when Alexandra's earlier convictions have borne fruit. Survival is no longer an issue for the Bergsons; instead, they must now find a way to live with their new prosperity. In *My Ántonia*, Jim Burden is spared this harsh, early phase of homesteading, since his grandparents had established themselves before his arrival. He is able to watch in relative comfort as Ántonia's family struggles to establish itself, a struggle that drives Mr. Shimerda to commit suicide and threatens for a time to transform the young Ántonia into little more than a farm animal.

Although both *O Pioneers!* and *My Ántonia* evoke the harshness of life for the early settlers, they initiate a process continued in *A Lost Lady* whereby the focus gradually shifts to later stages in the history of this new land. A comparison of the opening paragraphs of *O Pioneers!* and *A Lost Lady* suggests this change. Both novels begin by evoking a small town set upon the landscape. *O Pioneers!* begins with these sentences: "One January day, thirty years ago, the little town of Hanover, anchored on a windy Nebraska tableland, was trying not to be blown away. . . . The dwelling-houses were set about haphazard on the tough prairie sod; some of them looked as if they had been moved in overnight, and others as if they were straying off by themselves, headed straight for the open plain. None of them had any appearance of permanence, and the howling wind blew under them as well as over them" (3). Published ten years later, in 1923, the opening sentence of *A Lost Lady* evokes another Midwestern town, but it is an altogether more settled and peopled place: "Thirty or forty years ago, in one of those grey towns along the Burlington railroad, which are so much greyer today than they were then, there was a house well known from Omaha to Denver for its hospitality and for a certain charm of atmosphere" (3). Unlike Hanover in *O Pioneers!*, Sweet Water has achieved a degree of permanence; if it has already entered a period of decline, it has at least survived the harsh natural conditions of an earlier time. The first paragraph of *A Lost Lady* continues by introducing the many people to whom a house in Sweet Water was well known, thereby suggesting that it was intimately connected with the larger social world. By contrast, Hanover seems not only temporary but isolated. Finally, even the season is more propitious—it is summer, not the January of *O Pioneers!* Midway between these extremes stands *My Ántonia*. It begins with Jim Burden's account of his introduction to Nebraska farm life, and the experiences of the Shimerdas resemble those of the Bergsons in *O Pioneers!* But when Burden moves to nearby Black Hawk with his grandparents, his narrative becomes more concerned with the social opportunities available in such small towns than with the primary struggles continuing on the surrounding farms. After living in town to supplement her family's income, Ántonia herself famously returns to a farm; but Burden goes first to Lincoln and then to the great world beyond, in the manner of Niel Herbert and Marian Forrester in *A Lost Lady*. If Cather consistently celebrates life in early Nebraska in these novels—and especially the character of the individuals, her pioneers, who had the vision and courage to make lives there—her focus gradually shifts from the farms to the small towns, from the era of first rural settlers to the slightly later time of their successors living in nearby small towns.

This change is accompanied by a change in the females who are celebrated as figures of this life. Alexandra Bergson and Ántonia Shimerda are themselves pioneers. Alexandra's vision and tenacity are responsible for the success that she and her brothers eventually enjoy; if in the end she becomes something of a matriarch in a thriving farming community and is able to employ others to perform the many chores around a large farm, it is clearly implied that she had earlier performed them herself during the sixteen years that lapse between the first and second sections of the novel. Cather allows Ántonia's early ordeals to be more evident to readers of *My Ántonia,* who might thus join her young admirer, Jim Burden, in worrying that she is destined to be brutalized by life. Her life proves difficult, but in the end she too triumphs; if she is never as well off as Alexandra Bergson, she nonetheless stands at the center of a large and satisfied family. For Burden and Cather, the mature Ántonia eventually figures as the very emblem of Nebraska life: "She was a battered woman now, not a lovely girl; but she still had that something which fires the imagination, could still stop one's breath for a moment by a look or gesture that somehow revealed the meaning in common things. . . . She was a rich mine of life, like the founders of early races" (353).

Marian Forrester in *A Lost Lady* could scarcely be more different. She plays a role in Niel Herbert's mental life comparable to that played by Ántonia in Jim Burden's, but the reasons for her prominence are distinct. In this novel her husband, Captain Forrester, fills the role of revered pioneer, albeit as a builder of railroads rather than as a settler, and his active part in the settlement of the West is already over before the novel begins. Marian Forrester is more an emblem of the richness yielded by earlier efforts than a participant in them. The Forresters have no children, and it is impossible to imagine Mrs. Forrester doing farm work with either the satisfaction or the success of an Alexandra or Ántonia. As the Captain declines and eventually dies, her efforts to secure other financial means and ultimately to flee Sweet Water become increasingly frantic. She cannot survive in this small, relatively isolated town, much less on one of the neighboring farms. She is a creature of the wider world, of the resorts to which she and her husband at one time retired, and she is brought to this small town in the same manner and for similar purposes as the heavy furniture in their home. Without minimizing the satisfaction they provide one another, it seems possible to see Marian Forrester as foremost among her husband's rewards for having been a successful pioneer. For the young Niel Herbert, similarly stranded for a time in Sweet Water, she seems to represent both the fulfillment of an earlier era and the possibilities available in the wide world at the terminus of the Burlington railroad.

Although Marian Forrester's association with the accomplishments of the pioneers is decidedly different from Alexandra Bergson's and Ántonia Shimerda's, *A Lost Lady* focuses the particular concerns that transverse these three novels set in the Nebraska of Cather's childhood. *A Lost Lady* is written in the third person, but the narrative views matters most often from the vantage of Niel Herbert, who counts himself as fortunate for having been able to catch the last glimmerings of a heroic period before its decline:

> He had seen the end of an era, the sunset of the pioneer. He had come upon it when already its glory was nearly spent. . . . This was the very end of the road-making West; the men who had put plains and mountains under the iron harness were old; some were poor, and even the successful ones were hunting for rest and a brief reprieve from death. It was already gone, that age; nothing could ever bring it back. The taste and smell and song of it, the visions those men had seen in the air and followed,—these he had caught in a kind of afterglow in their own faces,—and this would always be his. (167–68)

Herbert's memories, like the novel itself, are structured by a series of stark polarities—old and new, honor and self-interest, courtly and bourgeois. The dramatic focus of the novel concerns what happens when Marian Forrester, a creature of the old order, is suddenly deprived of its resources and must make her way through a world now ruled on other terms.

It is the world of Captain Forrester that is lost in the course of the novel. Having earlier been instrumental in building the railroads that opened the West, the Captain retires to the small, then-prosperous town of Sweet Water. A series of illnesses eventually makes it impossible for the Captain to travel, thereby stranding his younger wife in a town increasingly showing signs of becoming a neglected backwater. Financial reversals also finally reach the Forresters. The Captain had invested heavily in a Denver bank that fails. His name among its directors had originally attracted deposits, for "it was the name which promised security and fair treatment to his old workmen and their friends" (85). When the time comes to settle accounts, the other directors, "promising young business men with many irons in the fire," refuse to take the losses themselves, arguing that they should be shared with the depositors.[1] Rather than having their trust in him abused, the Captain strips himself of money so that the deposits can be fully honored. As Judge Pommeroy, Niel's guardian and the Captain's friend, explains: "That was what a man of honor was bound to do. . . . With five of the directors backing down, he had either to lose his name or save it. The depositors had put their savings into that bank because Captain Forrester was president. To those men with no capital but their back and their two hands, his name meant safety" (86). In other words, Captain Forrester is brought low by the passage of time; as his physical condition deteriorates, a change in mores strips him of his financial well-being. The novel clearly implies that had this episode occurred earlier, or had the other directors been Forrester's contemporaries rather than "young business men," the Captain's actions would not have seemed anomalous, nor would they have been so singularly self-destructive.

Just as Captain Forrester's house becomes the property of Ivy Peters after the former's death, Peters himself is emblematic of the crass ascending world. Peters is an instance of a type in Cather's fiction; other avatars include Alexandra's brothers, Lou and Oscar Bergson in *O Pioneers!*, Wick Cutter in *My Ántonia*, and the Captain's young associates in Denver. Like Frank Shabata in *O Pioneers!*, whose accumulating resentments lead finally to the murders of his wife and Alexandra's brother Emil, these characters are motivated at bottom by *ressentiment:* "At the bottom of his heart Frank knew well enough that if he could once give up his grudge, his wife would come back to him. But he could never in the world do that. The grudge was fundamental. Perhaps he could not have given it up if he had tried. Perhaps he got more satisfaction out of feeling himself abused than he would have got out of being loved" (187). Niel Herbert speculates that once the Forrester place comes within his control Ivy Peters drained their marsh as much to assert his "power over the people who had loved those unproductive meadows" (102) as to turn a profit from them. Niel believes that Peters enjoys spiting others, that he presumes familiarity with the newly vulnerable Forresters as a way of compensating himself for earlier having been forced to feel inferior to them. Peters is fundamentally meanspirited; he resents the cultural authority that the Forresters seem to embody and takes pleasure in its increasing vulnerability.

Like his author, Niel Herbert has an instinctive revulsion for all that Peters represents, and he cannot help regretting the impotence of Captain Forrester and the old order he represents before the growing power of the new:

> The Old West had been settled by dreamers, great-hearted adventurers who were unpractical to the point of magnificence; a courteous brotherhood, strong in attack but weak in defence, who could conquer but could not hold. Now all the vast territory they had won was to be at the mercy of men like Ivy Peters, who had never dared anything, never risked anything. They would drink up the mirage, dispel the morning freshness, root out the great brooding spirit of freedom, the generous, easy life of the great landholders. The space, the colour, the princely carelessness of the pioneer they would destroy and cut up into profitable bits, as the match factory splinters the primeval forest. All the way from the Missouri to the mountains this generation of shrewd young men, trained to petty economies by hard times, would do exactly what Ivy Peters had done when he drained the Forrester marsh.[2] (102)

The terms in which this passage, representative of many others in *A Lost Lady*, casts this historical devolution should give one pause. Obviously Cather, like the American literary modernists generally, thinks the situation she regrets is the product of historical developments. Cather is clearly distressed by the tendencies of contemporary social life, seeing in them a diminishment of the satisfactions life can afford. It is also clear that she thinks the waning social order had afforded a quality of life that could not be duplicated by the ascending social arrangements. I take it that this combination of beliefs accounts in large part for the fond nostalgia that suffuses the texture of this fine novel. What brings me up short, however, are the terms in which Cather evokes the old order, which, we must recall, is that of the West during the latter part of the nineteenth century: the pioneers were "dreamers, great-hearted adventurers," "a courteous brotherhood," and their life was "the generous, easy life of the great land-holders." Captain Forrester, a former railroad man, is consistently rendered in terms that make him seem nothing less than aristocratic.

I submit that there is something inappropriate, something excessive about these characterizations of life in the Old West; as Dorothy Van Ghent has written, in this passage a reader can "feel here the hollow echoes of a prose beating out a thesis" (29). These phrases surely do not comport with my understanding of either social arrangements or the general tenor of life at that time and place; and since Cather elsewhere recorded the difficulties and even terrors experienced by early settlers, we cannot attribute this excessiveness to mere ignorance. Nor can we dismiss this inconsistency by attributing it exclusively to Niel Herbert, thereby converting it into further evidence of Cather's ironic indictment of his infatuation with the Forresters. Cather certainly mocks Herbert's excessive response to learning about Mrs. Forrester's affair with Frank Ellinger and his inability to understand her determination to continue living after her husband's death; but she shares his admiration for the Forresters, and expresses it in terms that carry over from *O Pioneers!*, *My Ántonia*, and other works where the possibility of irony is not at issue. I have come to take the inflated rhetoric in these descriptions as a measure of Cather's disenchantment with American society as it existed in the first years of the twentieth century. It is as if the degree of her disenchantment caused her, by some rule of compensation, to idealize the preceding age, the era of her own Nebraska childhood, the first alternative to the present scene that came to mind. Thus under the pressure of her condemnation of the present, the physical and social harshness of the earlier period is overridden in the service of her need to find relief.

As is the case with the other American literary modernists, Cather rejects the social order that assures the triumph of the bourgeoisie. Life in the new century seems somehow smaller, social contacts both more frequent and more abrasive. Cather holds out against this settling order a notion of what has been called the "heroic" phase of the bourgeoisie, the phase in which it was the ascending class, the period in which it busied itself acquiring the goods and capital that eventually led to its triumph. That is, she holds out a period during which great deeds seemed possible—the settling of the frontier, the building of the railroads—against one that seems to settle for "petty economies." As if that contrast were not enough, however, she goes on to clothe the earlier period in terms suggestive of feudal orders, thereby making the differences more striking. Among the deficiencies entailed by such descriptions, it seems to me that one of the most dire is the ascription to this rising class of qualities suggestive of a settled, stable social order, as if the early ranchers of the West were in all respects the equivalents of landed gentry in other countries and other times. Such descriptions altogether miss the frenzy of activity characteristic of the period, and therefore they fail to suggest the extent to which the accomplishments of men like Captain Forrester prepared the way for the new social order Cather so regrets (Schwartz).

The medieval hue in which Cather sees the previous era provides the further office of lending to the depiction not only a sense of stability but also the terms in which a viable community could be maintained. Those terms, however, are decidedly not egalitarian; they are paternalistic. If Captain Forrester is aristocratic in his virtues, so is he in his dealings with others. His generosity toward his former workers upon the collapse of the Denver bank is dictated by noblesse oblige. His sense of justice cannot be gainsaid; but the Forresters' aloofness in dealings with other residents of Sweet Water must also be acknowledged. Cather's initial description of two of Niel's contemporaries most clearly brings out this sense of social distance: "The Blum brothers regarded [Mrs. Forrester] humbly from under their pale, chewed-off hair, as one of the rich and great of the world. *They realized, more than their companions, that such a fortunate and privileged class was an axiomatic fact in the social order*" (14; my emphasis). When, many years later, Adolph Blum chances to witness Mrs. Forrester's assignation with Frank Ellinger, he does not reveal her secret; his mind, we are told, is "feudal" (63), and he accepts without question her right to do what she pleases. Obviously, then, we do not have to do here with an unfettered individualism that renders community impossible. However, Cather can seemingly imagine the possibility of community only by relegating masses of people to marginal classes and by falsifying actual historical conditions. We must be touching here on needs that are deeply frustrated, eager for resolution at any cost.

Niel Herbert does not believe that this change can be reversed and that men like Captain Forrester can be restored to their former prominence—"It was already gone, that age; nothing could ever bring it back" (168). At the same time, his aversion to Ivy Peters and all that he represents remains strong and keeps him from emulating his practices. I take it that Judge Pommeroy speaks for Cather when he advises his nephew on the choice of a career: "Son, I'm glad you want to be an architect. I can't see any honourable career for a lawyer, in this new business world that's coming up. Leave the law to boys like Ivy Peters, and get into some clean profession" (88).[3] We don't learn much about Niel's subsequent life and thus don't know whether he takes Judge Pommeroy's advice, but it is clear that the intervening years have done little to reconcile him with the terms of life represented by Peters. Instead, he draws strength from his memories of an earlier and better era. Years later, when "he was dull, dull and tired of everything, he used to think that if he could hear that long-lost lady laugh again, he could be gay" (67). He is of course deeply disappointed in her when their ways part, and his disillusionment is part of his more general dismay at the tenor of the world he must now inhabit: "But eventually . . . Daniel Forrester's wife returned to him, a bright, impersonal memory. He came to be very glad that he had known her, and that she had had a hand in breaking him in to life. He has known pretty women and clever ones since then,—but never one like her, as she was in her best days" (170).

In the final scene of *A Lost Lady,* set many years later, a chance encounter enables Niel to learn about Marian Forrester's life after leaving Sweet Water. He encounters Ed Elliott, a boyhood friend, in a Chicago hotel. Elliott had met her in Buenos Aires and, remembering Niel's special relationship with her, wants to tell him about her later life. She had married again, this time to a wealthy Englishman living in Argentina; they lived on a large ranch but regularly traveled to Buenos Aires on their private railroad car. Mrs. Forrester, in other words, had been restored to the conditions in which Niel first knew her. The location of her new life is critical; that her restoration occurs in Argentina rather than California, Chicago, or elsewhere in the new social world tells us something about the specific place she occupies in the imaginations of Niel Herbert and Willa Cather. The era of the pioneers might have passed in Nebraska, but Marian Forrester had made another life for herself on a new frontier in South America. She could be an adornment of that frontier, just as she had earlier adorned Sweet Water, because her second husband's wealth enables her to maintain commerce with the broader world, just as Captain Forrester's success had initially enabled them to sustain contacts with other members of what Cather renders as a pioneer aristocracy. The novel concludes with Elliott's and Herbert's expressions of pleasure at Marian Forrester's restoration.

We have seen that Niel Herbert draws upon his memories of the Forresters for sustenance as he makes his way in a world now presided over by people like Ivy Peters. Behind him is Willa Cather, and *A Lost Lady* is her elegy for that waning world, its mores and accomplishments. She seemingly shares Niel's aversion to contemporary life and, like him, draws comfort from memories of what she takes to have been a better time. When she was writing *A Lost Lady,* as when writing her other Nebraska novels and stories, Cather self-consciously evoked figures from her past, giving them in her fiction a status similar to what they held in her mental life. The figure of Marian Forrester, for instance, was based upon Mrs. Silas Garber, "the wife of the former governor of Nebraska and the leading lady of the town when Cather was growing up" (Woodress 340). As she explained in an interview with Flora Merrill: "*A Lost Lady* was a woman I loved very much in my childhood. . . . A character study of Mrs. Forrester would have been very, very different. I wasn't interested in her character when I was little, but in her lovely hair and her laugh which made me happy clear down to my toes. . . . The question was, by what medium could I present her most vividly, and that, of course, meant the most truly" (Merrill 77). As this passage makes clear, Cather was typically less interested in understanding such figures from her past than in reproducing in her fiction their effect upon her impressionable young mind. The stature that such figures possess in her fiction thus partially derives from the vantage from which the young Cather viewed them. Even if the culture were not taking a turn for the worse, it would have been difficult for people to measure up to these early impressions, or for those Cather encounters in later life to make a comparable impression on her. Be that as it may, Cather obviously shared Niel Herbert's conviction that life had been diminished when people like Ivy Peters replaced those like the Forresters. Having been drawn from her own recollections, her strongest and most characteristic fiction became a celebration of a passing way of life.

I believe that this conflict between declining and ascending ways of life is at the center of *O Pioneers!* and *My Ántonia* as well as *A Lost Lady*. The conflict is strictly implicit in the former. In *O Pioneers!* Alexandra's small-minded brothers are at most an annoyance, and not, like Ivy Peters, the agents of dramatic conflict; the novel is more concerned to celebrate the domestication of the land achieved by Alexandra and other immigrant settlers. However, even at the time of its publication in 1913, much less today, Cather's depiction of Alexandra served to remind readers how much their own lives were at variance from that won by Alexandra. The novel was striking precisely because the opportunities and values it celebrated already occupied such diminished places in society as a whole. The conflict between declining and ascending ways of life thus occurs largely outside the novel proper, between its fictional world and that occupied by its readers, who are invited by it to contemplate what had already been lost.

This conflict is internalized in *My Ántonia* by the intervention of Jim Burden. The narrator encounters Burden on a train crossing the plains. Both now live in New York, where he "is a legal counsel for one of the great Western railways" (x). Although Burden has made a life for himself elsewhere, he is something of a latter-day Captain Forrester: "He loves with a personal passion the great country through which his railway runs and branches. His faith in it and his knowledge of it have played an important part in its development" (x). The narrator implies that Burden's personal life has been less successful; at any rate, she does not care for his wife, who seems exclusively a creature of affluent eastern society. As the narrator and Burden cross the landscape of their childhood, their conversation "kept returning to a central figure, a Bohemian girl whom we had known long ago. More than any other person we remembered, this girl seemed to mean to us the country, the conditions, the whole adventure of our childhood" (x). Burden had recently sought a reunion with this person, and has subsequently been amusing him-

self by writing his recollections of her. The body of the novel purports to be Burden's effort. Burden concludes his long and loving
narrative by recounting his reunion with Ántonia after the lapse of
twenty years. He suspects that his fears that she might be changed
kept him away: "Perhaps it was cowardice that kept me away so long.
. . . I did not want to find her aged and broken; I really dreaded it.
In the course of twenty crowded years one parts with many illusions. I did not wish to lose the early ones. Some memories are re-
alities, and are better than anything that can ever happen to one
again" (327–28). Terence Martin suggests that Burden's reunion
with Ántonia serves to reconcile him to his present life (311). I believe that this overstates matters. Burden is obviously buoyed by his
visit with Ántonia and by the recognition of how she has fulfilled
his fondest expectations. However, he remains a character who has
parted with "many illusions." Burden is too little developed as a
character in *My Ántonia* to construe his present situation with much
confidence, but I have come to read him through Cather's later and
fuller characterization of Niel Herbert. That is, I understand him as
someone whose memories do not so much reconcile him with the
present as provide him with a means to endure it. His reunion with
Ántonia is thus destined to become another of those cherished
memories that sustain him through relations with others, including
his wife, whose way of life is so very different from Ántonia's. These
memories are compensations for a present that cannot provide either
Burden or the narrator with comparable satisfactions.

The latter thus both celebrate Ántonia's fecundity in contrast
with their own lives in another place. The fact that she is their contemporary suggests that what is at issue is the choice of a way of
life. They could and did choose a different course than Ántonia, and
their memories of her and all that she embodies at once suggest their
misgivings about their choice and sustain them in it. It is as if they
take comfort in the thought that the faith is being sustained elsewhere. In *A Lost Lady* Cather simultaneously relocates this choice
away from farm life and transforms it into a generational matter.[4]
These changes make plausible Niel's conviction that the era of the
pioneers is past. In *O Pioneers!* and *My Ántonia* Cather directly depicts the triumphs of the women who embody pioneer values; in *A
Lost Lady*, the Forresters are already in retirement when the novel
begins. Niel's reverence for the Captain rests on what the latter had

already accomplished, and he cannot locate anyone in his own generation who possesses comparable vision or comparable opportunities. Ivy Peters seems to represent Niel's own generation as thoroughly as Captain Forrester represented his own. If Niel is destined to live in meaner times, he considers himself fortunate to have at least glimpsed an other and better way of life in its decline; and he is determined to preserve and take comfort from his memories: "He had seen the end of an era, the sunset of the pioneer. . . . The taste and smell and song of it, the visions those men had seen in the air and followed,—those he had caught in a kind of after-glow in their own faces,—and this would always be his" (167–68). *A Lost Lady* thus reveals the degree to which memories of another era serve as an alternative to current ways of life throughout Cather's Nebraska novels.

II

In their celebrations of earlier times and mores, these novels are indictments of the way life had come to be lived in the first decades of the twentieth century. When Cather compares past and present, the latter is always found wanting. In her imagination, the open plains had at one time promised equally open opportunities for the people who had the vision and perseverance to make lives there. And she celebrates in her fiction the people who, in Jim Burden's terms, were responsible for transforming that land into a country, both farmers like Alexandra Bergson and railroad builders like Captain Forrester. In her fiction, the era of initial settlement coincides with the time of Cather's own childhood; the world and its inhabitants seemed to diminish as she aged. She nowhere suggests explicit reasons for this decline; she simply accepts it as a regrettable historical fact. Her recognition that life had been and so could be grander keeps her from acceding to contemporary conditions. Like Niel Herbert in *A Lost Lady,* she believes that this decline is irreversible, so she does not trouble herself or others by agitating for resistance against it. Instead, and rather than settling for the meager fare offered by the social conditions of her own day, in her fiction she recalls a past that never quite existed, elaborates with a charge of nostalgia a world calculated to reveal at every point the inadequacies of the present.[5]

Cather's decision in the teens to make use of her memories of her Nebraska childhood obviously marks a crucial moment in her career. "When I sit down to write," she said in a 1921 interview with Latrobe Carroll, "turns of phrase I've forgotten for years come back like white ink before fire. I think that most of the basic material a writer works with is acquired before the age of fifteen" (20). Whatever the general truth of the latter proposition, Cather's eventual reliance upon memory enabled her, beginning with *O Pioneers!*, to write some of her strongest and most characteristic fiction. The materials she drew on were frequently quite specific, enabling her biographers and critics to identify individuals from her early years who later served as models for her fictional characters. In this fiction, memory serves several functions. It is, of course, a source of material for several of Cather's most successful novels and stories. Within these fictions, it also operates as a source of satisfaction for many of her characters, a means by which they reconcile themselves to their portion in life. It is in this latter capacity that Cather's reliance upon memory becomes problematic. Perhaps because she felt bereft of other resources, she consistently tries the limits of memory by asking it to serve tasks well beyond its capacities.

There are at least three ways in which memory is unequal to the uses to which Cather would put it. First, memory is inherently faulty, given to lapses and excesses alike. We have seen that in *A Lost Lady* Niel Herbert and Cather are thoroughly disenchanted with the ascending world represented by Ivy Peters. Herbert, like Cather, considers himself fortunate to have glimpsed an earlier era and is determined to remain loyal to it. Memories of the Forresters will serve to brighten otherwise dull days, days that cannot provide him with comparable satisfactions. I earlier observed that Cather's depiction of the Forresters seems oddly excessive. It makes the time of initial settlement seem itself settled. Cather's decision to depict Captain Forrester in retirement perhaps renders this depiction initially plausible; but by emphasizing his repetitiveness in establishing his character, she undercuts his credibility as a representative of the pioneers, of those who were able and willing to break settled habits in order to establish new lives on the prairie. These purported memories, in other words, seem to be constituted as much by fantasy as by Herbert's or Cather's recollections.[6] The intermittent medievalism of allusions to the "feudal" Blums and aristocratic Forresters is only among the more striking indications that these memories have been decisively crossed by fantasy. The accuracy of such memories would not be an issue were the novel not claiming that the past offered a preferable way of life. In order to sustain that claim, one must do more than express one's dismay at current conditions; one must also present a credible depiction of the past. On that score, both Herbert and Cather fail in *A Lost Lady.* As they try to clothe themselves with memories against a cold world, they increasingly turn to fantasies about the past rather than genuine memories, as though the latter alone were not sufficiently warming. Their failures make the novel suspect as the product of the historical imagination; but they perhaps also contribute to the remarkable poignancy of its depiction of individuals desperate for consolation in a world they cannot otherwise abide.

Second, even in the best circumstances memory itself can only provide solace to generations that, so to speak, experience and survive the flood. If we accept Cather's claim that life was somehow fuller during the years of her childhood, we could accept her claim that it provides her with a means to buffer the shocks of a different and harsher social world. We would then consider her fortunate for having been born where and when she was, but it is hard to see what relevance her good fortune has for others, born in other places and at other times, including ourselves, her readers now. We have lived our entire lives since the ascendancy of Ivy Peters, and thus our memories cannot contain intimations of the earlier era she cherished. It is not, in other words, memory per se that promises relief for Cather, so that any pleasant memories from childhood would suffice; it is rather the fact (or presumed fact) that her childhood coincided with the era of the pioneers that renders her childhood memories particularly valuable in later years. A scene in *Shadows on the Rock* nicely contrasts with this happy circumstance. Pierre Charron, a pioneer at another time and place, is explaining to Euclide Auclair why he sought an opportunity to violate the seclusion of *la recluse de Ville-Marie,* who at one time had seemed destined to become his wife. The weather had been unusually harsh and it made Charron "wretched to think of her walled up there." "You see," he concludes, "there are all those early memories; one cannot get another set; one has but those" (211).[7] Charron's memories are not particularly happy and thus not invariably a resource in later life;

indeed, in this instance memories of his former fondness for the recluse serve to trouble him about her current condition. This incident demonstrates Cather's awareness that each person's memories are both contingent (upon the accidents of birth and experience) and invariable. Each of us must make do with those we possess; it was by her own account simply Cather's good fortune that her memories could serve as consolations in later times of need.

It is perhaps this recognition that accounts for the initially curious phrasing in the famous concluding sentence of *My Ántonia*. For more than three hundred pages Jim Burden has been recounting memories about Ántonia, memories that stretch back to their childhood and include his recent reunion with her after a lapse of twenty years. The reader by this point appreciates the importance of Ántonia in the mental lives of Burden and the nameless narrator. The final sentence can thus come as a shock: "Whatever we had missed, we possessed together the precious, the *incommunicable* past" (372; my emphasis). In what sense is this past incommunicable? It is clearly shared by the narrator, Ántonia, and Burden; and the latter has just devoted an entire novel to communicating to others, his readers, the meaning and continuing importance of this past in his current life. It is tempting to consider this term simply a rhetorical gesture at closure, or perhaps as a symptom of the lingering influence of Cather's early extremely romantic conception of art. However, I have come to read this passage in a way consistent with Charron's recognition. When Burden terms the past "incommunicable," he seems to be acknowledging that he cannot make that past the property of his readers, who have their own lives and memories and who, like Pierre Charron, "cannot get another set" of the latter. We can never possess the past that Burden relates in a way comparable to his own possession of it: we can know about it, can perhaps appreciate his reverence for it, but can never possess it in the manner we possess memories from our childhood (cf. Michaels 80). If *My Ántonia* is in some respects a celebration of the efficacy of memory, it finally also acknowledges its limits, limits that derive in part from the contingency of life and thus from the limited stock of memories any of us can later draw upon.

Finally, it must be observed that memory is a curious strategy for overcoming social estrangement. As Ivy Peters replaces Captain Forrester, Niel Herbert especially regrets a certain coarsening of social life. The dinner parties the two men preside over are obviously calculated to draw our attention to this consequence of the transition. It is difficult to see, however, how memory could rectify this regrettable fact. Niel's pleasant memories of earlier dinners at the Forresters' certainly do nothing to mitigate his dismay when he later joins Peters and others as Mrs. Forrester's guests; quite the contrary, the contrast serves chiefly to exaggerate his emotional distance from the others. The turn to memory usually functions in this way; as an individual falls back upon remembrances, he or she is increasingly distanced from immediate friends and neighbors. Memory isolates people; it does not bring them together. Thus it is no accident that we know so little about the subsequent lives of Cather's memory-artists, Niel Herbert and Jim Burden. *Lucy Gayheart* is in other respects a less successful novel, but at least in the final chapters it yields a fuller sense of how Harry Gordon's memories of Lucy became accommodated within his subsequent life. We know little about Herbert and Burden apart from the experiences that are the immediate occasion for *A Lost Lady* and *My Ántonia*. This lack of information is obviously a consequence of the narrative strategies used by Cather in these novels, and it is consistent with other novels written in this manner. In both novels there is the clear suggestion that their subsequent lives prove to be less than satisfying, that nothing and no one later measured up to the significant personages they had had the good fortune to know when they were young. They compensate for these later deprivations by recalling earlier and more rewarding encounters. When individuals routinely avail themselves of memories, however, they increase the distance between themselves and their immediate surroundings; they thereby contribute to the presumed thinness of the latter, and their inattentiveness makes it less likely that they will either find comparable resources to hand or be available for engagement with others—the individual preoccupied by reminiscences is scarcely a source of inspiration to his or her companions. The recourse to past satisfactions might be an explicable mental stratagem in these circumstances, but in the long run it seems more likely to compound rather than relieve the conditions it would redress.

In certain critical respects, therefore, memory is simply unable to perform all that Cather asks of it. She resorts to it in response to what she took to be a decline in social mores and the ways we live.

She apparently believed that during her childhood, American life, at least along the frontier, provided greater opportunities than it later would and that it had been peopled by individuals like Alexandra Bergson and Captain Forrester, who were especially able to appreciate and take advantage of such opportunities. The world that these pioneers labored to create seems meaner, and Cather considers the loss irreversible. If it seems to her futile to resist or to attempt reversing this decline, she would nonetheless call upon her memories of an earlier and better era as a means of cushioning her life in a world she otherwise regrets. As we shall see in the following chapter, Cather's reliance upon memory partially aligns her with other American literary modernists who located alternatives to regrettable contemporary conditions in the past. Many of the others, however, in one way or another identified that past as "tradition" and claimed that by stripping itself of traditional mores and institutions the culture had lost its way. "Tradition" can be defined in many ways, but most definitions make it clearly a cultural and thus a shared property, as distinct from memory, which is finally a personal matter. Although tradition and memory both point to the past, the fact that the former possesses a social dimension makes any claim about its absence more likely to produce an active call for its restoration. Cather, for instance, obviously shares with the Southern Agrarians an uncommon respect for the way of life presumably available on small farms. Unlike them, however, she is content to revere memories of that life, and she joins in no public agitation for its restoration. One might regret the cultural and political programs that result from such calls and doubt their viability, but at least they exist, and the cultural disquiet they represent does not so quickly run to the sort of quietism that is finally characteristic of Cather whenever she considers the apparent course of events. Cather's recourse to memory, in other words, seems destined to ensure that she will increasingly need to call upon its consolations, since she apparently believes that she has no recourse other than to stand by and let the cultural tendencies she regrets work their mischief unimpeded.

Nonetheless, there can be little doubt that Cather's decision in the early teens to draw inspiration from memories of her Nebraska childhood ultimately produced some of her strongest and most representative fiction. These memories gave her not only the material for some remarkable novels and stories, but they yielded as well the elegiac tone and episodic structure that became so characteristic of her subsequent fiction. Her decision, in short, was immensely productive. At the same time, we must acknowledge that this productiveness has limits that Cather herself did not consistently recognize, perhaps just because it otherwise yielded so much to her. Cather's memories provided her at once with a critique of and an alternate to modern American life; few others have been or remain so fortunate in their own experiences, and thus few others can directly profit by her example.

III

Since the workings of memory play a prominent role in the work of other American literary modernists, it might be helpful in appreciating its unique place in Cather's fiction to compare briefly its operations in the fiction of two somewhat younger contemporaries. Maxwell Geismar was among the first critics to remark on certain similarities between Cather and F. Scott Fitzgerald (166); the latter not only admired Cather, but at one time feared that he had inadvertently plagiarized from her. Among American literary modernists, memory is perhaps most prominent and most problematic in the fiction of William Faulkner. My purpose in the following pages is not to undertake a comprehensive account of the various accomplishments of these writers; I invoke them solely for the purpose of identifying through comparison the unique fictional uses to which Cather put memory.

In early 1925, as he was awaiting the publication of *The Great Gatsby,* F. Scott Fitzgerald wrote Cather expressing concern that she or others might construe a passage in his forthcoming novel as an instance of plagiarism. The passage in question occurs early in the novel, and it concerns the unusual promise that people heard in Daisy Buchanan's voice. Fitzgerald had come to recognize that this passage resembles one in *A Lost Lady,* which he had read with admiration, where Niel Herbert retrospectively contemplates Marian Forrester's eyes, which "seemed to promise a wild delight that he has not found in life" (172). In his letter to Cather, Fitzgerald explains that he had written his own passage prior to reading *A Lost Lady:* "Well, a month or two before I had written into my own book a parallel and almost similar idea in the description of a woman's charm—an idea that I'd had for several years. Now my own expression of this was neither so clear, nor so beautiful, nor so moving as yours but the essential similarity was undoubtedly there" (qtd. in Bruccoli 171–72). Cather replied in April, saying that she enjoyed reading *Gatsby* and attributed any similarities between the passages in question not to undue influence but to their efforts to endow these characters with similar qualities.

Fitzgerald was perhaps unusually sensitive to the appearance of plagiarism in these parallels because he was aware of how deeply his forthcoming novel was otherwise indebted to the example of Cather. Tom Quirk has written the most comprehensive and compelling analysis of this indebtedness. Cather's use of Jim Burden in *My Ántonia* and Niel Herbert in *A Lost Lady* might have initially suggested to Fitzgerald the advantages of using Nick Carraway as the narrator of his own manuscript. Quirk also suggests that Cather's early story "Paul's Case" and, more surprisingly, *Alexander's Bridge* might have influenced Fitzgerald's conceptions of *Gatsby*. The title character in the latter, like Gatsby, becomes involved in a self-destructive campaign to reclaim a lost love, an effort that partially involves the attempt to reclaim a former sense of himself. Quirk also observes that at a critical moment in *Alexander's Bridge*, a contemplative Bartley Alexander walks along a shore, while "red and green lights were blinking along the docks on the farther shore" (qtd. in Quirk 583). Quirk suggests, in other words, that Fitzgerald might have found in this passage from Cather's first novel the inspiration for what has become one of the most celebrated images in American literature—the green light on Daisy's dock, the green light toward which all Gatsby's aspirations are directed. "Gatsby believed in the green light," writes Fitzgerald in the conclusion of his novel, "the orgiastic future that year by year recedes before us" (182).

Whether or not one fully accepts Quirk's argument, there are clearly remarkable similarities of accomplishment and temperament uniting Fitzgerald and Cather. Daisy Buchanan's effect upon Gatsby resembles Marian Forrester's upon the young and impressionable Niel Herbert; differences in their ages and stations prohibit Herbert (as they don't Gatsby) from an overtly romantic involvement, but he is as intent upon preserving her image as Gatsby is in reviving his relationship with Daisy. In *A Lost Lady,* Niel Herbert simultaneously serves as the character most responsive to Marian Forrester and as the consciousness from which most of the action is observed. In *Gatsby*, Fitzgerald distributes these functions between Gatsby and Nick Carraway. As a result, the focus of Fitzgerald's novel is less upon the object that inspires Gatsby and more steadily upon the effect of that devotion. Carraway is as fascinated by Gatsby as the latter is by Daisy Buchanan; the use of Carraway thus enables Fitzgerald to make this effect the center of narrative attention, whereas the comparable center in *A Lost Lady* must be shared by Marian Forrester and Niel Herbert.

Like *My Ántonia* and *A Lost Lady*, *The Great Gatsby* is in an important way about different and conflicting ways of life. Unlike them, it is set largely in the East, and its moral norms, which are associated with the Midwest, remain largely implicit. Fitzgerald's novel thus reverses the strategy of presentation favored by Cather, who was inclined to celebrate certain waning ways of life and to allow that celebration to constitute an implicit criticism of ascending values. Cather's fiction is often least successful when it must characterize people and ways of life for whom she has little sympathy, such as Ivy Peters in *A Lost Lady*. Fitzgerald's decision to set *Gatsby* in New York is consistent with the greater allure that ascending ways of life broadly possess for him and his characters. The Buchanans, Gatsby, and Carraway are all drawn to New York; and if the lives they make there end in muddle and worse, and if in the end Carraway decides to return to the Midwest, they are clearly responsive to the promises of excitement and fulfillment seemingly made by the new era. Although Cather's Jim Burden and Niel Herbert also depart the Midwest for new lives, it is less clear why they do so; unlike Fitzgerald, Cather certainly never implies that they are positively drawn by extraordinary promises.

Gatsby himself is famously dedicated to the promise of an "orgiastic future." He understands that future as a version of the past, and believes that that future would be his if he could reclaim Daisy. When faced with Carraway's skepticism about the prospects for his success, Gatsby responds, "Can't repeat the past? . . . Why of course you can!" (111). And he spends himself in the effort. Cather's characters likewise recall objects of affection from the past, but they also believe that the past cannot be reclaimed—it can be recalled, it can be cherished as a source of continuing strength, but it cannot be restored. Cather's representative characters are thus able, as Gatsby is not, to settle for fond memories of the objects of their earlier affections.

Nick Carraway is the character in *Gatsby* who most nearly resembles counterparts in Cather's fiction. He narrates the novel from the Midwest, to which he returns in relief after Gatsby's death. Carraway's description of his native region seems calculated to mark its difference not only from the East but also from Cather's preexisting claims to this imaginative territory: "That's my Middle West—not the wheat or the prairies or the lost Swede towns, but the thrilling returning trains of my youth, and the street lamps and sleigh bells in the frosty dark and the shadows of holly wreaths thrown by lighted windows on the snow. I am part of that, a little solemn with the feel of those long winters, a little complacent from growing up in the Carraway house in a city where dwellings are still called through decades by a family's name" (177). This is the Midwest that Cather's pioneers made possible; it has already acquired a measure of apparent permanence that separates it on the one hand from the era of initial settlement and on the other from the seemingly relentless changes Carraway encountered in New York. Carraway's final allegiance to this Midwest, accordingly, contains little of Cather's reverence for her heroic pioneers. Furthermore, the narrative itself testifies to his continuing fascination with his recent experiences in New York. Carraway remains drawn to Gatsby by the enormity of the latter's aspirations, even though the latter seemingly "represented everything for which [he has] an unaffected scorn" (2). If *The Great Gatsby* resembles *My Ántonia* and *A Lost Lady* in being about a conflict between ways of life, the terms of that conflict are not quite Cather's; it also dramatizes that conflict more explicitly and especially explores the temptations posed by the ascending way of life. As *The Great Gatsby,* his other fiction, and most notoriously his life attest, Fitzgerald was responsive to those temptations in a way that Cather never was.

Memory proves to be as crucial to the well-being of Faulkner's characters as it is for Cather's. The reasons for its importance, however, are quite different. For Faulkner, the past constitutes an individual; as he explained at the University of Virginia: "No man is himself, he is the sum of his past. There is no such thing really as was because the past is. It is part of every man, every woman and every moment. All of his and her ancestry, background, is all part of himself and herself at any moment. And so a man, a character in a story at a moment of action, is not just himself as he is then, he is all that made him."[8] If individuals are their pasts, including the pasts of their families and regions, their conceptions of themselves obviously depend upon their abilities to retain this past—hence the central role played by memory in Faulkner's fiction. For Cather, on the other hand, an individual's early experiences obviously shape him or her in decisive ways; I have already cited her belief that "most of the basic material a writer works with is acquired before the age of fifteen." Cather also believes that she was especially fortunate in having been able in her youth to encounter the remarkable personages of a previous era. This good fortune enables her memories of this time later to serve as sources of strength through an era inhabited by few comparable people. Memory is thus important to Cather, but in a different and, it must be said, lesser way than to Faulkner.

Faulkner's characters respond to the importance of the past in several ways, two of which are especially relevant here. Some struggle to rid themselves of it and to begin their lives anew. This is the response of Thomas Sutpen in *Absalom, Absalom!* and of Flem Snopes in the Snopes trilogy. Such efforts are destined to fail; since Faulkner's characters in some sense are their pasts, efforts to deny the past prove to be self-destructive. Others strive precisely to remember. Faulkner's fiction contains many individuals, such as Rosa Coldfield and Quentin Compson in *Absalom, Absalom!,* who struggle to recall and reconstruct past events, sensing that these events will prove to have been consequential in making them and their lives what they are. Their efforts on behalf of memory are in their way heroic, requiring a measure of perseverance that has no counterpart in Cather. Memories seem to be readily accessible to Cather's characters, so that the tone of her fiction is not crossed by their tortured efforts to recall people and events from their past.

One way of describing the difference between the operations of memory in Cather's and Faulkner's fiction is to observe that in the former what is to be recalled is an era that is already lost, whereas in the latter the process of diminishment is still under way. The era of the pioneers is past, and the processes that brought it to an end might still be at work, but in her fiction Cather is frankly not concerned with their further consequences. Jim Burden and Niel Herbert might have gone from disappointment to disappointment in their later lives, but *My Ántonia* and *A Lost Lady* are less interested in their subsequent lives than in their original dispossession. If Ivy Peters, to use another example, must eventually yield the Forrester place to someone still less appreciative of it, that further devolution is to Cather of less moment than his replacement of the Forresters. The situation in Faulkner's fiction is quite different and is usually rendered under one of two distinct descriptions. Sometimes, as when speaking with students at Virginia in the passage quoted above, Faulkner describes the process in metaphysical terms. This is a fiction obsessed by time, by the speed with which each present moment seemingly slips into an ever more remote and expanding past. When this issue is foremost in Faulkner's fiction, memory becomes a means by which his characters can retain some sense of themselves; it becomes the site and sign of their integrity as persons. At other times the special urgency of Faulkner's fiction issues from specific historical circumstances. Faulkner wrote at a time when it was widely believed that the South, long thought to possess its own regional identity, was at last being transformed by being absorbed within the national social and economic order. In a sense, the issues involved in this transformation are similar to those envisioned by Cather in *A Lost Lady;* Ivy Peters can be considered another in Flem Snopes's swarm of distant relatives. Cather situates her fiction at a time when this transformation is an accomplished fact. In *Intruder in the Dust,* the Snopes trilogy, and elsewhere Faulkner chooses to depict this transformation of southern culture at times when it is under way. Since Faulkner regrets the direction of this change as thoroughly as Cather regrets the closing of the frontier, and since the outcome is still in doubt, at times he enlists his fiction in the service of resistance to it. Since the loss is not yet an accomplished fact, a certain and understandable urgency attends the efforts of those who remember and value an endangered way of life to resist further losses. The sometimes frantic urgency of Faulkner's prose, which can become especially intense when his narrators and characters try to recall what they are always in danger of losing, derives in large part from his conviction that the seemingly inevitable outcome of this transformation might still be avoided. Recollection in Faulkner, at least until *The Reivers,* does not consistently yield the measured calm and reassurance that it typically produces in Cather's fiction.

During the twenties and early thirties, when the reading public was still especially receptive to Cather, Faulkner wrote in relative obscurity. His claims to attention were established later, at a time when Cather's claims upon us were already in decline. I have sometimes thought that his overtly venturesome narratives have become especially valued in part because they apparently represent the best case for an American equivalent to experiments in fiction being conducted by his European counterparts. It would be unfortunate, however, if we allowed our admiration for his accomplishments to keep us from appreciating the different yet estimable accomplishments of writers like Cather, who seemingly tried the limits of narrative in another direction, by seeing how serene it could become while still holding our attention. Cather's most deliberate efforts in this direction occurred late in her career, especially in *Death Comes for the Archbishop* and *Shadows on the Rock,* the novels to which we shall now turn.

IV

Willa Cather first went to the Southwest in 1912 on a visit to her brother, Douglass. She proved to be as responsive to its landscape as she was to that of the more familiar Nebraska; she was also intrigued by the cliff dwellings and other evidence she encountered there suggestive of an earlier but dignified way life that was by then seemingly already lost. Both Judith Fryer and Sharon O'Brien have explored Cather's receptiveness to this new landscape; the latter even argues convincingly that her first visit in 1912 was instrumental in freeing Cather to write *O Pioneers!* (403–27). She would return to the region many times in following years and would write about it first in *The Song of the Lark* (1915) and later in the Tom Outland section of *The Professor's House* (1925). The latter represents Cather's attempt to repeat an experiment in form she had earlier conducted successfully in *O Pioneers!,* where she had grafted the story of Marie Shabata and Emil to that about Alexandra Bergson. In *The Professor's House* she uses Tom Outland and his excitement about the discovery of an abandoned cliff dwelling as a counterpoint to Professor St. Peters's increasing discomfort about the conditions of his and his

family's current life. Cather's imagination risked stridency whenever, as with Ivy Peters, she chose to depict explicitly the cultural
sources of her regret; and both portions of *The Professor's House*
become on occasion strident as she attempts to use this contrast to
account for St. Peters's emotional estrangement from what otherwise seem reasons for personal satisfaction. In *Death Comes for the
Archbishop* Cather reverts to her more successful mode; she presents
the exemplary life of Archbishop Latour as an alternative to contemporary mores, but allows its commentary on the latter to remain
largely implicit.

Death Comes for the Archbishop begins with a brief prologue. It
is set in the gardens of a villa high in the Sabine hills that look
out over Rome below. Three cardinals and a missionary bishop have
gathered for dinner and to discuss the latter's petition that a Jesuit
priest in his diocese along the Great Lakes be named to head the
anticipated Apostolic Vicarate in New Mexico, a territory recently
annexed by the United States. Although missionaries had first ventured into the region more than two hundred years ago and its inhabitants remained nominally Catholic, the bishop is worried that
religious observance there had become so slack as that it could
"prejudice the interests of the Church in the whole of North America" (7–8). The cardinals' "interest in the projected Vicarate was
tepid" (5), and their conversation demonstrates that their misplaced
knowledge about this vast territory and its inhabitants derives chiefly
from James Fenimore Cooper's novels. The disinterest of two cardinals and the personal interests of the third finally produce the
support the bishop seeks, but Cather makes it clear that none of the
three either knows or cares much about the condition of the church
so far from Rome. The prologue serves to explain to readers how in
the first chapter, set three years later, Jean Marie Latour will find
himself lost in central New Mexico. It also depicts the comparably
comfortable way of life the young priest has given up in order to
pursue his vocation.

Cather writes *Death Comes for the Archbishop* almost as though
she too were in residence at this villa in Rome and thus equally distant from the events she narrates. The book does not feel like a
novel. Cather's Father Latour is modeled upon Archbishop Lamy,
who was responsible for reviving the church throughout the Southwest in the later half of the nineteenth century. It loosely chronicles

various episodes in Latour's life beginning with his arrival in 1851, when local officials disputed his authority, until his death in 1889, when he was buried in the new cathedral that marked the culmination of his mission in the Southwest. In "On *Death Comes for the Archbishop*," Cather remarks that in writing the book she had "wanted to do something in the style of legend, which is absolutely the reverse of dramatic treatment" (9), and previous readers have called attention to resemblances between the novel and traditional saints' lives (Keeler; Rosowski 167–70; Stouck 129–49). If *Death Comes for the Archbishop* can usefully be conceived as a variant of the saint's life, it is clearly one that places little emphasis upon trials that might test the saint's devotion. Even in the Nebraska novels Cather had minimized the importance of plot, but not to the degree she would in this novel. Her characters rarely seem to feel pressed by time, and her readers are rarely caught up in suspense about the outcome of any episode. It is not lack of dramatic potential in the events of Latour's or Lamy's life that produces the unusual temporal sense of *Death Comes for the Archbishop:* Latour was shipwrecked in Galveston as well as lost in the desert when en route to Santa Fe; while there, he had to contend with renegade priests such as Father Martinez and with desperate men such as Buck Scales; and he had to conceive as well as oversee the construction of his cathedral. Cather might have seized upon any of these or similar events in order to dramatize Latour's life in the usual novelistic manner. Instead, she deliberately understates the dramatic potential of Latour's life—she mentions the shipwreck, for example, incidentally, relegating it to two passing sentences (24, 336), suggesting that her aspirations for this novel go in another direction.

As the event announced in Cather's title approaches, Archbishop Latour reflects upon his mental state: "He observed also that there was no longer any perspective in his memories. . . . He was soon to have done with calendared time, and it had already ceased to count for him. He sat in the middle of his own consciousness; none of his former states of mind were lost or outgrown. They were all within reach of his hand, and all comprehensible" (336–37). As Latour awaits his death, he calmly reflects upon the events of his life; the narrative follows his reflections and dispassionately reports that at the moment of his death the French priest was remembering a scene from the distant past, as he and his longtime companion, Father

Joseph Vaillant, prepared to leave their native Auvergne in order to take up their vocations as missionary priests in the New World. The explicit coincidence in these final pages between the consciousness of Latour and the narrator make it plain that the novel as a whole has been narrated from a similar vantage. That is, the reader of *Death Comes for the Archbishop* experiences Latour's life in the same way that Latour remembers it. Since Latour already knows the outcome of any episode, the sense of suspense has little place in his reminiscences. And since his life as a whole seems now accessible, he need not struggle to recall any particular episode; his recollections come with an ease and produce a satisfaction that have no counterparts in a Faulkner novel. The calm and affection with which the "Bishop was living over his life" (328) are precisely the qualities that characterize the novel as a whole. This is a novel seemingly written from the threshold of eternity, which puts the worry and urgency that can overtake life as it is initially lived into a perspective that makes them seem incidental.

If the curious attitude toward time in *Death Comes for the Archbishop* seems to derive from Latour's equanimity as he awaits death, his character is equally crucial to the tone of the novel. In *Death Comes for the Archbishop* Latour embodies many of the same accomplishments and attitudes that Cather had celebrated earlier in *O Pioneers!, My Ántonia,* and *A Lost Lady.* He is another of Cather's celebrated pioneers, a counterpart to Alexandra Bergson and Ántonia Shimerda, especially in their later years, when they are able to look with considerable personal satisfaction upon their thriving farms and family, respectively. Latour, because of his vocation, is more suited than Captain Forrester to represent similar attributes. I earlier observed the dissonance produced by asking the retired railway builder to serve simultaneously as the embodiment of pioneer virtues and of steadiness, as though the railroads were not party to changing frontier life in ways Cather regretted. Cather was shrewd enough to recognize that in Archbishop Lamy she had found a historical personage who was perhaps uniquely suited to her otherwise seemingly contradictory purposes. On the one hand, she wished to celebrate the pioneers—their vision, their perseverance, their accomplishments; on the other, she wished to portray them as being somehow more cultivated than later generations. The learned French priest is especially suited to these conflicting aspirations. It would have been possible when writing *Death Comes for the Archbishop* to stress the tension between Latour's European background and the conditions he endured in the Southwest, or to emphasize the hardships he endured; Cather occasionally mentions such incidents, but Latour's distress at such moments, as when he is otherwise exposed to hardships, is always in the end qualified and contained by his religious faith. The latter gives him and his actions an unusual degree of assurance. The lack of tension and narrative suspense that is so characteristic of this novel seemingly derives from the serenity with which Latour conducts his life. In an introduction to a collection of Sarah Orne Jewett's short stories, Cather identifies *The Scarlet Letter, Huckleberry Finn,* and *The Country of the Pointed Firs* as titles likely to be long read. "I can think of no others," she continues, "that confront time and change so serenely" ("Best Stories" 58). This is perhaps a curious criterion for identifying books destined for long lives, though one thoroughly consistent with Cather's preoccupation with the way her culture seemed to be changing. It is also an apt description of her accomplishment in *Death Comes for the Archbishop.* Of course the change at issue is the restoration of the church in the Southwest and not the waning of the pioneers; the novel is thus unique in Cather's canon for the way it focuses upon the period in which her pioneers make their mark. In *O Pioneers!* we initially see the Bergsons in a time of need, but Alexandra's triumph occurs in the sixteen presumably arduous years that elapse between parts II and III; in *My Ántonia* we watch Ántonia grow and seemingly lose her way, and she finally triumphs only after Jim Burden loses sight of her; and in *A Lost Lady* Captain Forrester is already in retirement when the novel begins. In her Nebraska novels Cather is not so much interested in the rigors her pioneers endured as in their eventual contentment. Archbishop Latour's faith gives him a comparable peace of mind from the beginning, and perhaps his serenity accounts for Cather's greater willingness to depict him as he goes about the business of restoring the church.

In *Shadows on the Rock,* Cather's next novel, the issue is not change but precisely the capacity to endure. It resembles *Death Comes for the Archbishop* in being based upon historical materials rather than Cather's memories, and it is probably more than coincidental that these materials are again both French and Catholic. Cather herself was not Catholic; in 1922, while on an extended visit with her family in Red Cloud, she and her parents had joined the Episcopal Church (Woodress 337). She was, however, a Francophile, and Edith Lewis reports Cather's delight at their chance discovery in 1928 of a thoroughly French culture on this side of the Atlantic when stopping in Quebec en route to their cottage on Grand Manan (151–63).

Shadows on the Rock is set in Quebec at the end of the seventeenth century. From the outset, as the last ships depart for France before the long winter sets in, the emphasis is upon the remoteness of this enclave and the stratagems its inhabitants must employ simply to survive. The small settlement of Quebec sat on a rock alongside the St. Lawrence River; it already contained shops, a hospital, churches, and a convent, but was surrounded by deep forests. The landscape here seems more overtly ominous than the open plains had initially appeared to Jim Burden and the Shimerdas: "The forest was suffocation, annihilation; there European man was quickly swallowed up in silence, distance, mould, black mud, and the stinging swarms of insect life that bred in it" (7). The novel focuses on a single year in the quiet life of a widowed apothecary in Quebec, Euclide Auclair, and especially on his young daughter, Cecile. Their encounters with customers and conversations with friends contain many interpolated stories, which collectively provide a sketch of life at the time throughout the province; we learn about conditions on an island farm, about the recluse of Montreal, about the hardships and injuries endured by the woodsman Frichette, about the growing excitement in the settlement as people await goods and news from France with the return of ships in the late spring, about the yearnings for France felt by many in this remote colony. People in Cather's Quebec must store up pleasant memories against future hard times in the same way they stockpile wood against the coming long winter. At times they seem conscious of this necessity even as they enjoy the experience. "The next time I am overtaken by a storm in the woods," explains the missionary Father Hector to Auclair during dinner, "this evening will be food and warmth to me. I shall see it in memory as plainly as I see it now. . . . How many times, out there, I shall live over this evening again" (173). *Shadows on the Rock* envisions a harsher life than *Death Comes for the Archbishop,* a difference that is perhaps suggested by the more primitive and penitential religiosity of the recluse and the Monseigneur l'Ancient, Old Bishop Laval.

In *Shadows on the Rock*, Cather again employs an omniscient narrator who often assumes, as earlier in *A Lost Lady*, the perspective of a young and impressionable character, in this case Cecile Auclair's. When Cecile visited the nursing nuns at the hospital, Mother Juschereau would often tell her stories about missionaries and martyrs. The nun recognized that Cecile's rapt attention was not indicative of a religious vocation: "She knew that her words fell into an eager mind; admiration and rapture she found in the girl's face, but was not the rapture of self-abnegation. It was something very different—almost like the glow of worldly pleasure" (46). The young girl's pleasure in the things and people about her resembles Archbishop Latour's, and it generally lends the novel a pleasantly affirmative tone; since Cecile is a child, the reader is prepared to accept the way the natural and supernatural are mingled in her mind. However, this narrative strategy risks becoming excessive and even at times cloying, as when Cecile exults, "Don't you like to know that the angels are just as near to us here as they are in France?" (151). Cecile is very much the product of Quebec proper, and she reacts with horror at the conditions she discovers on her long-awaited visit to a rural farm with Pierre Charron. The abundant wildflowers make Cecile initially think she is in paradise, but she recoils in disgust from the way the Harnois family lives—their food contains too much lard and the children are unkempt. Cecile has little of Ántonia's courage amidst such conditions. After a sleepless night, Cecile runs into the nearby fields: "She felt she had escaped forever from the Harnois and their way of living" (225). She begs Charron to take her back to Quebec early, and upon their return she prepares a meal for him as an expression of gratitude. As she works in her familiar kitchen she recalls her mother, who when dying had spoken to Cecile about the importance of the domestic duties she would be assuming. "You will see that your father's whole happiness depends on order and regularity, and you will come to feel pride in it. Without order our lives would be disgusting, like those of the poor savages" (28). As Cecile prepares this meal for Charron in her kitchen, she experiences a domestic epiphany: "These coppers, big and little, these brooms and brushes, were tools; and with them one made, not shoes or cabinetwork, but life itself. One made a climate within a climate; one made the days—the complexion, the special flavour, the special happiness of each day as it passed; one made life" (230). As Cather imagines life in colonial Quebec in *Shadows on the Rock,* she places similar emphasis upon the local legends and domestic arts that enabled these colonists to lend a modicum of order to lives created within otherwise difficult circumstances.

The Auclairs' lives are especially in need of such reassurance during the winter chronicled in the novel. There has been some thought that Cecile should return to France. Since Count Frontenac, who had been Auclair's patron even before they came out to Quebec, expected to be recalled to Paris, the Auclairs planned to return with him. However, the call never arrives, and instead the count's health declines and he dies, exposing the apothecary to a new isolation. When Auclair returns home after attending his patron, "he felt for the first time wholly and entirely cut off from France; a helpless exile in a strange land" (304). When Pierre Charron returns to Quebec to provide condolence for his friend, Cecile recognizes that his presence affords another sort of comfort: "He had not a throne behind him, like the Count (it had been very far behind, indeed!), not the authority of a parchment and seal. But he had authority, and a power which came from knowledge of the country and its people; from knowledge, and from a kind of passion. His daring and his pride seemed to her even more splendid than Count Frontenac's" (310).

Shadows on the Rock concludes with an epilogue, set fifteen years later, that celebrates the transition between the kinds of authority represented by the count and Charron. The authority and cultural institutions represented by the count were at one time critical in establishing European life in the New World. Without them, life there would remain, as Cecile discovered on her visit to a rural farm, little removed from savagery. In time, however, some colonists like Charron developed a local authority; Cather implies that he represents a natural (as distinct from an inherited) aristocracy. Charron, who seemingly combines traits that were distributed between Captain Forrester and Frank Ellinger in *A Lost Lady,* eventually marries Cecile, and their four sons are termed "the Canadians of the future—the true Canadians" (324). In the meantime, conditions have worsened in France, so that by the second decade of the eighteenth century anyone might already anticipate the cataclysms ahead. In the final paragraph the apothecary closes his shop and prepares to visit his daughter's home. Auclair "believed that he was indeed fortunate to spend his old age here where nothing changed; to watch his grandsons grow up in a country where the death of the King, the probable evils of a long regency, would never touch them" (325). During the course of the novel, in other words, the image of Quebec has been transformed from a remote, primitive outpost of French culture into a refuge for it, a place where it can remain stable and vital even as in France it enters a sustained period of turmoil and decline.

V

Cather's use of historical materials in *Death Comes for the Archbishop* and *Shadows on the Rock* represents a unique departure from her usual practices. (During her final years in the forties she worked on another historical novel, set in medieval Avignon and tentatively entitled *Hard Punishments;* Cather apparently never completed this manuscript, which Edith Lewis later destroyed at her request [Woodress 492–94; Kates].) Although these novels are set in different times and places, they suggest something of the specific qualities that Cather was also trying to evoke in her Nebraska novels. Archbishop Latour's Southwest in the latter half of the nineteenth century and the Auclairs' Quebec at the end of the seventeenth are, for her, obviously historical counterparts to her own memories of Nebraska life during the 1880s. These historical novels focus on characters who embody many of the same virtues that Cather admired in her Nebraska pioneers, but the interpolated stories attempt at least a sketch of life throughout these societies. It is the character of this life as a whole that particularly drew Cather. It was at least possible for her to imagine that people in these societies possessed an attachment to their personal and cultural pasts that was becoming increasingly rare in her own time. One of the striking features of these novels is the frequency with which their characters, who seem to inhabit comparably stable social worlds, nonetheless share her own preoccupation with the past and draw reassurance from their memories. The comparable stability of these societies derives largely from their inhabitants' respect for authority and consequent willingness to accept their own places within the social hierarchy. It seems that Cather was only able to imagine stable communities that were organized on traditional terms, and thus hierarchically. The authority of her protagonists is derived in various ways, including the vitality of Ántonia, the accomplishments of Captain Forrester and Pierre Charron, and the institutional responsibilities of Archbishop Latour and Old Bishop Laval. In every case, however, Cather characterizes such individuals in terms that suggest their worthiness to receive the deference generally extended them by others. The Mexicans and Native Americans of *Death Comes for the Archbishop* and the pious colonists in *Shadows on the Rock* are anticipated in Cather's fiction by the Blum brothers in *A Lost Lady*, who realized that "a fortunate and privileged class was an axiomatic fact in the social order."[9] Auclair explains to Cecile his affection for the dying Count in terms that recall Judge Pommeroy's admiration for Captain Forrester: "Since I was six years old, the Count has been my protector, and he was my father's before me. To my mother, and to your mother, he was always courteous and considerate. He belonged to the old order; he cherished those beneath him and rendered his duty to those above him, but flattered nobody, not the King himself. That time has gone" (302). The apothecary was willing to play his part in this scheme, and he was duly deferential to his betters and generous to those who, like Cecile's companion Jacques, were less fortunate. The stability of such communities, on the other hand, is threatened by the introduction of an Ivy Peters, who refuses to accept either his own designated place in the social order or the authority of his betters. Cather's attachment to traditional social forms and intermittent feudalism, in other words, apparently stems from her conviction that the acceptance of traditional authority was a necessary component of any stable community.

Actually, there has been from the outset a curious and inherently unstable irony in Cather's reverence for her pioneers. She seems to celebrate them for the world their efforts bring into being—for the way they change things—yet at the same time she characterizes them as adhering to fixed and traditional social values. This contradiction is perhaps why her novels characteristically marginalize their labor, preferring to depict them in full possession of their due. In the final paragraph of *Shadows on the Rock*, as we have seen, Auclair considers himself fortunate to be spending his old age in Quebec, "where nothing changed." Since elsewhere in this paragraph Auclair is fretting over apparently worsening political conditions in France, his sentiments are perhaps explicable; but they have the regrettable effect of drawing his own and the reader's attention away from the considerable changes implicit in the introduction of French culture to the Canadian wilderness. The peculiar quality of Cather's novels derives from her efforts to invest figures who were in fact responsible for producing a certain kind of life with attributes that make them seem to be inhabitants of thoroughly settled and unchanging social worlds, thereby minimizing the very accomplishments she would otherwise celebrate.

Cather's access to these other cultural moments was obviously different, and she relied upon various historical sources for information about life in these other times and places.[10] In *My Ántonia* and *A Lost Lady,* as we have seen, memory serves to reconcile Jim Burden, Niel Herbert, and their author to their subsequent lives. In *Death Comes for the Archbishop* and *Shadows on the Rock* it provides similar solace for various characters, but not for their author, who possesses no memories of life in these times and places. Lamy's Southwest and seventeenth-century Quebec are for Cather cultural moments that seemed to provide ways of life that are in important ways analogous to those available during her childhood on the Nebraska frontier. She seems to have derived the same satisfaction from contemplating these other cultural moments that she did from her recollections. I earlier observed that Cather's celebration of memory in her Nebraska novels served to limit the availability of such consolations, since few readers then and none now are so fortunate as to share her memories. Her discovery in these historical novels of comparable satisfactions in the contemplation of life in certain other times and places makes such satisfactions generally available to her readers, who enjoy equal access to the historical record. Readers who could not, because of the contingencies of their own lives, retire like Cather to memories of better times whenever their current lives become especially trying, could turn for consolation to the historical record. Cather's evocation and celebration of life in Lamy's Southwest and seventeenth-century Quebec thus potentially increase her readers', as well as her own, sources of satisfaction.

The remoteness of such cultural moments from conditions in the United States in the early decades of the twentieth century is precisely what makes them valuable to Cather. She celebrates them for the same reasons that she cherishes memories from her Nebraska childhood: they are moments in time that seem to be out of time; moments of unusual social stability and continuity, when people, like Euclide Auclair in *Shadows on the Rock,* could think "nothing changed," when one's life might be settled and serene. Cather sought out such moments because they contrasted sharply with her sense of what American social life had become in the early decades of the twentieth century. The latter was for her and other American literary modernists a period of unprecedented change and cultural decline. To contemplate the Southwest of Lamy and Latour constituted for her a temporary refuge from contemporary conditions; the depiction of that life, by demonstrating what lives might be like, constituted an implicit criticism of the opportunities available to Cather and her contemporaries. At the same time that these novels imagine an alternative to contemporary conditions, they provide little encouragement for believing that the latter can be significantly transformed. In *Death Comes for the Archbishop* and *Shadows on the Rock* Cather remains as pessimistic about prospects for restoring earlier ways of life as she had been in her Nebraska novels. She offers them to us as objects of contemplation rather than as calls to action. The unusual serenity of these novels perhaps owes something to her belief that such social conditions cannot be restored; had she thought otherwise, a hint of urgency might have troubled their tone, as it does in Faulkner's fiction. The settings of Cather's historical novels obviously differ from her better-known works set in Nebraska, and they might thus suggest increased access to comparable satisfactions, but these novels too are finally a form of revenge against a fretful, too-busy present that one would as soon forget.

After the publication of *Shadows on the Rock* in 1931, Cather reverted to her more characteristic materials and manner in her final three books of fiction. The stories in *Obscure Destinies* (1932) return to Nebraska and the frontier, as does *Lucy Gayheart* (1935), although its action is partially set in Chicago and at a somewhat later date. In her final novel, *Sapphira and the Slave Girl* (1941), Cather ventured further into her past and drew upon memories and family recollections from the Virginia her family left for Nebraska in 1883, when she was a young child. In a promotional brochure distributed by her publisher in 1926, Cather had written that her family came from "an old and conservative society; from the Valley of Virginia, where the original land grants made in the reigns of George II and George III had been going down from father to son ever since, where life was ordered and settled" (qtd. in Woodress 35–36). This passage illustrates again Cather's tendency to conceive of her own past as having been spent in especially stable cultural moments; she is disposed to consider any past as inherently more stable than the present. However, she set *Sapphira and the Slave Girl* in the years just prior to the Civil War, at a time when that stability was being shattered, and the novel turns on racial issues that would in part precipitate that conflict. Sapphira Colbert mistakenly becomes jealous of her husband's paternal relationship with a slave and in revenge arranges for an extended visit from her dissolute brother-in-law, believing that he is likely to rape the young black girl. Others recognize the girl's situation and arrange for her to escape to Canada by means of the Underground Railroad. The novel concludes with an epilogue, set twenty-five years later, that dramatizes the former slave's return to the scene of her earlier trials and her emotional reunion with her mother. Unlike the rest of the novel, which has an omniscient narrator, this concluding section is narrated in the first person. Although there is some dispute about the effectiveness of this shift (Hamner), readers generally agree in identifying this narrator as Cather herself. According to her biographer, the return to Back Creek of Nancy Till constitutes one of Cather's earliest and most vivid memories from childhood (Woodress 26, 481). It is of course more an accident of history than a matter of personal choice that in the final pages of her final novel Cather speaks in her own voice and relates this dramatic incident based upon a childhood memory. She had hoped to write other novels and indeed later made considerable progress on the lost *Hard Punishments,* but poor health and death intervened. However, since in her strongest and most representative fiction she was preoccupied by the attempt to make memory counteract the flow of history, the surprising first-person epilogue to *Sapphira and the Slave Girl* is perhaps an especially fitting as well as poignant close to her career.

3

ELIOT, TATE, AND THE
LIMITS OF TRADITION

Tradition is much more than the memory.
    Stevens, "Recitation," *Opus Posthumous* 115

ONE MORNING IN late June 1927, T. S. Eliot did not go as usual
to his office at Faber and Gwyer, the publishing firm where he
was a director. He went instead to a small church in Finstock, where
he was initiated into the Anglican Church. It was a private service,
and the small party accompanying Eliot did not even include his
wife.[1] At the time of his conversion, Eliot was arguably already the
most influential figure in literary London; through his poems, essays, and more recently as the editor of *The Criterion,* he was setting
a tone and direction that others took to be exemplary of modern literary practice and doctrine. Eliot announced his conversion in 1928,
in the now famous phrase from the preface to *For Lancelot Andrewes,*
describing himself intellectually as a "classicist in literature, royalist
in politics, and anglo-catholic in religion" (vii). We have perhaps become too familiar with this declaration to appreciate fully the shock
it delivered to his contemporaries, who had come to regard him as
an exponent of the most up-to-date. If the Sweeney poems and *The
Waste Land* were a provocation to many comfortable pieties, they
could nonetheless be celebrated within literary circles, by those who
shared Eliot's contempt for so much in contemporary life. Eliot's
declaration of faith, on the other hand, was a provocation directed
precisely at those with whom he had seemed to share so much.

The response was quick and predictable. Edmund Wilson reviewed *For Lancelot Andrewes* for the *New Republic,* calling Eliot
"perhaps the most important literary critic in the English-speaking
world" ("Eliot and the Church" 283). Wilson conceded that insti-

tutional religion had once served valuable social functions, but he could not imagine that large numbers of people could again convince themselves to accept religious belief, whatever the presumed social benefits. "You cannot have real Christianity without a cult of Jesus as the son of God," wrote Wilson. "But since it has plainly become anachronistic to accept the prophet Jesus in this role, it seems that we must reconcile ourselves to doing without both the churches and religion" (283). Despite his admiration for Eliot's literary accomplishments, Wilson could neither follow him into the church nor imagine that many others could again join him in that fellowship. The anonymous reviewer in the *Times Literary Supplement* observes that Eliot's religious convictions are in themselves unremarkable, "but from the author of *The Waste Land* [they are] at first sight astonishing, to say the least" ("Mr. Eliot's New Essays" 953). In his view, by accepting the authority of the church over that of personal experience, Eliot has unfortunately "abdicated from his high position."[2] In a published exchange about Eliot's later *After Strange Gods,* Ezra Pound was characteristically more pungent in dismissing his friend's new religious beliefs: "He is in fact treating the sickness of the age. His diagnosis is wrong. His remedy is an irrelevance" (559). Eliot surely anticipated and perhaps even courted such reactions, and they did not shake him from his new affirmations. In literary and intellectual circles, however, they left him in a position curiously similar to that of his persona in "Journey of the Magi," which he wrote shortly after converting. The speaker's satisfaction at having been present at the birth of Christianity is qualified by the way his new convictions have estranged him from his subjects, who now seem "an alien people" (100).[3] Eliot's journey to the Anglican Church, undertaken in what many thought to be the final days of institutional religion, was equally arduous; and if he drew sustenance from the fellowship he found there, his new beliefs estranged him to a degree from many intellectuals with whom he had otherwise made common cause.

It is widely agreed that Eliot's conversion marks a turning in his literary career. His poetry would continue to be remarkable for the degree of his speaker's yearning, but that yearning would henceforth be largely religious in character; he would continue to be interested in drama, but he would henceforth write, as well as write about, verse drama; and he would continue to write criticism and occasional prose, but he would henceforth address larger cultural issues as well as strictly literary topics. Thus in his "Preface to the 1928 Edition" of *The Sacred Wood*, Eliot remarks that he is now primarily interested in "the relation of poetry to the spiritual and social life of its time and of other times," whereas when writing these essays in the late teens he had been primarily concerned that poetry be approached "as poetry and not another thing" (viii). Eliot's conversion also draws attention to the lengths he and some contemporaries would go in turning to the past in an effort to locate resources that might ease the strains of modern social life. It is at least curious that a literary tendency that put such stock in formal innovation should simultaneously be so preoccupied by versions of the past. In addition to Eliot's England at the time of Bishop Andrewes, there is of course Pound's Provence, Yeats's Celtic Ireland, and the antebellum South of Allen Tate and his fellow Agrarians. The conservative cast of mind among these literary modernists is by now a critical commonplace (cf. Harrison). It seems that the critical animus among these writers was directed specifically at the present and recent past; their need to "make it new" was designed to unsettle contemporary tastes and was often inspired by their reading of earlier literary and cultural documents.

For many literary modernists the concept of tradition thus became invested with tremendous cultural significance. It was also defined variously. These definitions varied not only in terms of the particular national and cultural traditions that were invoked, but also in terms of the range or scope they were accorded. Pound's occasional advocacy of oriental literary practices necessarily pressed a different claim upon the attention of an American writing in the first decades of the twentieth century than did Eliot's celebration of metaphysical poetry. The former is simply an example drawn from the vast archive that one might admire and adapt to one's own language and purposes; the latter is immediately available as a measure to assess one's own purposes and achievement.[4] Likewise, it is one thing to isolate and champion a literary tradition and another to advocate an entire way of life. Pound's advocacy of the Noh theater, for example, is a different and, it must be said, lesser endeavor than the Agrarians' defense of southern culture.

In this chapter I want to investigate two representative efforts by American literary modernists to bring "tradition" to bear upon contemporary culture. I shall begin with Eliot, who in the late teens and early twenties was chiefly concerned with identifying and drawing upon the resources available within a specifically literary tradition. His conversion effectively brings this phase of Eliot's career to a close. He would thereafter continue to ask tradition to provide relief from contemporary conditions, but he would now define it more expansively so as to include social and religious institutions, practices, and beliefs. I shall not follow Eliot's career after he entered the church; instead, in the second half of the chapter I shall explore the Agrarian phase of Allen Tate's long career. As we shall see, the example of Eliot was decisive to Tate's poetry and social criticism. During the late twenties, at about the same time Eliot was reassessing his relationship to traditional British institutions and beliefs, Tate was actively repossessing his own southern heritage. Eliot himself would observe the similarities between these enterprises in the lectures he delivered at the University of Virginia in 1933, which were later published as *After Strange Gods*. Whereas Eliot would remain faithful to the beliefs he adopted in 1928 until his death in 1965, suggesting that for him at least they represented a viable solution to problems he had earlier articulated, Tate's advocacy of Agrarianism ceases abruptly in 1938, with the publication of *The Fathers*. Tate's defection from the Agrarian cause thus provides us, as the example of Eliot does not, with an opportunity to explore the shortcomings that some American literary modernists themselves identified in their various efforts to identify tradition—defined broadly as a way of life—as a resource in the task of making contemporary cultural and social conditions bearable.

I

The poems first published in *Prufrock and Other Observations* (1917) were written considerably earlier, while Eliot was still at Harvard and before he had finally resolved upon a literary career. They typically record impressions of urban life, both the squalor of the streets and tenements and the havens available to the cultivated classes. Some of the poems, such as the first two sections of "Preludes," are little more than vignettes, but they cumulatively suggest the dreary cast of this life:

> One thinks of all the hands
> That are raising dingy shades
> In a thousand furnished rooms. (13)

In these first poems, written in his early twenties, Eliot is not consistently able to grant his speakers much more than this keen eye; when they try to reflect upon these impressions, they typically either fall into easy dismissal, as in the final stanza of "Cousin Nancy," or reach for the evasive closure of another rhetorical register, as in the final line of "Rhapsody on a Windy Night."

The exceptions are "Portrait of a Lady" and the remarkable title poem. Like its more famous counterpart, "Portrait" is composed of recollected and anticipated encounters during the course of a year between the speaker and an unnamed lady. In large part because she is given more lines, the lady emerges more as a character in her own right than does her counterpart in "Prufrock." The repetition of phrase and line that would become characteristic of Eliot's verse, his means of evoking emotional intensity, is already on display in this early poem, where it occurs as often in the lady's lines as in the speaker's. The aging lady is of course both fatuous in her excessive cultivation and pathetic in her claims upon the speaker's attention.[5] In the first stanzas she expresses satisfaction in having secured so sympathetic a friend as the speaker; but by the final section, as he prepares to depart abroad, she continues to press her claims while conceding the emotional gulf between them:

> "For everybody said so, all our friends,
> They all were so sure our feelings would relate
> So closely! I myself can hardly understand.
> We must leave it now to fate.
> You will write, at any rate.
> Perhaps it is too late.
> I shall sit here, serving tea to friends." (11–12)

For his part, the speaker struggles to sustain his "self-possession" (the term or its variants are repeated three times) despite the lady's claims upon his attention and affection. The reader might wonder why he keeps returning to her home but otherwise requires no further explanation for the speaker's disinterest in the lady: between her cloying cultivation and her self-pity, she is simply not a person likely to become the object of anyone's affection. In "Portrait of a Lady," in other words, the speaker's emotional reserve seems both explicable and justified. The only genuinely discordant note occurs in the final stanza, when he wonders what might happen should she die while he is abroad:

> Well! and what if she should die some afternoon,
> Afternoon grey and smoky, evening yellow and rose;
> Should die and leave me sitting pen in hand
> With the smoke coming down above the housetops;
> . . . .
> Would she not have the advantage, after all? (12)

There is something distastefully cold about calculating such possibilities, and this final stanza thus suggests that there might be more to the speaker's reserve than the poem otherwise documents.

In "The Love Song of J. Alfred Prufrock" the dramatic situation is in one sense reversed. In this poem it is the speaker who would make claims on the affections of another and who fears that they will not be reciprocated. Except when Prufrock momentarily recalls her arms and perfume, the object of his emotions never comes into focus, as does the woman in "Portrait." Instead, she remains indistinct amidst an apparently more expansive urban landscape. "Portrait" rarely moves beyond the bric-a-brac of the lady's drawing room, whereas Prufrock's monologue evokes the streets along which he must pass in making his way to confront his love and "to force the moment to its crisis" (6). The "half-deserted streets," "one-night cheap hotels," and "lonely men in shirt-sleeves" provide a contrast to the gathering Prufrock prepares to attend, and they suggest something of his mood as he makes his preparations, but their distinctness also underscores the degree to which the presumed object of Prufrock's attention remains indistinct. Not only is this a love song that never gets sung, it is also a love song that fails to celebrate its object.

The famous refrain ("In the room the women come and go / Talking of Michelangelo") ridicules the cultural pretensions of the women Prufrock prepares to meet. As we have seen, the similar condemnation in "Portrait of a Lady" is credible; in "Prufrock," however, and precisely because the woman never emerges as a person in her own right, the ridicule finally feels like another rationalization Prufrock offers himself for his timidity. It is not her shallowness that deters Prufrock; it is instead his conviction that she will not return his affection: "That is not what I meant at all. / That is not it, at all" (6). He will ridicule others rather then provide them with opportunity to ridicule his balding head, thin limbs, and misunderstanding of their interest. For all the reader can know, Prufrock might be quite justified in his ridicule of the cultural pretensions of these people. This ridicule, however, is at odds with his obvious longing; it thus seems to be a way of letting himself down easily: it is as if he is telling himself that in the final analysis his timidity is not costing him much of value.

Demeaning the object of his affection in this manner is but one of the strategies Prufrock would employ to minimize his loss. He also would adopt a worldly air in order to convince himself that he already knows well enough the likely outcome of any action:

> For I have known them all already, known them all—
> Have known the evenings, mornings, afternoons,
> I have measured out my life with coffee spoons; (4)

If he knows this class of people and way of life so well, he is of course in a position to know the likely reaction to his declaration. And if that response is sure to be negative, why should he subject himself to certain disappointment? This line of argument appears to be decisive for Prufrock; in its midst the tense changes, suggesting that his decision has been made and the moment will be forgone. If his musings continue, it is only in an attempt to make himself more certain that perseverance could have come to nothing.

Neither of Prufrock's psychological ruses is in the end effective. Their failure is partially what makes the poem so moving, since if Prufrock had succeeded in minimizing his regret he could smugly get on with his life, finding his satisfactions elsewhere. But he cannot. His contempt at his own timidity finally overwhelms whatever ridicule he would heap upon those who are not paralyzed by the thought that others might think their appearance and desires ridiculous and who thus are able to participate in social life.[6] Prufrock freezes at the thought that others might slight him, and the poem is increasingly broken by fugitive mental images that indicate his self-contempt: "I should have been a pair of ragged claws / Scuttling across the floors of silent seas" (5). The final stanzas suggest that the mental struggle mounted in the poem has now subsided; they are characterized by a tone of quiet regret rather than the earlier nervous anticipation and bitter reproach of others and himself. For this moment at least, Prufrock regretfully resigns himself to a life apart, beyond both the chatter of drawing rooms and the songs of mermaids.

The psychological drama enacted in "The Love Song of J. Alfred Prufrock" accumulates considerable pathos. The understanding of the sources and consequences of Prufrock's pose of world-weariness is remarkably acute, especially when one recalls that Eliot was still in his early twenties when he wrote this poem. Such weariness would remain characteristic of Eliot's personae even into his later religious poetry. Edmund Wilson was among the first to comment upon it, when in *Axel's Castle* he reports impatience at its presence in "Ash Wednesday": "I am made a little tired at hearing Eliot, only in his early forties, present himself as an 'aged eagle' who asks why he should make the effort to stretch his wings" (130). The later poem, however, is a prayer, suggesting that Eliot and his persona have iden-tified a source of relief for their continuing anguish. There is no comparable agency on the horizon in "Prufrock"; accordingly, his situation seems irremediable. Although he lives in the midst of a modern city, Prufrock lives alone, without the fellowship afforded by interaction with others. His shaky self-esteem causes him to an-ticipate and shy away from potential slights from others; at the same time, he finds little comfort alone, since he must then face his own contempt at his timidity. Prufrock's presumed familiarity with the workings of the world ("For I have known them all already, known them all—") helps rationalize his unwillingness to press the issue, but it also means that he must live without hope that the future might somehow prove less dreary. Within the terms established by the poem, there seems to be no possibility that Prufrock will be released from his continuing and partially elected misery.

Most of the poems Eliot wrote later in the teens feel very differ-ent from "Prufrock"—more controlled and acerbic, they deflect at-tention away from the speaker. "Gerontion," on the other hand, is more in keeping with his earlier manner. This speaker is an old and lonely man regretting a life that has come to nothing. He has neither participated in the great events of his era nor sustained a passion that might have brought fulfillment:

> Here I am, an old man in a dry month,
> Being read to by a boy, waiting for rain.
> I was neither at the hot gates
> Nor fought in the warm rain
> Nor knee deep in the salt marsh, heaving a cutlass,
> Bitten by flies, fought.
> . . . .
> I have lost my passion: why should I need to keep it
> Since what is kept must be adulterated?
> I have lost my sight, smell, hearing, taste and touch:
> How should I use them for your closer contact? (29, 31)

If only because of his advanced age, Gerontion can lay greater claim to world-weariness than Prufrock, and perhaps for this reason the poem is altogether more somber, lacking even the earlier figure's self-deprecating humor. Gerontion has led the life that Prufrock still largely anticipates, and the outcome is appropriately sobering. In "Portrait of a Lady" the lady had emerged as a character in her own right, with a pathos of her own, however finally qualified; in "Prufrock" the object of affection is reduced to remembered gestures and scents, but otherwise indistinct; by "Gerontion" she is only a disembodied "you" addressed in absence. This progression underscores the isolation that troubles Eliot's various characters. They find it impossible to enjoy or even to imagine satisfying relations with others; they live life apart, unable even to share their misery with others.

Eliot, of course, is neither Prufrock nor Gerontion. He simply observes them, fixing them as definitively by phrase as the former worries might occur to him in the drawing room. Beyond the mockery that the fastidious Prufrock directs at himself is the gentle irony Eliot directs at him, beginning with the poem's title and the persona's justly celebrated name. However much he yet wished to accomplish, the still comparably young author of "Gerontion" had little reason to share the latter's despair at having lived to no purpose. Despite the distance between the poet and these personae, there is nothing in either poem to suggest how the misery of the latter might have been or still might be alleviated. Gerontion does retain some attenuated religious impulses, but there is nothing in the poem to suggest that they promise any more salvation than the deceptive gifts of history. It would not be in character or to much purpose for Eliot to imply that either of his creations should simply buck up; but no more sensitive and appropriate possibilities are insinuated either. Eliot was obviously able to imagine the plights of such individuals and to sympathize with them, but to this time in his life he was little more able to conceive of ways to alleviate such distress. However, by the time he wrote "Gerontion" in mid-1919 he was already beginning to formulate a possible remedy.

II

After Eliot's marriage in 1915 to Vivien Haigh-Wood and consequent decision to continue living in England, he was faced with the necessity of securing a livelihood. He initially taught school while completing his dissertation; in November 1916 he informed his brother Henry that he would cast about for other employment, explaining that while teaching "I am losing in every way. I have no time to pursue my literary connections, and overwork is telling on the quality of my production" (*Letters* 157). The following March he settled into a position at Lloyd's Bank, where he was to be employed for nearly a decade. In order to supplement his modest salary from Lloyd's, for several years in the late teens Eliot undertook to conduct courses under the auspices of various adult education and university extension programs.

Eliot had studied philosophy at Harvard; and although he had read widely, the pressure of preparing his classes forced him, as it has others, to develop a more extensive and more systematic knowledge of British literature. Both Michael Levenson (193) and James Longenbach (152–63) have pointed to the unexpected benefits Eliot would derive from his extension teaching.[7] Eliot's preparations for his lectures provided him with a more thorough and secure understanding of French and English literary history. Ronald Schuchard has made the syllabi and reading lists Eliot prepared for his courses more accessible to scholars. Eliot first delivered a series of six lectures on modern French literature, organized primarily around various reactions to romanticism; he later offered two year-long courses on Victorian literature; and, in 1918–19, he taught a remarkably comprehensive survey of Elizabethan literature. In retrospect, it appears that the immediate financial rewards were among the least important benefits Eliot was to derive from teaching these extension courses.

These benefits are most readily apparent in some of Eliot's best-known essays written during the late teens and early twenties. In "The Metaphysical Poets" (1921), he uses the publication of Grierson's anthology of metaphysical poetry as an opportunity to propose a sweeping thesis about the course of British poetry. He suggests that something "had happened to the mind of England between the time of Donne or Lord Herbert of Cherbury and the time of Tennyson and Browning" (247). He continues: "We may express the difference by the following theory: The poets of the seventeenth century, the successors of the dramatists of the sixteenth, possessed a mechanism of sensibility which could devour any kind of experience. . . . In the seventeenth century a dissociation of sensibility set in, from which we have never recovered; and this dissociation, as is natural, was aggravated by the influence of the two most powerful poets of the century, Milton and Dryden" (247). As the term "dissociation" itself suggests, Eliot considers this development regrettable. Whereas in the metaphysicals at their best "there is a direct sensuous apprehension of thought, or a recreation of thought into feeling" (246), thought and feeling subsequently and fatefully become separated, so that although "the language became more refined, the feelings became more crude" (247). What was once unified is now separate; both thought and feeling are diminished by their isolation from each other. "Tennyson and Browning are poets, and they think; but they do not feel their thought as immediately as the odour of a rose. A thought to Donne's mind was an experience; it modified his sensibility" (247).

I am less concerned with the plausibility or accuracy of Eliot's famous historical scheme than with the service it provided him. It is his early version of a historical explanation for more than the predicament of contemporary poetry. I have argued that American literary modernism was preoccupied by the deficiencies of its era, and that its practitioners typically understood those deficiencies to have been produced by specific historical developments. The "dissociation of sensibility" was Eliot's initial attempt at accounting historically for the specific qualities of modern life. His sketch reaches further back in time than most, locating the sources of the characteristic weaknesses of contemporary verse in the seventeenth century; it is likewise more abstract than most explanations proposed by his contemporaries, which is perhaps not surprising, given his training in philosophy. Eliot's historical sketch is first and most immediately concerned with the continuing devolution of British poetry. The essay concludes with Eliot's declaration that contemporary life seemingly necessitates that its poetry be *"difficult"*: "The poet must become more and more comprehensive, more allusive, more indirect, in order to force, to dislocate if necessary, language into his meaning. . . . Hence we get something which looks very much like the conceit—we get, in fact, a method curiously similar to that of the 'metaphysical poets' " (248–49). Eliot argues, in short, that the metaphysical poets provide models to which contemporary writers could profitably turn. If the latter were thereby able to produce a verse possessing the specific virtues found in metaphysical poetry, they would simultaneously meet the demands of contemporary social life and repair the separation between thought and feeling that had for too long and increasingly debilitated British literature.

During this period of his career, Eliot primarily undertook to write about strictly literary topics. The historical sketch he develops in "The Metaphysical Poets" is offered solely as a contribution to literary history. However, it contains crucial terms that make it available in principle for wider cultural purposes. It is, for instance, "the mind of England" that undergoes the dissociation of sensibility. That term is so vague and encompassing that one might have expected Eliot to document the dissociation of sensibility by drawing upon changes across a range of social and cultural realms. After all, if something as general as the mind of England changes, one would expect the consequences to be distributed widely. It is important to the argument I am advancing here that Eliot himself did not venture beyond literary history for evidence supporting his thesis. Whatever the potential broader implications of his thesis, in this phase of his career Eliot either carefully refrained from drawing them or displayed disinterest in them.

We have seen that Eliot believed that the example of the metaphysical poets could be useful to their counterparts writing in the early decades of the twentieth century. This is but a small example of the benefits Eliot came to believe writers might derive from attending to the literary heritage. "Tradition and the Individual Talent," first published in 1919, is Eliot's most celebrated statement on this subject. There he offers his well-known definition of tradition:

> It involves, in the first place, the historical sense, which we may call nearly indispensable to any one who would continue to be poet beyond his twenty-fifth year [Eliot at the time was twenty-nine]; and the historical sense involves a perception, not only of the pastness of the past, but of its presence; the historical sense compels a man to write not merely with his own generation in his bones, but with a feeling that the whole of the literature of Europe from Homer and within it the whole of the literature of his own country has a simultaneous existence and composes a simultaneous order. This historical sense, which is a sense of the timeless as well as of the temporal and of the timeless and of the temporal together, is what makes a writer traditional. (4)

Eliot believed that this historical sense is essential to the poet in part because the meaning and significance of any poet are not established in isolation but rather comparatively, in relation to the accomplishments of earlier poets. According to Eliot, at any given time "the existing monuments form an ideal order among themselves" (5). The new work does not simply augment this order; by suggesting new affiliations among the monuments, it instead forces a pervasive readjustment as it takes its place among them.

If we are to appreciate fully the place of this definition in Eliot's intellectual development, two features need to be stressed. First, it is exclusively literary. Eliot believes that the contemporary poet should possess a sense of Homer; he does not suggest that the poet should likewise be broadly conversant with ancient Greek culture and history. Thus when Eliot writes in these years about the crucial importance of the poet's "historical sense," he refers solely to the poet's sense of literary history.[8] Second, an individual does not acquire a tradition by being born at a particular time and place. When defined in this way, a tradition has little to do with the beliefs, customs, and folkways that people in a given culture share. It does not operate unconsciously, as if behind our backs. The tradition Eliot invokes here must be possessed consciously and can only be obtained "by great labor" (4). The letters Eliot wrote to family and friends during this period provide ample testimony to his own labor, as he devoted his evenings to various literary projects, including preparing his extension courses, after working each day at Lloyd's Bank.

Eliot believed that this labor would eventually benefit the poet in at least two ways. First, Eliot conceives of the poet's mind essentially as a machine that produces syntheses among otherwise disparate emotions, objects, and situations. He describes its operations in "The Metaphysical Poets": "When a poet's mind is perfectly equipped for its work, it is constantly amalgamating disparate experience; the ordinary man's experience is chaotic, irregular, fragmentary" (247). In "Tradition and the Individual Talent" he proposes the famous analogy equating the poetic mind with a chemical catalyst that causes elements to combine. At the same time, the historical thesis he advances regarding the dissociation of sensibility implies that our thoughts and feelings are progressively becoming more estranged from one another. It might then be that at no time in the past has the poet's task been either as difficult or as necessary for the culture at large. Eliot would nonetheless have the modern poet undo this dissociation and bring the various aspects of our lives back into alignment. Since poets have always striven to perform this task, modern poets can learn how best to do so by attending to the example of their predecessors. Thus in "*Ulysses*, Order and Myth," Eliot celebrates Joyce's use of myth: "It is simply a way of controlling, of ordering, of giving a shape and a significance to the immense panorama of futility and anarchy which is contemporary history" (177). Eliot obviously believed that Joyce's use of myth exemplified how modern writers could turn the literary tradition to their immediate advantage.

Eliot also turned to literary tradition seeking another and perhaps more personally pressing benefit. The disorder and separation he envisioned among each person's thoughts and emotions had their counterpart in relations among people. If poets could reunify the otherwise disparate aspects of their lives by drawing upon the literary tradition, perhaps they could at the same time reestablish social bonds. Eliot seemed to believe, as his comment about "the immense panorama of futility which is contemporary history" suggests, that modern social life was uniquely stressful, that people in his era were more fundamentally isolated from and at odds with one another than their counterparts at other times and places. This is the context in which I understand both Eliot's insistence in "Tradition and the Individual Talent" that at its best poetry is impersonal and his otherwise puzzling descriptions of the creative process. For Eliot, the poet at work becomes absorbed into the tradition he has previously labored so hard to acquire: "What happens is a continual surrender of himself as he is at the moment to something which is more valuable. The progress of an artist is a continual self-sacrifice, a continual extinction of personality" (6–7). This is the positive description; it emphasizes what the poet gains by means of this self-sacrifice. He later describes the progress again, this time emphasizing what the poet would thereby leave behind: "Poetry is not a turning loose of emotion, but an escape from emotion; it is not the expression of personality, but an escape from personality. But, of course, only those who have personality and emotions know what it means to want to escape from these things" (10–11).

It is initially difficult to know what Eliot means in this passage by "personality." It is clearly something disagreeable, something one would want to set aside, but Eliot's usage is so unusual that the term remains opaque. I have come to believe that the term refers to the condition Eliot depicts in "Prufrock" and "Gerontion." By "personality," in other words, Eliot seems to mean something like the extreme self-consciousness that is both a symptom and a cause of these characters' isolation (cf. Lentricchia, *Quartet* 259). Lacking responsive social worlds, Prufrock and Gerontion are necessarily thrown back upon their own resources; they inevitably come to doubt these resources, and thus to doubt their capacity to engage their worlds on mutually satisfying terms. Prufrock's mental state in particular feeds on itself, progressively increasing his timidity and self-contempt, in the end making his despair seemingly terminal. If Prufrock is indeed an emblem of what Eliot means by "personality," it is no wonder that he would welcome its extinction. In these terms, what is most personal is also necessarily what is most idiosyncratic and most painful. Writing impersonal poetry is thus a way for the poet to overcome these sensations by becoming absorbed within the literary tradition. In "The Function of Criticism," Eliot suggests that "between the true artists of any time there is, I believe, an unconscious community" (13). Thus at the same time and by the same process that the impersonal or traditional poet escapes the distractions of personality, he or she joins the fellowship of other artists. This community compensates "true artists" for the lack of such fellowship in modern social life; it is, perhaps, Eliot's image of what such life should be.

It is important to recognize that this community appears to be available only to writers, and among writers only to those who submit themselves to the labor of acquiring the historical sense. Although Eliot would later enlarge his definition of tradition, and thus increase the number of people who might share in its benefits, in the late teens and early twenties he typically refers exclusively to a literary phenomenon. He was constructing the means to redeem his own sorrows. It is impossible to imagine that those in the crowd crossing London Bridge in *The Waste Land* or a Prufrock could take advantage of this possibility. They are left to fend for themselves. However, the writer who imagines them, and who is able to transcend his own personality by drawing upon and being drawn into the literary tradition, would achieve a greater degree of fellowship than could be available to them in everyday life. Of course that fellowship would necessarily remain imaginary; the impersonal poet must be able and willing to settle for imagining him- or herself participating in an "unconscious community" with one's predecessors. The poet's interactions with them could never be as tangible as those that take place in the drawing room Prufrock prepares to enter. I am not belittling the services Eliot thought to obtain by apprenticing himself to the literary tradition; I only want to call attention to their relatively narrow limits. His own appreciation of these limits might have contributed to Eliot's subsequent decision to define tradition more broadly, a decision that completely altered the course of his life and career.

Longenbach comments on the change that Eliot's recognition of the importance of the historical sense works on his poetry: "Before 1917, Eliot's poetry and criticism reveal a scanty interest in history. The poems collected in *Prufrock and Other Observations* contain passing allusions to Eliot's favorite predecessors (Shakespeare, Dante), but it was not until he began to compose the quatrain poems collected in *Poems 1920* that an overpowering 'historical sense' became the structural principle of his verse" (155–56). The occasional use of traditional verse forms is one manifestation of Eliot's new appreciation of the literary tradition. His poems also become more relentlessly allusive. These allusions fulfill several functions.

They authorize the poet to give voice to concerns that are no longer merely personal, if only because they are articulated in another's words. Within each poem these allusions virtually enact a conversation that Eliot imagines might occur among writers, and it is not a conversation likely to occur in the drawing room Prufrock prepares to enter. It does not matter that few readers were likely to recognize the full measure of Eliot's indebtedness in these poems. The few who could would feel that they had been ushered into a select fellowship, thereby acquiring what modern life otherwise rarely makes available; the rest of us might at least sense that we were missing out on something, and some few might be provoked into putting ourselves to school so as to achieve an understanding of these otherwise puzzling poems. In one sense, however, whether or not readers can identify these allusions is beside the point. They enact a dialogue between Eliot and his predecessors, and their overriding function is to initiate the poet himself into that "unconscious community." When Eliot writes, in perhaps the most famous line of *The Waste Land,* "These fragments I have shored against my ruins" (69), he alludes to the process through which he hopes to be accorded membership in that community.

III

It should be clear that during the late teens and early twenties Eliot asked the literary tradition to do for him and other writers a great service. He looked to it most immediately for precedents, for examples of effective practice that could be adapted to or even incorporated within contemporary verse. More importantly, Eliot hoped during this period that the literary tradition could serve as a means for overcoming the debilitations of what he termed "personality." The latter is the excess of personal feelings produced in many people who are forced by modern social conditions to live isolated lives. "Personality," in short, seems to be the inevitable product of social conditions that are not conducive to establishing a sense of fellowship among people living at a particular time and place; it is what feelings blocked from their natural attachments to others produce instead. Eliot hoped that the literary tradition could provide the something "more valuable" within which the poet's personality could be absorbed. In other words, Eliot conceived the literary tradition as an imaginary community among writers that would provide what modern life otherwise could not. It was to be a substitute for what Eliot imagined had been the shared beliefs and shared lives available within traditional societies. Presumably people living in such societies had not been so troubled by what Eliot terms "personality," and impersonal poetry was to be the literary equivalent of such shaped lives. The special stresses of modern life were produced by the degree to which traditional institutions and practices had over time been weakened or displaced altogether, and Eliot's emphasis upon the literary tradition was an effort to have it alone do the work performed by a whole array of such institutions at other times and places.

Eliot's conversion in 1927 represents his implicit concession of the failure of this effort to piece together a usable tradition that would not require his assent to the institutional authority of church and state. Lyndall Gordon demonstrates in *Eliot's Early Years* that his interest in religion began much earlier and was in duration coextensive with his literary career. Religious longings, images, and allusions mark his poetry in the late teens and early twenties, perhaps most decisively in *The Waste Land;* but in these years he was trying to imagine their satisfaction outside religion in its usual institutional forms. He was trying, in short, to have literature do the work of religion. Eliot never explicitly repudiated this effort, thereby calling attention to his own later assessment of its worth. We can, however, sketch his implicit commentary on this stage of his career in several prose pieces written in the late twenties and early thirties.

Richard Shusterman has demonstrated how Eliot's conception of tradition changed after his conversion. In "Tradition and the Individual Talent," as we have seen, it is a body of literary knowledge that the poet acquires at great labor. When Eliot returns to this subject in *After Strange Gods* and subsequent writings, he defines tradition very differently. "What I mean by tradition involves all those habitual actions, habits, and customs, from the most significant religious rite to our conventional ways of greeting a stranger, which represent the blood kinship of 'the same people living in the same place'" (18). As Shusterman observes, by the early thirties a "real temporal community has replaced the ideal order of monuments" (160) celebrated in "Tradition and the Individual Talent." As Eliot

now defines it, tradition is something the people do inherit as well
as strive to acquire; and it extends far beyond literature per se, to
include even a people's conventional forms of greeting. Eliot would
still urge poets to become familiar with literary traditions, but those
traditions are not conceived as being independent from other aspects
of a culture; instead, they were a strand within an entire culture.
The poet's "historical sense" would henceforth need to be broadly
cultural.

Eliot's new sense of the interaction among and mutual support provided by various cultural institutions also figures in his polemic during the late twenties against humanism. His former teacher
Irving Babbitt is an explicit object of his criticism, but in retrospect it is possible to see these arguments as directed against his
own previous efforts to make the literary tradition autonomous. In
"The Humanism of Irving Babbitt," Eliot observes that the former
"is a stout upholder of tradition and continuity" (385). However,
Babbitt cannot assent to dogmatic religion and thus proposes humanism as a substitute for it. Eliot demurs. He too values the cultural documents that Babbitt would use to construct an independent humanism; but Eliot now believes that humanism has
especially flourished in periods when religion itself was strong. Soc-
rates and Erasmus might have criticized contemporary religious
practices, but they "were content to remain critics, and to leave the
religious fabric untouched" (386). Their humanism, in other words,
was finally in the service of religion and not, like Babbitt's, or like
Eliot's own previous veneration of the literary tradition, a substitute
for it.

Eliot identifies Babbitt's doctrine of the "inner check" as an especially vulnerable point in Babbitt's humanism.[9] With the dissolution of traditional authority in so many spheres of modern life, it
becomes increasingly necessary for individuals to curb themselves.
Eliot concedes the aptness of Babbitt's position in most cultural
realms, but he does not believe it can be extended to religious
restraints. The latter are by their very nature "inner," and not, as
Babbitt seems to think, chiefly impositions enforced from without:
"If a religion cannot touch a man's self, so that in the end he is
controlling himself instead of being merely controlled by priests as
he might be by policemen, then it has failed in its professed task. I
suspect Mr. Babbitt at times of an instinctive dread of organized

religion, a dread that it should cramp and deform the free operations of his own mind. If so, he is surely under a misapprehension"
(388). Not only does Babbitt mistake the inner nature of religious
restraints, but his rejection of them leaves him without a viable answer to the question of what people should "control themselves *for*"
(388). Eliot suspects that Babbitt would answer "civilization." He
then proposes a small experiment in thought of the kind that has
become common in philosophical discourse. Whenever Eliot tries to
concentrate mental attention on civilization per se, he finds that he
cannot focus on any specific object or accomplishment, unless it is
improved material conditions. The lesson Eliot draws from this experiment is that it is impossible for civilization per se to serve as the
end for which people will control their impulses. He believes that
only an explicitly religious end will serve, and thus "that it is doubtful whether civilization can endure without religion, and religion
without a church" (390).

Eliot believes that humanism itself could be a cultural good; he
objects only to the effort to convert it into a substitute for religion.
In "Second Thoughts about Humanism," he claims that it "makes
for breadth, tolerance, equilibrium, and sanity," and thus that it
serves as a valuable "mediating and corrective ingredient in a positive civilization founded on definite belief" (400). He also concedes that at any given time and place "a very small minority of
individuals" (401), including no doubt Babbitt, are able to live satisfactory lives informed solely by humanism. Such individuals, however, would always owe that privilege to the continuing authority
of the church among the majority of their contemporaries. Humanism, in other words, is made possible by religion and would itself
collapse should it attempt to replace the latter.

By the time Eliot wrote these essays in the late twenties, he recognized that humanism did not suffice for him. Although Irving
Babbitt is the primary object of Eliot's criticism, his arguments tell
as well against his own earlier effort to make the literary tradition
serve larger cultural and personal ends. For a period in the late teens
and early twenties, in other words, Eliot had himself advocated a
form of humanism, and thus these essays are implicitly exercises in
self-criticism. Whereas before his conversion Eliot asked the literary
tradition to provide him with a sense of community with other
writers, after his conversion he would find it in the communion of

the church. Likewise, whereas he earlier defined tradition narrowly, as knowledge of the literary heritage, he later defined it broadly, as the sum of cultural practices that collectively define a people living at a particular time and place. After having failed in his effort to make literature itself address the needs of modern life, Eliot was now prepared to assent to the authority of other traditional institutions within the community in which he lived. He now believed that the "immense panorama of futility and anarchy which is contemporary history" could only be redressed on the condition that the traditional institutions of church and state could be restored to their former prominence.

IV

In 1928 Eliot enlisted Allen Tate in his assault on Irving Babbitt and humanism; Tate's "The Fallacy of Humanism" was published in the July 1929 issue of Eliot's *The Criterion*. At the time Tate was a young and relatively unknown poet, but he was already under the elder poet's influence. Some years before, while still an undergraduate at Vanderbilt, Tate had championed *The Waste Land* against the reservations of other members of the Fugitive group, including John Crowe Ransom. Even as a young man Tate could be acerbic, and apparently his strident enthusiasm for Eliot's poem temporarily estranged him from Ransom. Several of the letters he exchanged with Donald Davidson during August 1923 refer to the "Tate-Ransom controversy" (Fain and Young 81–90), in which Tate's youthful enthusiasm for one mentor seemingly put him temporarily at odds with another. Although I do not believe that Tate's later decision to participate in the agitations of the Agrarians was motivated largely by the example of Eliot's own recent conversion, the latter could have served to confirm this redirection of his own energies. Like the later Eliot, the Agrarians believed that the difficulties of modern life could be attributed to the diminished authority of traditional institutions and ways of life. And like him, though with more directly political interventions, they sought to preserve and strengthen such institutions against the incursions of modern life. Of course the specific institutions and traditions that the Agrarians had in mind were very different from the church and state that the later Eliot revered, but the similarities between their ambitions are nonetheless striking (C. Brooks). As we shall see, the example of Eliot was obviously important to Tate during these years, and in *The Fathers* he adapted terms used by the elder poet in "Tradition and the Individual Talent" in his own depiction of the collapse of southern life. Tate's participation in the Agrarian effort effectively ceased in 1938, with the publication of his only novel.[10] *The Fathers* not only illustrates the virtues of traditional societies as Tate understood them, but also dramatizes, in the person of George Posey, Tate's final recognition that tradition cannot be reclaimed through individual acts of will.

Tate did not begin his literary career by celebrating the virtues of southern life. Late in 1925, after his arrival in New York, he took his native region to task for its lack of culture. The Old South, he wrote, was so preoccupied with the defense of its peculiar social and economic arrangements as to render serious intellectual life impossible, for "it could not afford to look at itself critically." More than fifty years after the Civil War, the situation had not substantially improved. "It is pretty much certain," wrote Tate in conclusion, "that the Southern variety of American writer must first see himself, if at all, through other eyes. For he of all Americans is privy to the emotions founded in the state of knowing oneself to be a foreigner at home" ("Last Days" 486). If history has made the southern writer a foreigner outside his native region, his vocation makes him a "foreigner at home." As a result, the serious writer from the South can only pursue his or her vocation in either physical or spiritual exile.

In December 1926 Tate would write the first drafts of "Ode to the Confederate Dead," a poem that seemingly inaugurates a changed attitude toward his native region and a new phase in his intellectual life. Events followed rapidly, as his letters to Donald Davidson indicate. At the beginning of March 1927, he writes Davidson that he has "attacked the South for the last time, except in so far as it may be necessary to point out that the chief defect the Old South has was that in it which produced, through whatever cause, the New South" (Fain and Young 191). Two weeks later he writes with plans "regarding a Southern symposium of prose," and makes clear that he has already been in correspondence with John Crowe Ransom about what would become *I'll Take My Stand* (195). In April he announces to Davidson that he has signed a contract to write *Stonewall Jackson, the Good Soldier: A Narrative,* which appeared the following year (198). Over the course of little more than a year, in sum, Tate transformed his attitude toward the South, and from his outpost in New York he made himself over into one of its more outspoken apologists.

Eliot was important to Tate throughout his career, but especially during the formative 1920s; and it is hard to imagine "Ode to the Confederate Dead" achieving its final form without the examples of "The Love Song of J. Alfred Prufrock" and "Gerontion." The image of the "blind crab" and the line "Like an old man in a storm" seem to be allusions to Eliot's poems. The title, like Eliot's for "Prufrock," is askew: the poem does not so much commemorate the Confederate dead as confess its persona's inability to understand the roots of their devotion to an idea. The speaker in "Ode to the Confederate Dead" is Tate's Gerontion. As he stands in the Confederate cemetery, before rows of headstones whose inscriptions are being lost to erosion, he cannot comprehend the intensity of belief that sent the dead laid out before him to their ends:

> Turn your eyes to the immoderate past,
> Turn to the inscrutable infantry rising
> Demons out of the earth—they will not last.
> Stonewall, Stonewall, and the sunken fields of hemp,
> Shiloh, Antietam, Malvern Hill, Bull Run.
> Lost in that orient of the thick-and-fast
> You will curse the setting sun.
>
>> Cursing only the leaves crying
>> Like an old man in a storm
>
> You hear the shout, the crazy hemlocks point
> With troubled fingers to the silence which
> Smothers you, a mummy, in time. (21)

These old soldiers are twice dead: physically, of course, but also dead in the lives of their descendants, who, like the persona, cannot understand them and thus cannot model their own lives after their example. The speaker recognizes that the gallant charges that cost these soldiers their lives must have been more meaningful than the leaves now blowing among the graves, but he lacks the terms for understanding the difference between them. For him, now, the confusions of battle and of swirling leaves are fully comparable, the former no more explicable than the latter. "Ode to the Confederate Dead" is, in short, a poem about the predicament of the modern man who has lost touch with history and who is accordingly caught in the coils of his own consciousness, and I cannot read it as being other than utterly despairing.

Tate attached obvious importance to this poem. He reworked it several times, especially during the years of his Agrarianism, and did not finally abandon it to its final form until after more than twenty years of tinkering (cf. Kingsley). The poem is also the subject of his remarkable exercise in self-criticism, "Narcissus as Narcissus." Nonetheless, it is odd that "Ode to the Confederate Dead" should begin Tate's new preoccupation with the South and its traditions. Tate obviously looked to the southern heritage to provide the same service Eliot initially sought in the literary tradition and later secured in the institutions of the Anglican Church. They both sought, in Eliot's bland phrase, "something which is more valuable" ("Tradition" 7) within which they could overcome the isolation thought to be characteristic of modern life. Although they appeal to different traditions with correspondingly different implications for daily life, both poets seek in them the means for restoring to their own era a sense of shared purpose. However, the speaker of Tate's "Ode" despairs of understanding the Confederate dead, much less of having the heritage they represent inform his present life. How will Tate accomplish what the speaker of his most famous poem cannot?

Tate provides an answer in 1930, at the conclusion of his contribution to *I'll Take My Stand,* "Remarks on the Southern Religion." The citizen of the modern South can no more find access to his tradition ready at hand than can the speaker of "Ode to the Confederate Dead." Therefore, the modern southerner can only "take hold of his Tradition," writes Tate, "by violence."[11] Like Eliot at the time he wrote "Tradition and the Individual Talent," Tate here emphasizes the strenuousness of the task facing the would-be traditionalist. His language suggests the paradoxical nature of the task. In his final paragraph, Tate describes the paradox facing the southerner: "He must use an instrument, which is political, and so unrealistic and pretentious that he cannot believe in it, to re-establish a private, self-contained, and essentially spiritual life" (174–75). Public and political means, in other words, must be employed to achieve an essentially private and spiritual end.

Tate obviously follows his own prescription, putting himself to school in his tradition by writing biographies of Stonewall Jackson and Jefferson Davis. Despite such efforts, however, the degree to which a modern man can make himself over in the image of tradition is open to question. According to Tate, the quality the modern man most envies in his traditional counterpart is the latter's presumed serenity, which is largely the product of an abiding conviction that his way of life is the only one imaginable. He accepts his tradition unquestionably and does not conceive of himself as having made a choice in the matter. The modern, would-be traditionalist, on the other hand, knows only too well that other beliefs and ways of life are possible, and he chooses a tradition from among them. In binding himself to a tradition, he must do consciously what the traditional man does without thinking. He believes in the value of a heritage, but he must set aside his own as a citizen of the modern world in order to appropriate one he judges workable. He must, in other words, do a violence to the continuity of his own life in order to achieve the desired sense of wholeness and serenity; and perhaps the ardor characteristic of the convert simply reflects the manner in which he has had to dispatch his own previous existence. Be that as it may, the would-be traditionalist inevitably puts himself in a bind: he wills to believe what his models believe unconsciously; he seeks serenity through violence; and although he values continuity, he must break with his own past in order to align himself with one he thinks more serviceable.

A successful and enduring conversion, as Tate well knew, requires a change in more than one's beliefs and incidental ways of living. It requires as well the cultivation of social institutions appropriate to such beliefs, for in their absence one's peace of mind would constantly be tried by the lack of fit between one's way of life and the lives of one's fellows. The wholeness for which modern man envies his traditional counterpart is not simply a matter of the individual life, but rather extends to the compatibility among the economic, political, and religious institutions within which that life is lived. "Traditional men," writes Tate, "are never quite making their living, and they never quite cease to make it" ("What Is a Traditional Society?" 556). They secure their livelihoods, in other words, in ways altogether compatible with everything else they do; as a result, one cannot really tell where their economic activities leave off and other activities begin. Everything they do and believe is of a piece; and their beliefs and practices are fully compatible with those of their neighbors. Thus the would-be traditionalist is obliged to seek out or create the institutions appropriate to the tradition in question. The tradition in Tate's case was that of the Old South, and since its institutions were in danger of disappearing altogether from the scene, he joined, however reluctantly, in a public agitation for their preservation.[12] The violence to which Tate refers in "Remarks on the Southern Religion," accordingly, is not only political in nature but also the violence to one's inclinations and sensibilities necessitated by such political acts. That Tate willingly subjects himself to this violence testifies to the seriousness of his new convictions.

V

Obviously, I do not think it appropriate to term either *I'll Take My Stand* or Agrarianism in general as primarily literary in character. It seems to me a curious compliment we sometimes pay our writers when we try to preserve their efforts by suggesting that they should not be taken literally, but only as literary images. We thereby deny the seriousness of their original claim to attention. Tate's contributions to *I'll Take My Stand, Who Owns America?,* and *The American Review* cannot today be taken seriously as proposals for social action, and whatever interest they retain derives largely from other sources; nonetheless, it seems important to acknowledge that they were written with that hope in mind.[13]

Tate and his fellow Agrarians were deeply disturbed by the quality of modern industrial life, and fearful that it was in the process of becoming the norm even in their own, at the time comparably little touched, region of the nation. Tate urges that the man of letters resist being drawn into the manifold dissociations characteristic of intellectual life in an industrial world:

> He must not be committed to the illiberal specializations that the nineteenth century has proliferated into the modern world: specializations in which means are divorced from ends, action from sensibility, matter from mind, society from the individual, religion from moral agency, love from lust, poetry from thought, communion from experience, and mankind in the community from men in the crowd. There is literally no end to this list of dissociations be-

cause there is no end, yet in sight, to the fragmenting of the western mind. ("Man of Letters" 13)

It is an article of faith among the Agrarians that these regrettable developments are, like the rise of industrialism itself, the inevitable products of an economy increasingly governed by the market. The market favors large producers and thereby creates a demand for an industrial workforce, drawn in part from rural communities. In becoming a part of the industrial sector, these workers, living now among strangers, are not only without means of production and the avenues of assistance available in stable communities composed of friends and families; they are also increasingly vulnerable to the whims of the market and the possibility of being displaced by machines.[14] A harsh calculus of profit and loss seemingly dictates the terms of life available within a market economy, with the result that precariousness becomes a standard feature of modern life.

In the end, the Agrarians consider the market economy too high a price to pay for whatever material benefits it might seem to bring. Their campaign against the encroachments of the market into the South began in the late twenties, but it took on a new urgency and force in the following decade, when, with the onset of the Depression, the entire nation had to find a means for securing the livelihoods of its citizens. The expansion of the market into the South still had its advocates, but the Depression made them easy targets for Tate's irony. In a 1934 review of *Culture in the South,* Tate writes that one of its contributors, Broadus Mitchell, "stands alone in wishing to bring the Southern factory and financial system to the chaos that has overtaken the North" ("View" 428). Why should the South follow the example of the North, if doing so means breadlines, factory closings, and bank failures? If the widespread depredations of the thirties temporarily lend credence to Tate's Agrarianism, we must recall that he came to it earlier, during the relative affluence of the late twenties. The object of his animus is the market itself, and the Depression only seemed to confirm his conviction of its inherent evils.

Tate recognizes that the current market system has been in the making for quite some time. In "Notes on Liberty and Property," he writes that since 1787 American history has been marked by a struggle in which small landowners have steadily been worsted by big, corporate ownership. In *Jefferson Davis: His Rise and Fall* Tate offers his economic version of the "dissociation of sensibility." He traces the origins of the Civil War back to Europe and the Reformation, and suggests that the war "was the second and decisive struggle of the Western spirit against the European—the spirit of restless aggression against a stable spirit of ordered economy—and the Western won" (301). Tate obviously regrets this victory. Even after its defeat the South retained a measure of economic independence; at the least, a significant portion of its population earned its livelihood off the land. But the market continued to encroach upon the South, so that even this residual autonomy now seemed endangered. The Agrarians, Tate among them, put on the gray to defend their native region by attacking the depredations brought about by the market and simultaneously defending the dignity of rural life.

Tate's contribution to the Agrarian enterprise invokes a particular conception of traditional society. "The traditional society," he writes, "is based upon property, and property means not only ownership but control; not only economic privilege but moral obligation; not only rights but duties; not only material welfare but moral standards" ("Liberalism and Tradition" 208–09). When individuals own and control their own means of production, they recognize the sources of their livelihoods in nature and thus come to respect the land and animals they cultivate. Furthermore, such individuals possess a degree of freedom unknown to their industrial counterparts. Lacking the means of production, industrial workers must depend for their livelihoods upon the goodwill of employers and the impersonal whims of the market. If they are shoemakers and the market is glutted, they are likely to be unemployed whatever their skills or needs. The small farmer, by way of contrast, can produce pretty much whatever he needs himself, or survive by bartering goods and services with his neighbors. The industrial worker can hand on to his children only his own worry as to how to secure their livelihood; the small yeoman farmer, on the other hand, can hand on not only title to the land itself but also knowledge about its proper husbandry.

Obviously, Tate's traditional society is composed chiefly of independent farmers. Since its members live and work on a single tract of land, their lives are not subject to the dissociations that have overtaken the inhabitants of the modern world, whose lives are divided between home and workplace, family and fellow workers, producers and consumers. The independent farm, accordingly, provides a material basis for a unity of life not otherwise possible. Furthermore, since they retain title to the land and possess the knowledge to work it, Tate's independent farmers suffer little coercion from the market. They bring goods to market as and when they wish, not out of material need. As a result, they might lack some of the amenities available within other societies, but Tate believes that the resultant security and stability are certainly worth that price.

Tate concedes that the perfect traditional society, as he construes it, never existed. "We are wasting our time," he writes, "if we suppose that St. Thomas, religious authority, the Catholic Church, were more than approximations of a moral ideal by certain men at certain times under certain conditions" ("Liberalism and Tradition" 211). He argues, nonetheless, that his conception of the traditional society serves as a crucial point of reference, what Wallace Stevens might call a necessary fiction. It conceives of an ideal condition toward which we can aspire and assists us in seeing where, and by how much, particular lives and social arrangements fall short. Tate's defense of southern ways and institutions depends upon his claim that they more nearly approximate this ideal than do other current arrangements. Thus to his mind they deserve defense against the derision of others, and protection against further encroachments on the part of the market economy.

In the midst of this defense, Tate often writes as though the South had been and remains an embodiment of the perfect traditional society. He has a penchant for constructing polar oppositions (traditional versus modern, South versus North, agricultural versus industrial, symbolic versus angelic) and a talent for polemic. When he engages in the latter, as he does in all his Agrarian pieces, Tate's rhetoric can obscure the fact that he retains throughout the period a lively sense of the South's deficiencies as a traditional society. In his 1929 biography of Jefferson Davis, for instance, Tate writes that the South withdrew from the Union in order "to perpetuate a stable and deeply rooted way of living" (48); some pages previously, however, Tate accurately characterizes the Lower South as "expansive, unbound by strong local tradition," and "pushing toward an empire" (18, 19). In "Remarks on the Southern Religion," Tate argues that the South never developed a religion compatible with its way of life; it was "a feudal society without a feudal religion" (166). In "The Profession of Letters in the South," Tate returns to a point he had made earlier, in "Last Days of the Charming Lady," at a time prior to his adherence to Agrarianism: "It must be confessed that the Southern tradition has left no cultural landmark so conspicuous that the people may be reminded by it constantly of what they are. We lack a tradition in the arts; more to the point, we lack a literary tradition. We lack even a literature" (520). Even in Tate's mind, as we can see, the South approximates the traditional ideal most imperfectly: it was never as stable, as cohesive, and as supportive of culture as it should have been.

Although he does not develop it himself, we can piece together from Tate's Agrarian essays an argument that the South was early on fatally inflicted by influences it would subsequently resist. In his "Remarks on the Southern Religion," he suggests that the disastrous Jamestown settlement provides "a symbol of what later happened to this country": "It was a capitalistic enterprise undertaken by Europeans who were already convinced adherents of large-scale exploitation of nature, not to support a stable religious order, but to advance the interests of trade as an end in itself" (166–67). As it happens, settlers in the South found soil and climate conducive to agriculture, and many set about becoming the sort of independent farmers Tate so admires. Others, however, took these same conditions as an opportunity to produce cash crops on an enormous scale. The Lower South was settled in response to the continuing market demand for cotton. The institution of slavery emerged as a means for providing sufficient labor for the plantations, which amounted to agricultural factories. Tate nowhere addresses the moral questions posed by slavery, but he believes that it had an adverse effect upon the entire society. Because the slaves worked the land, the plantation owners rarely developed the attitude toward it Tate attributed to traditional societies ("Profession" 525). Its orientation toward the market thus kept a significant portion of the South from acquiring several of the attributes Tate particularly values in traditional societies. It could even be said, within the terms of Tate's own analysis, that the tensions between North and South that he traces in such a partisan manner arose not so much between societies organized according to different economic principles as they did between factions within a single market economy, and that the Civil War was fought by rival capitalists.

VI

If his analyses make it possible to extrapolate such conclusions, Tate himself never draws them. In his eyes the market remains the source of social ills; and in order to inveigh against its growing influence in the South he minimizes the extent to which it had a hand in shaping the very institutions he would now defend. Perhaps the fact that the South had been, in its own way and from the beginning, participating in the larger market system helps explain its continuing vulnerability. The extrapolations demonstrate that in Tate's mind the lines separating North and South are frequently not as clear-cut as his polemical writings suggest. Had the lines been sharper, he might have been able to conduct his defense of the South without resorting to the necessary fiction of its approximation of the perfect traditional society.

Tate's contributions to the Agrarian cause during the thirties become increasingly remote from a defense of the South per se. The transition occurred in two ways. First, in his early biographies of Stonewall Jackson and Jefferson Davis, published in 1928 and 1929, respectively, he is by the very nature of his topics involved in southern apologetics. By the mid-thirties, however, in pieces like "Liberalism and Tradition" and "What Is a Traditional Society?," Tate's position becomes more abstract. His prose is no less forceful, but he now argues for the virtues of a traditional society, wherever and whenever it might have existed, and the South itself figures much less prominently in his argument. Likewise, his essay of 1936, "Notes on Liberty and Property," argues for the importance of individual ownership and control of property. Its conclusions are compatible with positions he takes elsewhere on independent farming and the traditional society, but their relevance can hardly be confined to the South, or even to agriculture. If Tate's argument is correct, it would apply equally to the North and to the South, to farmer and shopkeeper alike.

By the mid-thirties, therefore, Tate's writings on social issues lose their original provincial cast (cf. M. O'Brien 152). It might be thought that this change only represents a new rhetorical strategy, an attempt to win a wider and more responsive audience. Shortly thereafter, however, Tate completely ceases to write on broad social issues and instead confines himself to more properly literary topics. His one novel, *The Fathers,* completed and published in 1938, brings the Agrarian phase of his career to a close. It depicts events occurring just prior to and during the early days of the Civil War and provides an account, utilizing Tate's recently acquired abstract terms, of the forces leading to that conflict. The novel thus nicely brings together different versions of Tate's Agrarianism; more importantly, *The Fathers* also suggests why Tate would thereafter abandon Agrarianism.

The Fathers is narrated by an elderly doctor, one Lacy Buchan, and it concerns his recollections of events that occurred fifty years earlier and led to the devastation of his immediate family (cf. Carpenter, Holman). The novel opens in 1860, with preparations under way at Pleasant Hill, the Buchans' plantation, for the burial of Lacy's mother; by its conclusion little more than a year has lapsed, but what remains of the family is in disarray: the plantation house has been burned by Union soldiers; Major Buchan is dead by his own hand, and his son Semmes at the hands of his brother-in-law; Susan, Lacy's sister, is deranged by grief and rage; Lacy and his remaining brother are scattered in defense of the Confederacy. An entire way of life has been laid waste.

Lacy wants to understand the causes and implications of this disaster, so his recollections rarely stray from events involving his immediate family. His reflections employ a language familiar to readers of Tate's recent prose, particularly "Liberalism and Tradition" and "What Is a Traditional Society?," thereby making the fate of the Buchan family available as an instance of what was befalling the South in general. Lacy attributes to his family and their way of life at Pleasant Hill all the qualities that Tate elsewhere finds the hallmarks of traditional societies, above all its "impersonality," a term Tate apparently defines in the same way as Eliot. The Buchan family is initially unsettled and finally devastated by the introduction into it of George Posey, who marries Susan. His restless energy, acumen for business, and above all his tendency to take everything personally make Posey the antithesis of traditional values and ways of life. An episode related early in the novel brings out these differences. Posey cannot bring himself to attend his mother-in-law's burial, apparently because it puts him in mind of his own mortality. His departure causes Lacy to reflect: "My new brother George had needed intensely to leave, to escape from the forms of death which were, to us, only the completion of life, and in which there could be nothing personal, but in which what we were deep inside found a sufficient expression" (22–23). Posey's behavior repeatedly confounds the Buchans, who can neither understand nor stop it. To the adolescent Lacy, however, Posey possesses the allure of a romantic figure: "In my boyish delight I would have any day followed him over a precipice, just for his bidding" (10). In the end, Posey takes the entire Buchan family and its way of life with him over a precipice, but he retains the loyalty of his young admirer even as Lacy witnesses the destruction Posey is visiting upon his family.

The reader knows little about Lacy's life during the subsequent fifty years, but the few facts we learn clearly suggest his continuing allegiance to Posey. He becomes a doctor, lives for a time in Posey's Georgetown home, and apparently never marries. That is, this last of the Buchans makes no effort to revive the fortunes of his family or to re-create the life of his father at Pleasant Hill. He might regret the passing of that life, and particularly the manner in which it came about; however, like Cather's Niel Herbert in *A Lost Lady*, Lacy believes that it was doomed. Thus he believes that even if George's marriage to Susan could have been stopped, or Semmes kept from killing Yellow Jim, or any event in the long accumulation of tragedies could have been averted, the life of the Buchans at Pleasant Hill would have been destroyed "in some other way" (5). Its time had passed and was now as irretrievable as the era of the pioneer in *A Lost Lady*.

Lacy's conduct in this respect contrasts sharply with Tate's own, especially during the years immediately prior to his writing of the novel. We must ask why. The answer involves Lacy's long relationship with Posey, and in particular in what he learns from watching the actions of his friend. As a youth Lacy had been caught up in admiration of the romantic figure Posey cut against the background of plantation life, but even then he had recognized certain deficiencies in Posey's character—for instance, his embarrassment at witnessing a bull about his business, and his inability to attend the burial of Mrs. Buchan. Subsequent events would provide ample rea-

son for Lacy to moderate this early adulation; but he nonetheless
writes, in the final, revised lines of the novel: "As I stood by his
grave in Holyrood cemetery fifty years later I remembered how he
restored his wife and small daughter and what he did for me. What
he became in himself I shall never forget. Because of this I venerate
his memory more than the memory of any other man" (306–07).
Posey introduces Lacy and the entire Buchan family to life in the
modern world. He might be an exemplary citizen of that world, but
Lacy knows, at least in retrospect, that Posey's life was always and
necessarily a trial. Citizenship in the modern world does not bring
with it the peace of mind enjoyed by Major Buchan, for it is a world
that delivers its shocks directly upon the unprotected nerves of its
inhabitants. Although he is thoroughly a creature of the modern
world and, accordingly, impatient with the practices of Pleasant
Hill, Posey seeks an alliance with the Buchan family as a means of
securing release from peculiarly modern torments. Lacy reflects:
"What Semmes gave to him was what he most needed but never
could take: Semmes gave him first of all Susan, and then . . . he tried
to give him what the Poseys had lost: *an idea, a cause, an action in
which his personality could be extinguished,* and it seemed as if George
had succeeded in becoming a part of something greater than he:
the Confederate Cause" (179–80; my emphasis).

In several respects this passage strikes me as being among the
most telling in *The Fathers.* Its phrasing, especially in the emphasized
portion, calls to mind Eliot's "Tradition and the Individual Talent,"
demonstrating that Tate in the thirties continued to work under the
elder poet's influence. Although Tate defines "tradition" broadly as
a way of life, in a manner completely compatible with Eliot's definition after his conversion, in this passage he adapts Eliot's earlier and
more restrictive phrasing to his purposes, thereby melding different
phases of Eliot's intellectual life. As a result, Tate has Posey looking
to the Buchans to provide the same services that during the late
teens and early twenties Eliot had sought from the literary tradition
and which he would finally receive as a communicant in the Anglican Church—namely, relief from the conditions of the modern
world. Being a citizen of the modern world is obviously not the
same thing as being comfortable within it.

The reader of *The Fathers* learns that Posey's hopes are misplaced.
He is impatient with Major Buchan's management of Pleasant Hill.

When control of the plantation comes to him, he restores it by introducing modern business methods. He aids the Confederate cause and continually risks his life in providing it with necessary supplies, but he retains only contempt for the posturing of his new comrades-in-arms. "Your people are about to fight a war," he once declares to Lacy's cousin John. "They remind me of a passel of young'uns playing prisoner's base" (166–67). Whatever his longings to the contrary, Posey cannot bring himself to accept the ways of the Buchans and the South. He might desire to extinguish his personality in some larger cause, but the cause cannot be so patently foolish and doomed.

What is more, his efforts in that direction all come to violent ends. If, as Lacy believes, Posey seeks to escape the modern world through his relationship with the Buchan family, his efforts paradoxically result in the devastation of that family. Semmes is first disowned by his father and then killed by Posey himself; Posey is estranged from his wife, who seems permanently deranged by the family's ordeal; and Pleasant Hill is destroyed and Major Buchan dead by suicide as a result of Posey's contemptuous dismissal of Union soldiers. Life at Pleasant Hill might have been faltering before Posey's arrival, and it might, as Lacy believes, have been doomed to collapse sooner or later; but there can be no doubt that Posey hastens its destruction or that he contributes toward making its demise particularly violent.

Lacy, of course, is a witness to Posey's efforts. I suggest that he reads in them two lessons. The first concerns the inability of citizens of the modern world to live by the dictates of a traditional society. They cannot, by dint of will alone, make themselves over into something they are not. The mark of the modern world is ineradicably upon them. The second concerns the violence that must result from such doomed undertakings. Taken together, these lessons would account for Lacy's apparent resignation, during the fifty years since the events he recounts, to the loss of Pleasant Hill and the way of life it represents. His recollections are themselves testimony to the fondness with which he continues to regard that life, but one can simultaneously regret and accept such a loss. George Posey introduces Lacy to the modern world; once the introductions are made Lacy cannot reclaim the innocence of his childhood. Like his mentor and friend, he too is henceforth a citizen of the modern world, and he learns from his elder's example about the futility of attempting to reclaim his lost patrimony.

Lacy is not the only one instructed by Posey's example. Tate is also. It has become something of a critical commonplace to identify Tate's brother, Benjamin, as a likely source in Tate's life for the character of George Posey (cf. Squires 145). Although I am not in a position to comment either way on the aptness of that attribution, I find remarkable similarities between Posey and Tate himself. Both were citizens of the modern world, but neither could be at peace with it. In a memoir Tate writes about the outbreak of World War I: "I could not know that August 5, 1914, was the end of the nineteenth century, and that four years later, when I entered college, I would be in a new world so different from the old that I would never quite understand it, but would be *both of it and opposed to it the rest of my life*" ("Lost Traveller's Dream" 17; my emphasis). This passage obviously establishes parallels between the situations of Tate and Lacy Buchan: in each case, war marks a transition between old and new worlds. It also makes clear, however, that despite his confusions and regret, Tate, like Posey, was a citizen of the new order. His early impatience with the culture of the South resembles Posey's with the management of Pleasant Hill, and both are signs of their common citizenship in the modern world.

Both Tate and Posey are as much opposed to the modern world as they are of it. Both would like to relinquish their citizenship. According to Lacy, Posey seeks to do so through his alliance with the Buchan family and the southern cause. Something like the same motivation underwrites Tate's Agrarian activities during the decade or so prior to the publication of *The Fathers*. Although both Posey and Tate look to the life of the Old South as a means of securing relief from modern conditions, in the end both find that life defective. Posey believes Pleasant Hill mismanaged and the Confederate army unprofessional. He finds the modern world intolerable, but he is too much its creature to accept the obvious inadequacies of the only available alternative. It is his tragedy that he can live at peace with neither world. The same must finally be said about Tate. He initially champions the ways of the South as a preferable alternative to the fragmentation and estrangement he thinks characteristic of the modern world. His opposition to that world continues unabated, but he increasingly opposes it in the name of an abstraction ("traditional society") and less in that of any specifically southern heritage. One suspects that he resorts to the more abstract argument out of a recognition that in the end the South is not a viable alternative. In *The Fathers*, Major Buchan, despite his obvious dignity, is certainly not equal to the task of preserving his way of life.

Major Buchan holds a place in the thematics of *The Fathers* comparable to that held by Captain Forrester in Cather's *A Lost Lady*, and the representations of both figures are remarkably similar. The obvious affection and dignity Cather and Tate vest in these figures derive finally from their presumed status as singular survivors of declining ways of life. Both are creatures of repetition and habit—the Captain's toasts and stories, the Major's morning rituals; traits clearly meant to link them to once stable and now waning ways of life. As the patriarch of Pleasant Hill, Major Buchan is a more fitting embodiment of a settled social order than Forrester, the retired railroad builder. In Cather's terms, both are members of that "courteous brotherhood" of a previous era, men "strong in attack but weak in defence, who could conquer but could not hold" (102). Their advanced age is perhaps representative of their incapacity but is not its cause. Instead, changes in mores have rendered them unable to resist or even to comprehend their younger, now economically more successful, adversaries. The Major is disarmed when Posey simply fails to recognize his rebuke for giving Lacy a gun, and later when Posey declares his intention to marry the Major's daughter, rather than asking the Major's permission to do so. After a stroke, Forrester is reduced to sitting in the sun as Peters manages his property, ruefully acknowledging to Niel that Peters "ain't overly polite" (115). Likewise, in *The Fathers* the former patriarch of Pleasant Hill eventually relinquishes the management of the family plantation to his son-in-law and suffers the indignity of being told by the overseer that he is no longer master of his own family plantation (272). If in these generational conflicts Posey is described in more favorable terms than Peters, that fact is attributable to Lacy's and Tate's sympathy for Posey's dilemma in contrast with Niel Herbert's and to Cather's unqualified contempt for everything Peters represents.

I have come to understand the depiction of Posey in *The Fathers* as Tate's oblique commentary on his own efforts as an Agrarian. Accordingly, I suggest that in Posey's failure to achieve relief from the modern world through his relationship with the Buchans, Tate acknowledges, if only to himself, the only possible outcome of his Agrarianism. His discontent with the modern world makes him long for a fading alternative to it; but Tate, like Posey, is finally too much a creature of the modern world to be content with the life available within traditional societies.

Two features Tate attributes to traditional life largely account for its appeal to him: its serenity and its coherence. Neither would be available to Tate. The presumed serenity of the traditional man derives from a conviction that his own ways are the only ways; the tradition operates through him unconsciously.[15] The would-be traditionalist, on the other hand, knows only too well that choices are to be made; he desires, in fact, to be relieved of this necessity. Once the need to choose has been recognized, however, the serenity of a Major Buchan cannot be attained, even if one consciously chooses just what Major Buchan would choose unconsciously. The serenity of a Major Buchan also has sources in the presumed compatibility among the various aspects of his life, and between his own life and the lives of his neighbors. In some measure, therefore, the benefits the would-be traditionalist seeks require the widespread adoption of his social program and the cultivation of compatible social institutions. Otherwise, his peace of mind would continually be tried by individuals and institutions operating according to different principles. By 1938 the failure of Agrarianism as a political program had long been clear to Tate. Since its benefits to individuals always depended upon its political success, Tate could no longer spend his energies in a cause so clearly lost. In its depiction of Major Buchan and Pleasant Hill, *The Fathers* fondly evokes a way of life that had unfortunately been weakened from within and could not sustain itself against incursions from without. The novel, accordingly, brings Tate's Agrarianism to a close.

VII

Eliot, Tate, and other American literary modernists shared a conviction that American life had recently become unusually stressful. They differed in their specific descriptions of these new cultural strains, their sense of their causes, and thus in their sense of how the situation as a whole might be redressed. That conviction, however, included and was shaped by a belief that life had not always been so harsh, that at other times and places societies had not subjected their members to these new difficulties. If these strains were new or had recently become exacerbated, it would seem to follow that one could locate their causes by identifying corresponding changes that had led to the weakening or displacement of earlier cultural institutions or practices. This conviction, in other words, contains a predisposition to believe that possible solutions can be found by surveying the cultural record and then restoring the appropriate institutions or practices. This was only a predisposition or bias; as we shall see in the following chapters, other alternatives were both conceivable and energetically invoked. However, it is no accident that several American literary modernists sought to combine literary innovation with cultural conservatism. The innovative aspect of their work represented a firm rejection of current and recent literary practices; the conservative aspect represented their belief that literature and the culture as a whole could be restored by adapting one or another traditional form to contemporary needs. If many American literary modernists believed that the tradition or the past held possible remedies for contemporary literary and cultural ills, they conceived of "tradition" in varying ways; these differences proved consequential not only for their literary practice but also for the larger social programs implied by their work. In this chapter I have attempted to suggest this diversity by outlining two representative attempts to make tradition serve critical literary and cultural ends.

For a time during the late teens and early twenties Eliot attempted to address these issues in strictly literary terms. His poetry in those years articulates a deep and abiding sense of the insufficiencies of the terms seemingly available for living meaningful and satisfying lives. Fellowship might be difficult to find in current social life, but in his prose Eliot suggests that the writer can join an "unconscious community" of true writers by sacrificing his dubious freedoms to the impersonality of the creative process. Of course one must put oneself to school in order to acquire knowledge of the literary tradition and the historical sense; but in the end a simple change of belief and attitude is thus held to promise relief. This phase of Eliot's career is marked by an incommensurability between the difficulties he senses and the solutions he would employ. We can characterize this discrepancy in two ways. The poetry implies that the inadequacies of contemporary life are widespread, affecting people in all walks of life, whatever their social station. Eliot's initial solution, however, is seemingly only available to the more culturally and literarily inclined; others are left to their own devices. Furthermore, it is odd that an individual's change of belief or attitude, however profound, could in itself be thought adequate to the dimensions of the problems illustrated by Eliot's poetry. Eliot's early humanism, in other words, is in many respects similar to Cather's effort to memorialize a passing cultural moment. It is an individual accommodation to a pervasive social change, not a form of resistance to it.

Eliot's conversion in 1927 could be seen as simply such a change in belief and thus as another form of individual accommodation. I want to argue, however, that more was at issue in Eliot's conversion than his assent to a set of traditional beliefs. His conversion also implicitly acknowledges that such beliefs are dependent upon certain institutional arrangements for their preservation and fulfillment. Eliot did not simply become religious or even Christian; he became a communicant in the Anglican Church, and thereafter assented to its doctrines and institutional forms. The traditional authority of that church in his adopted homeland and thus its historical compatibility with other English institutions were themselves compelling reasons for his choice. We have already seen that Eliot's definition of "tradition" changes after his conversion; his later emphasis upon an entire way of life reflects his new appreciation of the interrelation between personal beliefs on the one hand and social formations on the other. The Anglican Eliot would also address topics that were less specifically literary; he would, for instance, urge his contemporaries to reconsider their indifference to traditional institutions, suggesting that the latter afforded a bulwark within and against an otherwise debilitating social world. Although he would subsequently make his own religious and cultural convictions clear, Eliot rarely undertook such work with missionary zeal. It is unclear whether he was ever very hopeful that such overt proselytizing would meet with genuine success, that traditional English institutions of church and state could ever again become

robust and regain their earlier authority. Even their residual authority, however, afforded Eliot a welcome haven in an otherwise seemingly inhospitable world.

Although Allen Tate and the other Agrarians were religious to
varying degrees, religion was neither their primary concern nor central to their eventual program. They could find little to celebrate in
a social order seemingly governed increasingly by a market economy,
and so mounted a defense of the southern way of life against further
encroachments by the market. Like the later Eliot, and perhaps partially inspired by his example, they recognized the interdependence
of ideas and social arrangements. This recognition made their agitations from the first more directly political and thus more explicitly
dependent upon their success in converting others to their cause.
The economic hardships of the thirties might seem to have made
their platform initially plausible, but in the end they were able to
convince few others, even in the South, to accept it. After a few
years of fitful activity, Agrarianism as a cause was already exhausted
by 1938, when Tate was completing *The Fathers,* and its participants
were already drifting off to follow their individual inclinations.
Tate's novel suggests that he recognized, at least in retrospect, that
Agrarianism was doomed from the start. Like George Posey, Tate
was himself too much a product of the modern world to have ever
accepted a thoroughgoing traditional alternative to it. His irritation
at that world might for a time have tempted him to believe otherwise, but finally he was himself no more ready to accept forty acres
and a mule as his portion in life than were his largely unresponsive
fellow citizens during the thirties.

More than a decade later, in 1950, and perhaps still partially due
to the influence of Eliot, Tate would convert to Catholicism. More
than twenty years earlier, in a 1929 letter to Donald Davidson written as plans for *I'll Take My Stand* and the whole Agrarian movement
were still being made, Tate had confided: "I am more and more
heading toward Catholicism. We have reached a condition of the
spirit where no further compromise is possible" (Fain and Young
223). This comment introduces a brief account of Tate's current
work in progress, "The Fallacy of Humanism," which Eliot would
publish in *The Criterion* later that year. The entire Agrarian phase
of Tate's career thus represents an interlude between his dawning
attraction to Catholicism in 1929 and his eventual conversion in

1950. Although Tate's conversion might have been in part inspired by Eliot's, it would necessarily possess a different resonance. Eliot's conversion tied him more intimately to the history and life of his adopted country; it was part of a broader suit for membership in English life. Tate's eventual conversion to Catholicism, on the other hand, would further estrange him from his native region, whose traditions and ways of life he had earlier defended at some cost to his own temperament. Whatever else his conversion to Catholicism meant to Tate, it clearly represented an attempt to draw upon the resources of yet another and older tradition. It thus illustrates again for us the diversity among the ways American literary modernists would define and use the past when attempting to redress the strains of social life in their own era.

4

HARLEM AND THE LIMITS
OF A TIME AND PLACE

I was in love with Harlem long before I got there.
    Langston Hughes, "Early Days" 312

W
HEN RALPH ELLISON'S nameless protagonist in *Invisible Man* emerges from a subway and steps for the first time into Harlem, he reenacts what is, by 1952, a familiar scene in African-American fiction:

> I had never seen so many black people against a background of brick buildings, neon signs, plate glass and roaring traffic—not even on trips I had made with the debating team to New Orleans, Dallas or Birmingham. They were everywhere. . . . Then at the street intersection I had the shock of seeing a black policeman directing traffic—and there where white drivers in the traffic who obeyed his signals as though it was the most natural thing in the world. Sure I had heard of it, but this was *real.* My courage returned. This really was Harlem, and now all the stories which I had heard of the city-within-a-city leaped alive in my mind. (158–59)

Several of the specific figures Ellison uses to represent his protagonist's initial reaction to Harlem are familiar. When Angela Murray in Jessie Fauset's *Plum Bun,* first published in 1928, walks through Harlem for the first time, "she was amazed and impressed at this bustling, frolicking, busy, laughing great city within a greater one" (96). The scene forces Angela to acknowledge that "Harlem was a great city, but after all it was a city within a city" (98), and she would make her new life in the broader metropolis. In Rudolph Fisher's "The City of Refuge," first published by *Atlantic Monthly* in 1925, King Solomon Gillis initially arrives in Harlem like Ellison's narrator on the subway. Gillis too is momentarily overwhelmed by the number and apparent prosperity of Harlem's residents; the fugitive is transfixed, however, by the sight of an African-American policeman directing traffic: "[There] stood a handsome brass-buttoned giant directing the heaviest traffic Gillis had ever seen; halting unnumbered tons of automobiles and trucks and wagons and pushcarts and streetcars; holding them at bay with one hand while he swept similar tons peremptorily on with the other; ruling the wide crossing with supreme self-assurance. And he, too, was a Negro!" (4). Gillis, Angela Murray, and Ellison's narrator all journey to Harlem because of the stories about it that began circulating among African Americans in the 1910s, and all are surprised to find those stories seemingly confirmed by their first impressions. Their subsequent experiences in Harlem would complicate and qualify these initial impressions, but Harlem itself remains in these works a unique locus, and by midcentury Ellison must bring his narrator there to complete his veiled fictive history of African-American life.

James Weldon Johnson's celebratory history of Harlem, *Black Manhattan*, was published in 1930. "Throughout coloured America," Johnson declares, "Harlem is the recognized Negro capital" (3). He begins *Black Manhattan* with accounts of the earliest African-American presence in New York City, dating back at least to 1626, but the book as a whole concentrates on the recent establishment of Harlem as the national center for African-American life. African Americans in New York had previously lived primarily in midtown, and the move to Harlem during the teens was motivated largely by the availability of modern housing: "At the beginning of the year 1917 Negro Harlem was well along the road of development and prosperity. There was plenty of work, with a choice of jobs, and there was plenty of money. The community was beginning to feel conscious of its growing size and strength. It had entirely rid itself of the sense of apology for its existence. It was beginning to take pride in itself as Harlem, a Negro community" (231). The lure of Harlem in the early years of this century drew African Americans from throughout the nation, as well as immigrants from the West Indies and Africa. Between 1915 and 1930, the black population of New York City increased from 91,709 to 327,706, with most living in Harlem (Wintz 14). In a 1925 article with the feel of an anthropologist's report, Chester Crowell describes the behavior of newcomers to Harlem for the mainstream readers of the

Saturday Evening Post: "As he learns more about his new community, he begins to take vast pride in the achievements of his neighbors. Presently he feels a sincere pride in his race, a pride that makes him wish to go about his business with quiet dignity" (94).

Black Manhattan chronicles this growth and the sense of possibility it simultaneously reflected and fueled; but later chapters concentrate more on recent cultural contributions by African Americans. "The most outstanding phase of the development of the Negro in the United States during the past decade," writes Johnson, "has been the recent literary and artistic emergence of the individual creative artist; and New York has been, almost exclusively, the place where that emergence has taken place" (260). By the time *Black Manhattan* was published the Depression was already under way, and Harlem would soon come to signify something other than an ample present and a better future; in 1930 Johnson himself resigned from his position as general secretary of the NAACP and left Harlem for Fisk University, in Nashville, Tennessee.

Black Manhattan had its origins in Johnson's contribution to Alain Locke's *The New Negro,* and several paragraphs in the earlier essay, entitled "Harlem: The Culture Capital," reappear unchanged in the later book. Locke's 1925 collection is usually considered a manifesto for what has come to be called the Harlem or New Negro Renaissance. In this chapter I want to investigate several of the central figures and texts of the Harlem Renaissance and demonstrate their compatibility with other variants of American literary modernism. American history gave Locke, Jessie Fauset, Langston Hughes, and other African-American contributors to the Harlem Renaissance little to be nostalgic about and little wish to revive fading traditional ways of life.[1] African Americans brought to Harlem their churches, music, and other cultural resources from their lives in the South, but they came in search of fuller lives. Their alternatives to social arrangements otherwise decried broadly were immediately at hand, everywhere on the busy sidewalks of Harlem, the unofficial capital for a people who, until its emergence, had none. The confidence and hopes for the future that we earlier identified in Van Wyck Brooks's *America's Coming-of-Age* seemingly crystallized a decade later among African Americans, and they were seemingly abetted by World War I, the very experience that seemingly dampened the prospects for better ways of life among many of their white contemporaries. In these years African-American writers used various cultural strategies to express solidarity among black Americans. These expressions are the counterparts to the images of viable communities so crucial to other variants of American literary modernism. For a people scarcely fifty years removed from slavery, a people still widely stigmatized and subjected to legal and social discrimination, such images were at once a claim upon their own dignity and a rejoinder to those who would continue to deny them any dignity. Many of these writers were drawn to Harlem, and the city-within-a-city provided them with a cultural apparatus in the forms of opportunities to collaborate, outlets for their work, and the prospect of an interested readership, both black and white. I shall look initially at Locke's own contributions to *The New Negro*, and then at some of the fiction and poetry that would seem to realize his claims. In these years there was a broad curiosity about African-American life, as at least a narrow segment of the broader society seemingly believed that it provided cultural resources not otherwise available in the United States. In this chapter, however, I am less interested in what various aspects of African-American life in the twenties might have meant to their white contemporaries, such as Carl Van Vechten and others who made pilgrimages to the rent parties and famous nightclubs in Harlem, than in the significance vested by African Americans themselves in these same cultural possibilities.

I

Alain Locke was born in 1886. His parents were both teachers, and he grew up in comfortable middle-class homes in Philadelphia and nearby Camden, New Jersey. After graduating from Philadelphia's Central High School and its affiliated two-year teacher's college, Locke matriculated at Harvard College in 1904. When he graduated in 1907 he became the first African American to be awarded a Rhodes Scholarship for graduate study at Oxford University. After undertaking further study in Berlin, Locke joined the faculty at Howard University in 1912. He was invited to serve as master of ceremonies for a 1924 dinner given by *Opportunity*, a magazine sponsored by the National Urban League, to recognize the publication of Jessie Fauset's first novel, *There Is Confusion*. This occasion marks for many the beginning of the Harlem Renaissance, and it led to an invitation to Locke from Paul Kellogg, the editor of *Survey Graphic,* to serve as guest editor for a special issue to be devoted to Harlem. The Harlem number was published in March 1925; a revised and expanded version was published by Boni and Liveright later that same year as *The New Negro.*

In his several introductions to sections of *The New Negro,* Locke argues for the emergence of a new spirit among African Americans, and he uses the fiction, poetry, drama, and essays he includes in the volume to document his claims. This new spirit has emerged, according to Locke, amidst and partially as a consequence of vast demographic shifts. He identifies three especially salient factors: a population shift from South to North, movement from countryside to city, and the emergence of class differentiation among African Americans, so that "to regard and treat the Negro *en masse . . .* is becoming with every day less possible, more unjust and more ridiculous" (6). In various urban centers and especially in Harlem, African Americans from many different backgrounds and with distinct ambitions have come to live side-by-side: "Hitherto, it must be admitted that American Negroes have been a race more in name than in fact, or to be exact, more in sentiment than in experience. The chief bond between them has been that of a common condition rather than a common consciousness; a problem in common rather than a life in common. In Harlem, Negro life is seizing upon its first chances for group expression and self-determination. It is—or promises at least to be—a race capital" (7). The experience of living in close proximity with one another allowed African Americans to be newly conscious of themselves as a people and proud of their collective accomplishments. "This deep feeling of race is at present the mainspring of Negro life. It seems to be the outcome of the reaction to proscription and prejudice; an attempt, fairly successful on the whole, to convert a defensive into an offensive position, a handicap into an incentive" (11).

Writing at a time not long after a series of violent racial incidents and when segregation was still legally sanctioned, Locke nonetheless terms as "the most unsatisfactory feature of our present stage of race relationships . . . the fact that the more intelligent and representative elements of the two race groups have at so many points got quite out of vital touch with one another" (9). There was obviously contact enough between white employers and their African-American employees, and even in some workplaces between manual workers of both races. Locke specifically regrets the comparable lack of interaction between the intellectual and professional classes of both races. He senses that this situation is just beginning to improve: "There is a growing realization that in social effort the co-operative basis must supplant long-distance philanthropy, and that the only safeguard for mass relations in the future must be provided in the carefully maintained contacts of the enlightened minorities of both race groups" (9). The fact that these interactions occur between "the enlightened minorities of both race groups" does not alone assure their productiveness; the participants must further be able and willing to engage one another. The likelihood that they would encounter condescension or worse has too often caused African-American participants in such exchanges in the past to operate behind a "spite wall" and to allow "social discrimination to segregate [them] mentally" (9), thereby depriving themselves of access to the best current thought. Locke believes that such intellectual consequences of the social situation of African Americans are being overcome primarily by the New Negro's new confidence and drive toward self-expression. If, as we saw, Locke believes that the initiatives that are producing the New Negro came initially from the masses, he also clearly believes that they cannot reach fruition until and unless they are now guided by the social and intellectual elites of both races. When he observes that "much of this reopening of intellectual contacts has centered in New York" (10), he seems to have squarely in mind the racial coalition headed by W. E. B. DuBois at the NAACP and DuBois's own commitment to leadership by what he called the "talented tenth."

Locke believes that for the most part the "Negro mind reaches out as yet to nothing but American wants, American ideas" (11–12), but he warns that it might turn to more radical solutions should its aspirations be unduly frustrated. At the same time, the international population of Harlem makes African Americans aware of broader responsibilities: "One is the consciousness of acting as the advance-guard of the African peoples in their contact with Twentieth Century civilization; the other, the sense of a mission of rehabilitating the race in world esteem from that loss of prestige for which the fate and conditions of slavery have so largely been respon-

sible" (14). Locke documents the emergence of these international
interests with references to the pan-African congresses organized by
W. E. B. DuBois and to Garveyism, and locates their animating center in Harlem. "The pulse of the Negro world," he writes, "has begun to beat in Harlem" (14).[2]

Writing in 1925, Locke could not know how these new international interests might most productively manifest themselves in the
years ahead: "Our greatest rehabilitation may possibly come through
such channels, but for the present, more immediate hope rests in
the reevaluation by white and black alike of the Negro in terms of
his artistic endowments and cultural contributions, past and pro-
spective" (15). Locke argues that African Americans had already for
generations contributed not only to the economy but also to the
culture of the American South, even if the pervasiveness and value
of the latter contribution had yet to be acknowledged. He is confident that new artistic contributions will be recognized: "A second
crop of the Negro's gifts promises still more largely. He now becomes a conscious contributor and lays aside the status of a bene-
ficiary and ward for that of a collaborator and participant in American civilization. The great social gain in this is the releasing of our
talented group from the arid fields of controversy and debate to the
productive fields of creative expression" (15). Locke seems to believe that defensiveness and resentment among African-American
writers and artists may frequently have compromised their work in
the past, but that the new spirit of racial pride and solidarity among
the generation that has recently come of age permits them equal
access to cultural self-expression. "Our poets have now stopped
speaking for the Negro—they speak as Negroes" (48). Locke writes
with obvious pride and excitement about the accomplishments of
a new generation of African-American writers, who have rapidly
achieved more broad recognition for their work than previous
African-American writers received in their lifetimes. "It has
been their achievement also to bring the artistic advance of the Negro sharply into stepping alignment with contemporary artistic
thought, mood, and style. They are thoroughly modern, some of
them ultra-modern, and Negro thoughts now wear the uniform
of the age" (50).

Locke celebrates the artistic accomplishments of the New Negro
for several reasons. He values them in themselves, simply as artistic

contributions to the culture. He also believes, however, that they "should in turn prove the key to that revaluation of the Negro which must precede or accompany any considerable future betterment of race relationships" (15). When the broad public acknowledges that fiction and poetry written by African Americans is every bit as worthy of acclaim as that written by their white contemporaries, it will be more difficult to justify any differentiation in the treatment of the races. The recognition of artistic equality should produce social and economic equality. Locke thus enlists African-American artists and writers in the broader struggle for racial equality, but he does not ask or even especially want them to address that struggle directly. Indeed, he claims that the sense of racial solidarity available in Harlem releases African-American writers from the "self-consciousness, rhetoric, bombast, and the hampering habit of setting artistic values with primary regard for moral effect—all those pathetic over-compensations for a group inferiority complex which our social dilemmas inflicted upon several unhappy generations" (48). Social equality would be a by-product of the cultural contributions of individual New Negroes, not necessarily their polemical goal; and it would flow from the respect they won for the race as a whole by means of their artistry, not from the force of arguments they mount on behalf of social and economic justice. With the sense of equality already in evidence everywhere on the bustling streets of Harlem, African-American writers, according to Locke, have in one sense been liberated from obligations to the race and, in another sense, been enabled to render it a greater, albeit indirect, service by winning broad respect for their literary merit.

II

As the editor first of the special Harlem number of *Survey Graphic* and then of *The New Negro,* Locke eagerly assumed the role of spokesperson for the rising generation of African-American writers. He was not alone in assigning special significance to the cultural work accomplished by the writer, even though his own contributions in this regard now typically overshadow those by others, black and white. It will repay our effort to situate Locke's several introductions in *The New Negro* within the broader discourse in which it participates.

In 1922 James Weldon Johnson published the first edition of his *The Book of American Negro Poetry*. Johnson's cultural ambitions for the anthology are clearly stated in his introduction: "The final measure of the greatness of all peoples is the amount and standard of the literature and art they have produced. The world does not know that a people is great until that people produces a great literature and art. No people that has produced great literature and art has ever been looked upon by the world as distinctly inferior. . . . And nothing will do more to . . . raise his status than a demonstration of intellectual parity by the Negro through the production of literature and art" (9). Johnson's prose possesses a directness and force that Locke rarely achieves, but he places a similar responsibility upon African-American writers, who are to legitimate the cultural worth of the race as a whole. Elsewhere in the introduction Johnson claims that African Americans are responsible for "the only things artistic that have yet sprung from American soil and been universally acknowledged as distinctive American products" (10)—namely, the Uncle Remus stories, spirituals, the cakewalk, and ragtime. These cultural products, however, are rarely considered equivalents of traditional Western literary forms, and so *The Book of American Negro Poetry* is meant to demonstrate that African Americans are comparably accomplished in these arts as well. When he was preparing the first edition of his anthology in 1921, Johnson did not have available to him work by Countee Cullen and Langston Hughes, who figure prominently in Locke's *The New Negro* and whose work would largely come to be definitive of the Harlem Renaissance, and he claims to have prepared a second edition in 1931 largely for the purpose of including them.

Locke concludes his general introduction to *The New Negro* with this sentence: "And certainly, if in our lifetime the Negro should not be able to celebrate his full initiation into American democracy, he can at least, on the warrant of these things, celebrate the attainment of a significant and satisfying new phase of group development, and with it a spiritual Coming of Age" (16). Locke's capitalization calls attention to the final phrase, and it feels like a deliberate allusion to Van Wyck Brooks's *America's Coming-of-Age*.[3] As it happens, Brooks and Locke were classmates at Harvard; and Jeffrey Stewart reports that Brooks, Locke, and the future poet John Hall Wheelock took lunch at the same table in Commons during their first year in Cambridge (38). In May 1925, when Locke was preparing the Liveright version of his collection for publication, Brooks was among a distinguished panel of judges for the first literary awards sponsored by *Opportunity.*

Locke's argument and tone in *The New Negro* share several features with Brooks's in *America's Coming-of-Age.* Both set writers crucial cultural tasks. For Brooks, as we saw in the first chapter, American writers to date have been too complicitous with the culture as a whole and thus have neglected to provide it with means to link its professed values with its everyday activities. He clearly expects writers to create the necessary linkages. Locke provides less historical background, but he gives the writer an equally crucial social task; the young writers just coming of age need to demonstrate the full artistic potential of African Americans, thereby demonstrating the worthiness of the race as a whole to be treated with the same respect accorded to other Americans. Brooks and Locke seem equally confident, though in retrospect the reasons for their optimism are different. Locke's introductions in *The New Negro* name many accomplished and promising African-American writers, and the anthology includes representative examples of their work. Neither in *America's Coming-of-Age* nor in *Letters and Leadership* does Brooks mention specific writers or works that would seem to be the basis for his apparent confidence that the cultural situation he analyzes so energetically will soon be overcome. Indeed, when Brooks in later reviews and books comes to write about the work of his contemporaries, his disappointment is obvious, making it seem that he subsequently felt that his earlier confidence in their likely accomplishments had been misplaced. Locke, in short, can introduce us to his younger generation, whereas Brooks can only attempt to call his into existence in the belief that the time is right.

When Brooks, Locke, Johnson, and others write about the role of the writer on the current scene, they frequently invoke other instances of cultural nationalism, especially in Ireland. In *Letters and Leadership,* for instance, Brooks alludes several times to Manzini's Italy by way of illustrating how a writer can meld a region into a people. In a late chapter he declares, "Ireland and America really are alike in that they inherit a dominant academic tradition colonial in essence, having its home in centers of civilization remote from the springs of a national life which has only late come into its own consciousness" (91). While Brooks was affiliated with *Seven Arts* in the teens, it ran a series of articles on emerging cultural tendencies in "Young Japan," "Young Spain," "Young India," and "Youngest Ireland," including Brooks's own "Young America." *Survey Graphic* devoted special issues to Mexico and Ireland prior to the Harlem issue edited by Locke; Paul Kellogg advertised the forthcoming Harlem issue by comparing it to the earlier special issues: "Writers, poets, artists, professional men, social workers, [in Harlem] express a social and cultural ferment which is as interesting in its way as the resurgence of Celtic Ireland or the revival of native culture in Mexico" (qtd. in Chambers 113). Finally, when James Weldon Johnson, in his introduction to *The Book of American Negro Poetry,* was discussing the difficulties of using dialect for the African-American poet, he declares, "What the colored poet in the United States needs to do is something like what Synge did for the Irish; he needs to find a form that will express the racial spirit by symbols from within rather than by symbols from without, such as the mere mutilation of English spelling and punctuation" (41). Locke draws on these same examples when he writes that "Harlem has the same role to play for the New Negro as Dublin has had for the New Ireland or Prague for the New Czechoslovakia" (7).

When Locke and Johnson draw African-American writing into the matrix of cultural nationalism, they clearly demonstrate their awareness of possible models for the cultural resurgence among African Americans that they wish to document and abet. They write shortly after the flowering of Irish literature early in this century and the establishment of a free Irish state. The stage Irishman was as much a stock comic figure in British literature as the African American was in the popular minstrel shows. In both cases, dialect was already assigned a place within the repertoire. What drew Johnson and Locke to the example of the Irish is their writers' apparent success in tapping both a deep folk tradition and a broad Irish audience. Synge wrote as an Irishman and explicitly to the Irish, as well as to others who share their interests. As we have already seen, for Locke it was important that the New Negro wrote as a Negro, not on behalf of Negroes.

The political success of the Irish is perhaps another reason for Locke and Johnson to be optimistic about the prospects for African Americans, but neither wished for political independence for African Americans, and neither mentions the political turmoil in Ireland that accompanied the literary production. It is extremely doubtful that Synge and the other Irish writers of the time would themselves, whatever the force of their writing, have led to the establishment of a free Irish state. The fact that the example of Ireland was also available to Brooks as a way of conceptualizing the continuing dependence of American literature as such upon the English tradition suggests that the situation of African-American writing is more complicated than that in Ireland. The latter could at least appeal to a known indigenous tradition, whereas African Americans were only beginning to become aware of possible African cultural roots. The Irish sought political independence, whereas African Americans primarily sought equality, but within the existing political framework. Identity politics was crucial in both movements (and in Brooks's charge to the American writer), but Locke and Johnson thought to break the logic of that position short of its seemingly logical conclusion. African-American writers were to demonstrate their worthiness to be full citizens, not to sue for citizenship in another, racially homogeneous, nation. Marcus Garvey and others were urging the latter course during the twenties, and it is crucial to acknowledge that Locke and Johnson consciously rejected it in favor of a more moderate position. Instead, they would have African-American writers contribute to American life and culture by drawing upon the African-American experience and their own native talents to produce a literature that would be enjoyed and admired by all Americans.

III

The range of texts produced by African Americans during the twenties is among the most remarkable features of the Harlem Renaissance. There was the experimental novel, such as Jean Toomer's *Cane;* more overtly conventional novels, such as Jessie Fauset's *Plum Bun;* as well as genre novels, such as Rudolph Fisher's *The Conjure-Man Dies* and *The Walls of Jericho.* Countee Cullen chose to write within and to master conventional poetic forms, whereas Langston Hughes opted for more open forms and frequently ran the risks that Johnson had identified in the use of dialect. Claude McKay had published a volume of poetry before coming to the United States from

Jamaica. His first publication in this country was in *Seven Arts,* and his fiction and poetry are usually claimed for the Harlem Renaissance, but his inclusion further complicates efforts to identify a common denominator or project informing the movement as a whole. Locke was for many years a publicist for African-American cultural activity, and his eagerness to seize on any plausible evidence of it perhaps explains his willingness to enlist such a range of writers and work. However, this range presents a difficulty for later historians and critics wishing to understand this burst of creative activity, and especially for those who, like myself, suspect that it might best be understood within the broader, contemporaneous phenomenon of American literary modernism. It is hard enough to intuit a common project for Jessie Fauset and Langston Hughes; it is accordingly more difficult to understand how their project is compatible with that of a Willa Cather or Wallace Stevens, both of whom were living in Greenwich Village during the years that Harlem was emerging several miles to the north as an African-American cultural center.

It might, of course, be possible to argue that the Harlem Renaissance should be recognized as an isolated phenomenon, with its own causes, resources, and cultural significance. Certainly African Americans possess their own special history in this country, one making it more difficult for them simply to assume their full citizenship. Accordingly, the statements made by Eliot and Pound when they became expatriates, and later by the former when he became a British citizen, are different from the statements made by Richard Wright and James Baldwin when they chose to live abroad. Certainly, too, African-American writers must be conscious of the likely racial composition of their readership in ways that white writers need not be. When Willa Cather, in *A Lost Lady,* allows Judge Pommeroy, in describing the actions of the other Denver bank directors to Marian Forrester, to say, "By God, Madam, I think I've lived too long! In my day the difference between a business man and a scoundrel was bigger than the difference between a white man and a nigger" (76), she is presumably not concerned about the reactions of any possible black readers, nor qualifying the respect she would have her readers feel for Niel Herbert's uncle. African-American writers rarely assume such impunity. These factors alone might tempt us to assume that the cultural energies now identified as the Harlem Renaissance cannot or should not be assimilated within the roughly contemporaneous phenomenon I am calling American literary modernism.

I shall argue that we should resist that temptation. The similarities already identified between Alain Locke's argument for the emergence of the New Negro and Van Wyck Brooks's earlier call to a new generation of writers in *America's Coming-of-Age* suggest that both looked to writers to fulfill similar cultural agendas. The broader cultural maturation that Brooks foresaw for the nation as a whole took a more specific form for African Americans, and Brooks himself no doubt would have neither recognized nor appreciated the degree to which a Langston Hughes thought to answer his call to the younger generation to reconnect American values and everyday practices. However, Brooks's own limitations need not keep us now from noticing the similarities between *America's Coming-of-Age* and his former Harvard classmate's introductions in *The New Negro*. Locke is less interested in the fate of the nation as a whole than in the place allotted to African Americans within the United States. That place hitherto had been marginal at best. Locke argues, however, that several large demographic shifts have enabled Harlem to emerge as a thriving and cosmopolitan city within a city. Its emergence, in turn, affords a new measure of racial pride and solidarity among its residents. Locke senses this new pride and optimism among the younger generation of African-American writers, and he charges them with producing a literature so strong that it will, by its very existence, serve to disprove any argument against full equality for all African Americans.

African-American writers in the twenties used various strategies to represent this new sense of racial solidarity. Representations of Harlem itself figure prominently in their work. "Both the time and the circumstances of its creation," argues Huggins in his *Harlem Renaissance,* "made Harlem symbolize the Afro-American's coming of age" (13). These representations provide more than a chance setting for the fiction and poetry of the time. In a single image Harlem both crystallized the richer future that African Americans imagined might soon be available to them and enacted their identification with the people of Harlem. This identification is crucial to this literature, since it articulates the racial solidarity that Locke took to be characteristic of the New Negro: to celebrate Harlem is to celebrate African Americans. These celebrations of racial solidarity are the counterpart in the Harlem Renaissance of the possible viable communities identified in other variants of American literary modernism. As we saw in the second chapter, Cather imagined that an earlier moment in our history made available stable and functioning communities affording their members mutual respect and support. She believed that such communities were no longer available—there were now too few Blum brothers, who respected class distinctions, and too many Ivy Peters, who took pleasure in flouting them—and considered herself fortunate that she could comfort herself in their absence by means of her memories of an earlier and better way of life. The cold weather, unaccustomed bustle, or absence of former neighbors back home in the South might all occasionally tempt Harlemites to regret their new lives in New York; but Harlem typically held them, largely because it represented new possibilities for African Americans. According to Locke, Harlem embodied their new consciousness of themselves as a people and, for a time at least, came closer to providing them with modern housing and other amenities of modern life than did other locations within the country. Living in Harlem enabled some African Americans to consider themselves less a subjugated people than, according to Locke, as "the advance-guard of the African peoples in their contact with Twentieth Century civilization."

Writers of the Harlem Renaissance articulated this new confidence in various ways, a fact that contributes to the diversity already acknowledged among their works. Some chose primarily to represent the African-American middle class. This strategy harkens back to earlier works by African-American writers, as well as to the political programs advocated by Booker T. Washington and W. E. B. DuBois. Representations of the lives and accomplishments of the "talented tenth" were to evidence the worthiness of African Americans for full citizenship in the same way as the literary accomplishments of African-American writers. The persistence of this strategy is still evident in the ways critics write about DuBois, Locke, Countee Cullen, and Jessie Fauset. It seems impossible to mention these writers without making reference to their remarkable educational accomplishments; such references document their achievements and, by implication, the potential accomplishments of other African Americans. This strategy typically minimizes the presumed differences between African Americans and other segments of the population, concentrating instead on the unique problems faced by individuals who in most respects share the same ambitions as their contemporaries but who, because of their race, are not afforded the same opportunities. Another, though initially less familiar, literary strategy that emerged during the Harlem Renaissance involves the representation of other segments of African-American life. This is the strategy that was pursued by Claude McKay in *Home to Harlem,* by Langston Hughes, and by Sterling A. Brown. It accepted and even celebrated the differences in the specific values and cultures developed by African Americans and implicitly argued that these differences represented the specific contributions that African Americans might make to the culture as a whole. This strand of the Harlem Renaissance often risked the use of dialect, whereas the former usually deployed a diction comfortably within standard, or even elevated, English. The initial reception of this strand was frequently controversial among African Americans; in his review of *Home to Harlem,* for instance, DuBois declared that reading the novel made him feel in need of a bath (202), and in a summary article Locke characterized McKay as a "spiritual truant." In retrospect, these works are often considered more definitive of the Harlem Renaissance than those written by Cullen or Fauset, which can seem, by comparison, more conventional, less venturesome, and less distinctively African American. Certainly some contemporary white readers were more intrigued by this second strand, which could be taken as evidence of an indigenous alternative to cultural forms that seemed either oppressive or played out. Representations of Harlem itself figure less prominently in the fiction of Zora Neale Hurston and the poetry of Sterling A. Brown, thereby loosening the connection between the city-within-a-city and the upsurge of African-American literary production. In its place, representations of the African-American folk—rural as well as urban, working class as well as middle class—are not mediated by figures of Harlem. I shall argue, however, that the emergence of Harlem provided the literary apparatus that supported Hurston's and Brown's work and empowered them to identify with rural African Americans, thereby enacting a racial pride and community that functions in their work in the same manner in which figures of Harlem function in the work of their contemporaries.

IV

Jessie Redmon Fauset was the literary editor for *The Crisis,* the NAACP journal edited by W. E. B. DuBois between 1919 and 1926, years when its monthly circulation reached 100,000 households. In that capacity she met many aspiring young African-American writers and was able to introduce the more promising and accomplished to her readers. She published Langston Hughes's "The Negro Speaks of Rivers," for instance, a few short months after he graduated from high school in Cleveland. In *The Big Sea,* Hughes would later write that Fauset was one of "the three people who midwifed the so-called New Negro literature into being" (218)—Charles Johnson, the editor of *Opportunity,* and Alain Locke being the other two. In the early twenties, Fauset also edited and wrote for *The Brownies Book,* a short-lived children's magazine for which DuBois had great hopes. Her first novel, *There Is Confusion,* was published in 1924, and would be followed by three others: *Plum Bun* (1928), *The Chinaberry Tree* (1931), and *Comedy: American Style* (1933).

Although Fauset lived in Harlem from 1919 to 1940 and was one center of its literary activities, of her four novels only *There Is Confusion* and *Plum Bun* are set primarily in New York, the former in the early years of Harlem's emergence and the latter only occasionally venturing north of Central Park. Her fiction is primarily concerned with exploring the seeming antinomies involved in living in the United States as simultaneously black and a member of the cultured middle class. Throughout much of *Plum Bun,* Angela Murray, Fauset's heroine, attempts to bypass this dilemma by achieving the satisfactions available to the latter while passing as white. She had been initiated into this possibility by her mother while still a child. The two would be mistaken for white when they shopped in Philadelphia on Saturdays, and the young Angela mistook the reasons for her mother's obvious pleasure during these excursions:

The daughter could not guess that if the economic status or the racial genius of coloured people had permitted them to run modish hotels or vast and popular department stores her mother would have been there. She drew for herself certain clearly formed conclusions which her subconscious mind thus codified:

First, that the great rewards of life—riches, glamour, pleasure,— are for white skinned people only. Second, that Junius and Virginia [her father and younger sister] were denied these privileges because they were dark. (17–18)

Fauset wrote these lines while living in Harlem, that is, in an environment that afforded African Americans direct access to "the great rewards of life," as Angela understood them, in their own neighborhoods. Had the Murrays lived in the Harlem of the twenties, in other words, Angela's mother need not have relied on her skin color for access to such pleasures, and the young Angela herself might have been spared the conclusions she drew on the streets of Philadelphia.

From a very early age, Angela wanted nothing so much as to be free—free to enjoy these pleasures glimpsed on Saturday excursions, free from restraints imposed by Jim Crow laws, free from tiresome talk about racial betterment. Fauset arranges the plot line of *Plum Bun* to permit Angela an unusual degree of freedom. Angela's desire for freedom has a special resonance for an African American, and it cannot simply be dismissed as inappropriate without a careful definition of freedom, its uses and inevitable limits. Although by no means wealthy, the Murrays are able to provide a secure home for their daughters and to educate them for careers as teachers. Fauset also arranges for the elder Murrays to die conveniently, thereby at once providing Angela with a modest inheritance to finance her quest for freedom and the emotional independence that makes her decision to pass less immediately loathsome. When Angela prepares for a new life in New York a few months after her parents' deaths, she explains her decision to her sister in these terms: "Why should I shut myself off from all the things I want most,—clever people, people who do things, Art, . . . travel and a lot of things which are in the world for everybody really but which only white people, as far as I can see, get their hands on. I mean scholarships and special funds, patronage" (78). Angela abandons her darker-skinned sister, but siblings usually pursue their own lives, and her decision to pass does not as directly involve rejecting her family and heritage as it would were her parents still alive. Fauset seems to be conspiring with Angela to make the latter's decisions as explicable and acceptable as possible.

Once in New York, Angela settles into a leisurely routine centering on art classes at Cooper Union. The classes introduce her to other New Yorkers, including another young African American who studiously maintains some distance between herself and her otherwise white classmates. Angela is eventually courted by a wealthy young white man, Roger Fielding. Fielding obviously does not know that Angela is African American; it is enough for him to know that she comes from a family of little social consequence, and as such would never be accepted by his father as a potential daughter-in-law. Angela might be willing to deny her heritage, but Fielding is unwilling to risk his inheritance, and so he proposes to a surprised Angela that she become his mistress. Her scruples and ambition initially keep Angela from accepting his proposition, but she eventually convinces herself that there is no good reason to resist and thus consents to the relationship he seeks.

Throughout this long, central series of episodes racial issues generally recede from the novel. In one scene, Angela is embarrassed and angry when Fielding reveals his bigotry by directing that an African-American family be ejected from a restaurant where he is dining with Angela; for the most part, however, Fauset seems more interested in using this relationship to demonstrate that the options of even white women are more limited than Angela had previously imagined. The freedom that Angela sought by passing as white, in other words, proves to be less capacious than she had imagined, and it is doubly ironic, given Angela's insistence on freedom, that Fielding invokes the rhetoric of "free love" in his pursuit of her. Angela has an inkling about such matters amidst the initial pleasure in her new life in New York:

> She was seeing the world, she was getting acquainted with life in her own way without restrictions or restraint; she was young, she was temporarily independent, she was intelligent, she was white. She remembered an expression "free, white and twenty-one,"—this was what it meant then, this sense of owning the world, this realization that other things being equal, all things were possible. "If I were a man," she said, "I could be president," and laughed at

herself for the "if" itself proclaimed a limitation. But that inconsistency bothered her little; she did not want to be a man. Power,
greatness, authority, these were fitting and proper for men; but
there were sweeter, more beautiful gifts for women, and power of
a certain kind too. (87–88)

As Fielding's lover, Angela is immediately "possessive"; if she defines herself by means of this relationship, it becomes important that
she be able to give a full account of his activities (203). Fielding,
however, increasingly resents any display of her possessive interest.
He rebukes her for calling him at home. When she replies that he
calls her, he replies, "Of course I do, that's different. I'm a man"
(228). "The conversation about the telephone left an effect all out
of proportion to its actual importance; it represented for her the
apparently unbridgeable difference between the sexes; everything
was for men, but even the slightest privilege was to be denied to a
woman unless the man chose to grant it" (229). Later, after Angela
has broken off her relationship with Fielding, she reassesses her decision to seek fulfillment by passing in New York. With the exception
of a single incident, she does not believe she has caused any injury;
moreover, she reasons, "if she had been a boy and had left home no
one would have a word of blame, it would have been the proper
thing, to be expected and condoned" (308). Angela's reassessment
of her actions glosses over the question of passing—a young male
might be expected to leave home and seek his fortune elsewhere, but
it is not clear that he would be expected to pass, or that his actions
would be condoned if he did; her affair with Fielding, however,
makes Angela painfully aware that her freedom is circumscribed as
much by her gender and class as by her race, since at no point does
she reveal to Fielding that she is African American.

Instead of the fulfillment that Angela sought by passing in New
York, she eventually recognizes that her new life is extremely lonely.
At one point she acknowledges to herself that "life which had
seemed so promising, so golden, had failed to supply her with a
single friend to whom she could turn in an hour of extremity"
(234). She had imagined herself becoming the hostess of a salon,
but she in fact lives in a small Greenwich Village apartment and has
very few friends. The temporal dimension of *Plum Bun* is rather
faint, so the reader is likely as surprised as Angela when she recog-

nizes that she has been in New York nearly three years and still lacks a circle of close friends. Angela's isolation in Greenwich Village is underscored by occasional comparisons to the life being led by her sister, who has also come to New York and is living in Harlem. "Virginia, without making an effort, seemed overwhelmed, almost swamped by friendships, pleasant intimacies, a thousand charming interests" (241). Virginia and another teacher had rented an apartment on 139th Street, and "it seemed to Angela well worth an effort to live in this beautiful block with its tree-bordered pavements, its spacious houses, its gracious neighbourliness" (242).[4] It occurs to Angela, in other words, that her sister has willy-nilly acquired many of the accoutrements of the good life, the very things Angela set such stock in. The life of the dark-skinned Virginia, in short, is in many respects richer than the life Angela has been able to forge by passing as white in Greenwich Village. Perhaps the color line is not now the obstacle to personal fulfillment that Angela has been assuming it need be.

At the conclusion of *Plum Bun*, Angela jeopardizes a fellowship to Paris she wins for her painting by announcing her ancestry when the other winner, an African American, is denied the prize because of her race. Her declaration feels uncharacteristic, but it is actually at least her second self-sacrificial decision, since she has previously relinquished a growing affection for Anthony Cross when she recognizes that he is already engaged to her sister. "No," she explains to him, "I took her sister away from her [when she initially departed for New York and decided to pass]; I won't take her lover" (305). Fauset rewards Angela for her forbearance by giving her the trip to Paris and then, in the final paragraph, by reuniting her with Anthony Cross, who comes to Paris as a Christmas present from Virginia. In other words, Fauset withholds from Angela the satisfactions that she so fervently seeks precisely until she willingly relinquishes her claims on them.

Before she initially departs for New York, Angela has a conversation with Virginia in which she tries to explain her pending departure:

> "Now be practical, Jinny; after all, I am both white and Negro and look white. Why shouldn't I declare for the one that will bring me the greatest happiness, prosperity, and respect?"

"No reason in the world except that since in this country public opinion is against any infusion of black blood it would seem an awfully decent thing to put yourself, even in the face of appearances, on the side of black blood and say: 'Look here, this is what a mixture of black and white really means!' " (79–80)

Virginia's argument seems to be Fauset's own. Aside from the restrictions it imposed upon her, being an African American is seemingly an incidental fact about Angela. It provides her with no special talents or liabilities, no broader allegiances or debts; Fauset simply presents her as a talented, headstrong young American woman literally indistinguishable from the throngs of other young women intent upon making lives for themselves in New York. Virginia would have (and Fauset does have) Angela stand against public opinion and demonstrate that African Americans are Americans after all, and that at least some among them have the same middle-class aspirations, talents, and values as their white counterparts. "The matter of blood," Angela later says to her sister, "seems nothing compared with individuality, character, living"; it is an issue only "because this country of ours makes it so important" (354). If Roger Fielding and others can continually assume that Angela is, like them, white, it is because she is like them in every way that should matter. *Plum Bun* might be in most respects a quite conventional sentimental novel, but it quietly puts into question an assumption that seems deeply embedded in our culture about the crucial influence of race in the shaping of individual character.[5]

Given Fauset's apparent desire to minimize the presumed importance of race, it is not surprising that she makes so little of Harlem in *Plum Bun*. Near the end of the novel, however, there is a brief episode that is scarcely integrated into the fabric of the novel as a whole. Angela is emerging from the depression and intense loneliness that overwhelm her after she learns about Virginia and Anthony's relationship. The passage begins with a surprising paean to Harlem: "Harlem intrigued her; it was a wonderful city; it represented, she felt, the last word in racial pride, integrity and even self-sacrifice. Here were people of the very high intellectual type, exponents of the realest and most essential refinement living cheek by jowl with coarse or ill-bred or even criminal, certainly indifferent, members of their race" (326). The scene shifts to Maude's, a hairdressing shop in the heart of Harlem to which Angela would occasionally accompany Virginia, largely to listen to the other patrons talk among themselves. The clientele in Maude's documents the mixture of classes that has just caused Angela to marvel. Maude herself possesses "an air of real refinement" (327). She is originally from Texas but has since traveled to London and Paris and is as conversant about her trade "as any hairdresser in the vicinity of the Rue de la Paix or on Fifth Avenue" (327). The other patrons in Maude's, by way of contrast, are people that Angela would otherwise avoid; not only are they black, but Fauset's use of dialect in rendering a few snippets of conversation suggests that the speakers are southern and less educated than Angela. When it is explained that one patron is returning to Texas, another exclaims, "Child, ain't you learned that you don't never own no property in Texas as long as those white folks are down there too? Just let those Ku Kluxers get it into their heads that you've got something they want" (327–28). Angela recognizes the speaker "as the epitome of the iron and blood in a race which did not know how to let go of life" (328).

This is one of few passages in *Plum Bun* that focus on Harlem life proper, and the only one that expresses sentiments more common in other works from the Harlem Renaissance, from the celebration of Harlem itself in the initial paragraph to Angela's final admiration for the determination illustrated by the ungrammatical patron in Maude's. In her own, perhaps misguided, way, Angela has illustrated a comparable determination. Like the woman who will never return to Texas, she displays the courage to kick herself free from the security available in the only life she has known to seek greater satisfactions in New York City. Angela seeks her new life downtown, while passing as white, whereas the patrons in Maude's and thousands like them in the first decades of this century seek their new lives uptown, in Harlem. Since *Plum Bun* concludes immediately after Angela and Anthony Cross are reunited in Paris, readers can only guess how and where they might live thereafter. It seems apparent, however, that neither will deliberately pass, whether in Paris or New York; and it is at least plausible to assume that if they returned to the United States, they would choose to live in Harlem, where Cross has been living all along, even while he was passing for white as an art student at the Cooper Union. Angela has learned, during her occasional excursions to Harlem, like her visits to Maude's, that Harlem makes available to African Americans the refinement she desires, even if it must exist adjacent to coarseness. Had the Murrays lived in Harlem instead of Philadelphia when Angela and Virginia were children, Angela and her mother would not have needed to pass for white on their Saturday shopping excursions, since that city-within-a-city contained "the bustle, excitement and fashion" (17) that her mother craved and that were only available at that time and place in predominantly white sections of Philadelphia. When Angela learns to appreciate the determination and resilience articulated by the ungrammatical speaker in Maude's, she learns to recognize and admire qualities available everywhere on the streets of Harlem, qualities she too possesses in abundance.

Jessie Fauset's contributions to the Harlem Renaissance are considerable if oblique. She is intent on demonstrating that African Americans are in no crucial ways different from their white contemporaries. The African American, she would declare in her foreword to *The Chinaberry Tree,* "is a dark American who wears his joy and rue very much as does the white American" (xxxii). The accident of her skin tone aside, these fundamental similarities are the reasons that Angela can pass for white so effortlessly. She need not learn another language or in other ways prepare herself for living as a white person: such a life simply releases her from the obstacles to fulfillment that a nation that makes too much of race places before people of color. Miss Powell and Angela Murray are gifted enough to win prizes for their paintings in open competition with white art students. Their accomplishments do not signify for Fauset any special artistic endowment possessed by African Americans. Instead, they represent the cultural recognition that Alain Locke predicted for the younger generation in *The New Negro:* "The especially cultural recognition they win should in turn prove the key to that revaluation of the Negro which must precede or accompany any considerable further betterment of race relationships" (15). Fauset and some of her contemporaries, such as Countee Cullen and Georgia Douglas Johnson, chose to seek this recognition by demonstrating a mastery of conventional forms already in wide circulation. If African Americans demonstrated comparable facility with these forms, or so the implicit argument runs, they would have another reason to think well of themselves, and the broader society would have more difficulty whenever it tried to conceive of them as essentially different, other, inferior.

V

The argument made by Fauset and others that African Americans are fundamentally similar to their white contemporaries requires them to represent or at least to celebrate only those aspects of African-American life that explicitly support it. The acknowledgment of differences, even minor differences in language usage, opens the possibility that these differences might be taken as evidence for deeper differences that would falsify the claim to similarity, and hence to equality. The need to defend claims of similarity thus establishes limits to possible representations of African-American life. Even in the scene set in Maude's, where Angela Murray and Fauset herself seem most receptive to the virtues possessed by people with diverse backgrounds, Fauset apparently feels a need to establish Maude's credentials by commenting on her personal refinement and by comparing her with Parisian and Fifth Avenue hairdressers. The dapper Alain Locke had as thoroughly assimilated middle-class values as Fauset, but he also knew that the new confidence emerging in Harlem during the twenties was partially produced as various groups of African Americans found one another there. He, like Fauset, was a certified member of DuBois's "talented tenth," but he recognized that in the demographic shifts responsible for the emergence of the New Negro, "it is the rank and file who are leading, and the leaders who are following. A transformed and transforming psychology permeates the masses" (*New Negro* 7). This recognition perhaps made him more receptive than Fauset to the potential worth and obvious dignity of cultural practices that differed from established middle-class norms. His New Negro is characteristically less defensive than Fauset about the standing of African Americans, more ready to celebrate their specific differences and thus their specific contributions to American life as a whole.

A passage in Ellison's *Invisible Man* illustrates the attitudes that some middle-class and upwardly mobile African Americans had regarding others of their race. It occurs early in the novel, while

Ellison's narrator is attending a historically black college. He is serving as a driver for a white trustee during his visit to campus; they
pass some sharecroppers' cabins, which remind the narrator of the
students' discomfort whenever the sharecroppers sang "their primitive spirituals" in the college chapel for white visitors: "We were
embarrassed by the earthy harmonies they sang, but since the visitors were awed we dared not laugh at the crude, high, plaintively
animal sounds Jim Trueblood made as he led the quartet. . . . I
didn't understand in those pre-invisible days that their hate, and
mine too, was charged with fear. How all of us at the college hated
the black-belt people, the 'peasants,' during those days! We were
trying to lift them up and they, like Trueblood, did everything it
seemed to pull us down" (47). Such instances suggest that loyalties
to class, or at least to the class to which one aspired, were stronger
among some African Americans than racial loyalties. One could not
allow oneself to admire the spirituals for fear that it would mark one
as different from other members of the middle class and so inferior.
The ambitious students recognize that the white visitors take this
music to be uniquely African American, but the students' aspirations seemingly depend upon denying that they are fundamentally different from the white visitors. The "peasants" who produce
this music are thus transformed into obstacles to racial betterment as much as potential beneficiaries of it. During a performance,
Ellison's narrator and his classmates feel that they have more in common with their white guests than with Trueblood and the other
singers; but the white guests are able to enjoy the performance, partially because they need not simultaneously worry that their enjoyment jeopardizes their class standing. Claims that African Americans were little different from other Americans, in other words,
introduced differences among African Americans and potentially
alienated some from their own heritage and people.

The emergence of Harlem as a "race capital" in the early decades
of this century eased for some the felt need to minimize the specificity of African-American cultural practices. It offered African
Americans better living conditions than they had typically enjoyed,
and its rapid growth seemed to promise even greater prosperity in
the years ahead. "We have tomorrow / Bright before us / Like a
flame," writes Langston Hughes in a passage that Locke cites in *The
New Negro* (5) to illustrate his own confidence in the immediate

future. On the streets of Harlem, African Americans from rural southern states came to know one another, as well as African Americans native to New York and immigrants from the West Indies and Africa. They were able to achieve, in Locke's terms, a "common consciousness" and "a life in common." The poems of Langston Hughes and Sterling A. Brown articulate divergent celebrations of the African-American people. Neither was subject to the embarrassment and fear felt by Ellison's narrator before specifically African-American cultural products such as the sorrow songs or blues music. Indeed, both wrote about segments of African-American life that the "talented tenth" might well have wished ignored. Both made extensive use of dialect, thereby risking, as James Weldon Johnson had warned as recently as 1922, inadvertently invoking available racial stereotypes that would undercut the dignity they were investing in their speakers. Hughes's poetry, now as then, is the better-known, but his use of dialect is more casual than that of Brown, who, as an amateur folklorist, had made a careful study of rural African-American speech. Hughes and Brown insist upon the specificity of African-American life and are not embarrassed by the "earthy harmonies" of the sorrow songs, by rural juke joints, or by the ungrammatical speech of some African Americans. Their poetry is informed by an unapologetic identification with the African-American people as a whole, and it celebrates a quality that Fauset's Angela Murray comes to appreciate only while listening to the patrons in Maude's—the "iron and blood in a race which did not know how to let go of life."

Langston Hughes's first appearance in a national journal could hardly have been more auspicious. Jessie Fauset published his "The Negro Speaks of Rivers" in the June 1921 issue of *The Crisis.* Hughes was nineteen at the time and had written the poem the previous summer, when crossing the Mississippi by train on his way to visit his father in Mexico. He writes as "The Negro" and claims a reach of experience scarcely possible for someone who had graduated from high school in Cleveland only a month earlier. It might be said that Hughes would subsequently devote his long career to living up to the claims implicitly made in his youthful poem, written, he claims in *The Big Sea,* in about fifteen minutes. Throughout his long and productive career, in his most representative poems

Hughes would speak less as *the* African American and more in the voices of individual African Americans.

Hughes is clearly among the younger generation that Alain Locke had in mind in *The New Negro,* and the anthology contains nine of his early poems, including "The Negro Speaks of Rivers." Hughes's first collection, *The Weary Blues,* appeared in early 1926, just a few weeks after *The New Negro;* the title poem had won first prize in the 1925 *Opportunity* awards for which Van Wyck Brooks served as a judge. Many of the poems in *The Weary Blues* are about Harlem and its residents, but it and they are typically viewed from the outside, and at times it is unclear whether the speaker lives there or even whether he is African American. The brief "Young Prostitute," for instance, is an imagistic rendering of the title and concludes: "Those kind come cheap in Harlem / So they say" (33).[6] "Those" distances the speaker from his subject, who is also at least aware of what others, presumably less sympathetic outsiders, say about Harlem's young prostitutes. In the title poem, the blues are evoked at several removes, as the speaker recounts an earlier visit to a Harlem nightclub:

> Droning a drowsy syncopated tune,
> Rocking back and forth to a mellow croon,
>   I hear a Negro play.
> Down on Lenox Avenue the other night
> By the pale dull pallor of an old gas light
>   He did a lazy sway. . . .
>   He did a lazy sway. . . .
> . . . .
> I heard that Negro sing, that old piano moan—
>   "Ain't got nobody in all this world,
>   Ain't got nobody but ma self.
>   I's gwine to quit ma frownin'
>   And put ma troubles on the shelf." (50)

The traditional blues lyrics Hughes incorporates within the poem (he claims in *The Big Sea* that "The Weary Blues" represents his introduction to the blues [215]) are mediated for the reader first by the performer and then by the speaker. The difference in diction between the interpolated song and the speaker establishes a distance between them, and the latter's need to identify the performer twice as an African American leaves his own racial identification ambiguous. The speaker could be one of the many whites in the twenties who frequented Harlem clubs, some of which were segregated, as an African American. At the same time, the poem as a whole dramatizes the way both the musician and the speaker are captivated by this music. The poem might be said to be about the power of traditional blues music to speak to a broad public, thereby overcoming barriers otherwise erected by race, class, and background.

Other poems in *The Weary Blues,* such as "To Midnight Nan at Leroy's" and the wonderful "Song for a Banjo Dancer," evoke Harlem's nightlife more exuberantly, and Hughes was perhaps encouraged by the favorable response to the volume to work more consistently in that direction. Both Fauset and Locke reviewed *The Weary Blues* favorably. The proper Fauset singled out "Song for a Banjo Dancer," which she had earlier published in *The Crisis,* for special mention; she appreciates its articulation of carpe diem conventions within African-American dialect, concluding that "though I am no great lover of any dialect I hope heartily that Mr. Hughes will give us many more such combinations" (41). Locke predicts that "if Hughes should turn more and more to the colloquial experiences of the common folk whom he so intimately knows and so deeply loves, we may say that the Negro masses have found a voice, and promise to add to their natural domain of music and dance the conquest of the province of poetry. Remember—I am not speaking of Negro poets, but of Negro poetry" (44–45).

Hughes put together a second collection quickly. *Fine Clothes for the Jews* (1927) contains both new poems and some that he had chosen not to include in *The Weary Blues* the previous year. It is a comparably large volume, with fifty-six poems grouped into six sections. The logic governing the groupings is elusive, but it seems that Hughes seeks to suggest a panorama of working-class African-American life. *Fine Clothes for the Jews* begins and ends with sections entitled "Blues" and "And Blues," respectively; in between are sections devoted to "Railroad Avenue," "Glory Halleluiah," "Beale Street Love," and "From the Georgia Roads." Few of the poems are explicitly set in Harlem; instead, I would argue that Hughes has been empowered by Harlem to identify more broadly with the African-American people. "Laughers" is little more than a catalog of laborers ("Dish-washers, / Elevator-boys, / Ladies' maids") who are nonetheless "Dream-singers all,— / My people" (27). The individual poems in the "Railroad Avenue" section are largely about—and at times spoken by—people who hold such menial jobs and the cynicism they develop to survive them.

The free verse and occasional imagistic poems in *Fine Clothes for the Jews* closely resemble those included in *The Weary Blues*. More extensive use of dialect and the prominence of poems modeled on the blues tradition make Hughes's second collection distinctive. If "The Weary Blues" illustrates the hold that the traditional blues can exercise over an audience, in these poems Hughes would claim that power for his own poems. The blues poems in *Fine Clothes* are about economic hardship and, especially, love gone bad; the personae are as likely to be female as male. Here are the first and fourth stanzas of "Young Gal's Blues":

> I'm gonna walk to the graveyard
> 'Hind ma friend Miss Cora Lee.
> Gonna walk to the graveyard
> 'Hind ma dear friend Cora Lee.
> Cause when I'm dead some
> Body'll have to walk behind me.
> . . . .
> When love is gone what
> Can a young gal do?
> When love is gone, O,
> What can a young gal do?
> Keep on a-lovin' me, daddy,
> Cause I don't want to be blue. (123)

There was a vogue for the blues in Harlem nightclubs and on "race" records during the twenties. By drawing on the blues for so many of his poems in this period, Hughes was participating in this broader interest. He was dignifying the "folk" form as an equivalent of the high cultural resources available to the poet. He was also identifying himself as a poet with blues performers and the African-American cultural matrix within which their common art arose.

The third section in *Fine Clothes,* "Glory Halleluiah," contains nine religious poems. Hughes himself was not particularly religious; an episode in *The Big Sea* recalls his almost immediate regret for having capitulated to pressure at a revival meeting when he was twelve and declaring himself saved without experiencing the requisite vision (18–21). A notorious later poem, "Goodbye Christ," would complicate Hughes's career; religious people would resent it as sacrilegious, and when he excluded it from later collections, others would accuse him of currying favor with conservative readers. However, "Prayer Meeting" resembles "The Weary Blues" in that the speaker recounts someone else's religious sentiments:

> Glory! Hallelujah!
> The dawn's a-comin'!
> Glory! Hallelujah!
> The dawn's a-comin'!
> A black old woman croons
> In the amen-corner of the
> Ebecaneezer Baptist Church.
> A black old woman croons—
> The dawn's a-coming! (35)

Other poems in this section, such as "Feet o' Jesus" and "Moan," are similarly direct, but articulated from the perspective of the "black old woman" in "Prayer Meeting." Another poem written at about the same time but not collected until *The Dream Keeper* (1932), "Ma Lord," nicely illustrates Hughes's capacity to present religious speakers without mediation or irony:

> Ma Lord ain't no stuck-up man.
> He's a friend o' mine.
> When He went to Heaben,
> His soul on fire,
> He tole me I was gwine.
> He said, "Sho you'll come wid Me
> An' be ma friend through eternity." (107)

The second line above derives directly from a familiar spiritual, but its presence does not establish a distance between the speaker and its source, as in "The Weary Blues"; instead, it suggests just how thoroughly the poem as a whole is articulated within that cultural matrix. Such poems demonstrate that Hughes, whatever his personal reservations about their beliefs, is as able to identify with the religious sentiments of some African Americans as he is with their more secular, earthy neighbors.

The only segment of the African-American community conspicuously absent from *Fine Clothes* would seem to be the "talented tenth," that is, precisely that segment that had, whether through good fortune or concerted effort, begun to assume many of the values and habits pervasive in the surrounding white community. In "To Certain Intellectuals," an early poem published originally in the *Messenger* and not included in either of Hughes's first two collections, he again draws on the gospel refrain used in "Ma Lord," but to a different end:

> You are no friend of mine
> For I am poor,
> Black,
> Ignorant and slow,—Not your kind.
> You yourself
> Have told me so,—No friend of mine. (43)

No poems in *Fine Clothes for the Jews* angrily draw such lines within the African-American community, but it is nonetheless telling that, with the possible exception of Hughes himself, the "talented tenth" are so thoroughly absent from the volume. Hughes associated with and depended upon members of this class as he went about the business of establishing his literary career. However, *Fine Clothes* instances his determination to identify with "my people," and he understood that term to refer to the common folk, the ladies' maids, cooks, porters, and crapshooters, and to the cultural practices, such as the blues, that they had invented.

The mood of the volume, like that of the blues, is usually grim, and occasionally it turns violent. "I beats ma wife an' / I beats ma side gal too," says "Bad Man," who offers no explanation other than, "It keeps me from feelin' blue" (112); and in "Hard Daddy" the female speaker wishes that she could fly, then "I'd fly on ma man an' / I'd scratch out both his eyes" (124). Aside from "Ma Man," the penultimate poem in the volume, in *Fine Clothes* there is little of the exuberant sexuality that appears more frequently in *The Weary Blues*. Throughout the volume, Hughes adapts the idiom and folk blues tradition for the making of his own poems, with the intent of restoring the latter to the originating context; "I bring you my songs, / To sing on the Georgia roads" (122). In other words, Hughes wants these poems to be not only *about* African Americans,

but also to be *for* them as additional equipment for living. If, as in
"Misery" (77), African Americans sometimes turn to the blues to
ease their pain, then Hughes would have his poems available to serve
a similar purpose. The title "Lament over Love" seems to catch him
in the midst of this transformation (69). The poem is a lament
over a love gone bad; but the word "lament" is intrusive, no more
compatible with the diction of the poem than the term *carpe diem*
would be in "Song for a Banjo Dancer." At such moments, as in
many less successful free verse and imagistic poems, we can glimpse
the writer Hughes's ambitions for the largely oral materials he
gathers, his effort to turn them to identifiably literary ends. Such
moments also demonstrate that Hughes's identification with "my
people" has been produced by a labor that is typically obscured by
its success. Hughes worked to produce his seemingly artless poems,
and the most successful are typically those that obscure his effort
most completely.

VI

Sterling A. Brown began publishing poems in 1927, the same
year Knopf issued *Fine Clothes for the Jews;* his first collection, *Southern Roads,* was published five years later. Brown's poems superficially
resemble those that Hughes collected in *Fine Clothes for the Jews:*
both often draw on folk traditions for their forms, both extensively
use dialect, and both clearly articulate their respect and affection for
less privileged members of their race. Brown's dialect poems, however, often prove to be more difficult for speakers of standard English to enter; the diction is less familiar, the lines rougher and less
predictable. At the time *Southern Roads* was published, Brown and
Alain Locke were both on the faculty at Howard University. In his
review, Locke welcomed his younger colleague's volume as initiat-
ing "a new era in Negro poetry." Not only does Brown use dialect
accurately and adroitly, but he has also "dared to give the Negro
peasant credit for thinking" ("Sterling Brown" 51), thereby reaching "a sort of common denominator between the old and the new
Negro" (53).[7]
Brown's poetry is not usually included in discussions of the Harlem Renaissance. His omission from such discussions no doubt con-

tributes to his subsequent dismissive attitude toward the centrality of Harlem as the locus for literary activity in these years: "The New Negro is not to me a group of writers centered in Harlem during the second half of the twenties. Most of the writers were not Harlemites; much of the best writing was not about Harlem, which was the show-window, the cashier's till, but no more Negro America than New York is America" ("New Negro" 57). Brown himself visited New York infrequently during these years, and his strongest poems scarcely mention Harlem. I want to argue, however, that the energy and confidence newly available to African Americans within discourse about the emerging city-within-a-city empowered Brown's own poetic itinerary. That itinerary took him south from his native Washington, where he listened to and recorded the speech, stories, and music of rural African Americans. It is not, in other words, a contingent, accidental fact of literary history that Brown begins writing poems drawing upon and celebrating the resourcefulness of the black folk shortly after the emergence of Harlem seemingly inaugurates a new day for African Americans. Those materials, after all, had been available for many years, but African-American poets typically shied away from them, preferring instead to write using recognizably literary forms and diction. The new social and cultural confidence that Locke reports and instantiates in *The New Negro* makes it possible for Brown and others to put these folk materials to literary uses. Brown's own project was self-consciously modeled on the example of Yeats, Lady Gregory, and Synge, who a few years earlier had begun rehabilitating the stage Irishman and dignifying Irish speech ("Literary Parallel"). The image of Harlem is necessarily northern and urban; but Locke, Hughes, and even Fauset identify its particular strength in the range of peoples drawn to it, including people like those represented and celebrated by Brown.

"Ma Rainey" is in many respects comparable to Hughes's "The Weary Blues" and can serve to suggest the characteristic differences between the poets. The poem is seemingly set in the South, not in Harlem; and it does not make itself available, as Hughes's poems sometimes do, for easy celebrations of the African American as vital primitive. The entire poem is written in dialect, whereas in "The Weary Blues" Hughes confines dialect within the few interpolated lines from the blues song. The poem is about the celebrated blues singer's hold on her audience and is built around a contrast between its behavior before and after she sings:

> Dey comes to hear Ma Rainey from de little river settlements,
> From blackbottom cornrows and from lumber camps;
> Dey stumble in de hall, jes a-laughin' an' a-cacklin',
> Cheerin' lak roarin' water, lak wind in river swamps.
>
> An' some jokers keeps deir laughs a-goin' in de crowded aisles,
> An' some folks sits dere waitin' wid deir aches an' miseries,
> Till Ma comes out before dem, a-smilin' gold-toofed smiles
> An' Long Boy ripples minors on de black an' yellow keys. (62)

The above stanzas constitute the second of four sections in "Ma Rainey." The two stanzas in the following section are addressed directly to the performer, as though expressing the audience's wishes for her performance:

> O Ma Rainey
> Li'l an' low;
> Sing us 'bout de hard luck
> Roun' our do';
> Sing us 'bout de lonesome road
> We mus' go. . . .

In the final section, the persona neither observes the audience's reaction, as he had observed its gathering earlier, nor places himself among the audience and speaks on its behalf, as he had in the third section. Instead, he largely turns the fourth and final section of the poem over to someone else, and quotes this other person's effort to describe the reaction to Rainey's rendition of "Backwater Blues." The poem concludes with these lines, which immediately follow a few interpolated lines from the blues song:

> "An' den de folks, dey natchally bowed dey heads an' cried,
> Bowed dey heavy heads, shet dey moufs up tight an' cried,
> An' Ma lef de stage, an' followed some de folks outside."
>
> Dere wasn't much more de fellow say:
> She jes' gits hold of us dataway. (63)

Rainey thus transforms a noisy, rambunctious crowd into a sorrowful audience. Of course the audience came precisely to experience this transformation, in the expectation that Rainey would, by getting "way inside us, / Keep us strong." Neither the speaker nor the person who shares this incident with him can explain her power, her capacity to articulate their own grief, and must settle for expressing wonder and gratitude for it.

One of the hallmarks of Brown's poetry is its generosity of spirit. "Sister Lou" imagines the death and passage to heaven of an old woman who has worked hard all her life. It is addressed directly to Sister Lou, and urges her to make it a leisurely passage and to settle comfortably into eternal life. "Sporting Beasley" also concludes by imagining the title character's possible entrance into heaven. Beasley is a dandy who, away from work, where he must endure "the snippy clerks" he serves, asserts his dignity by means of an outrageous wardrobe and strut. The final stanzas are a mock prayer on Beasley's behalf:

> Oh Jesus, when this brother's bill falls due,
>   When he steps off the chariot
>   And flicks the dust from his patent leathers with his silk
> handkerchief,
>   When he stands in front of the jasper gates, patting his tie,
>
> And then paces in
> Cane and knees working like well-oiled slow-timed pistons;
>
> Lord help us, give a *look* at him.
>
> Don't make him dress up in no night gown, Lord.
> Don't put no fuss and feathers on his shoulders, Lord.
>
> Let him know it's heaven.
>
> Let him keep his hat, his vest, his elkstooth, and everything.
>
> Let him have his spats and cane
> Let him have his spats and cane. (109–10)

It is easy and common enough to ridicule figures like Beasley, who work so hard at calling attention to themselves. The speaker cannot but be drawn by the spectacle of Beasley's passage through his world. He knows, however, that the costume and performance likely represent Beasley's sole claims to self-respect and the admiration of others. One might wish that this were not so, that a Beasley would have other and more substantial means to demonstrate his worth to himself and others. Instead of expressing this regret, Brown simply and generously wishes for Beasley a heaven that he himself would recognize as such.

"Sporting Beasley" is an instance of Brown's comic poetry. "Glory, Glory" and the Slim Greer poems are others. Comic exaggeration is their most common trope. In "Glory, Glory," Annie Mae Johnson is a female Beasley, and when she "condescends to take the air," such crowds gather to witness her passage that the city comes to a stop. "Aaanh, Lord, when Annie Mae lays it down, / If you want to take the census proper, better come around" (234). The Slim Greer poems chronicle Greer's adventures along the color line: improbably passing while living with a white woman, abiding by Jim Crow laws in Atlanta dictating that blacks only laugh in telephone booths, and finally in hell, which he discovers to be nothing other than the American South. When he reports this last discovery to St. Peter, he is summarily dismissed:

"Git on back to de yearth,
    Cause I got de fear,
You'se a leetle too dumb,
    Fo' to stay up here. . . . " (92)

These poems celebrate the resourcefulness of those lower down. There is no pretense that in the struggles of life the odds against them are anything but long; nonetheless, they manage to survive, even at times to triumph, and by so doing they encourage others in their struggles.

Few of Brown's poems are set in Harlem or even refer to it in passing. It is the Mecca in the poem with that title, where a woman from South Carolina and a man from Martinique find one another (105). In "Harlem Happiness," the persona recalls an evening with his lover, "that night at least the world was ours to spend" (166). In "Negro Improvement League," the speaker wonders "what new dreams could now convoke / My gullible and naive folk" (167) into participating in one of Marcus Garvey's parades. In Brown's poetry, Harlem is as often a snare as a figure of a haven or a better future. "Maumee Ruth" angrily mourns an old woman who dies alone, ignored by her son and daughter who are living in Harlem, using cocaine and alcohol:

To cut her withered heart
    They cannot come again,

Preach her the lies about
  Jordan, and then

Might as well drop her
  Deep in the ground,
Might as well pray for her
  That she sleep sound. . . . (24–25).

The remarkable "When de Saints Go Ma'ching Home" is Brown's tribute to the blues singer Big Boy Davis. It received first prize in the 1927 *Opportunity* awards. It is also an oblique commentary on Brown as poet, figured in his representation of the blues singer. Davis apparently concluded his concerts by playing the familiar spiritual, his mother's favorite, identified in Brown's title. As Davis sang the spiritual, "he would see / A gorgeous procession to 'de Beulah Land,'— / Of saints"; these saints ascending to heaven were not nameless strangers, but Davis's friends. The second section of the poem consists of six stanzas, each describing one of the marchers, including his grandfather:

"An' old Grampa Eli
Wid his wrinkled old haid,
A-puzzlin' over summut
He ain' understood,
Intendin' to ask Peter
Pervidin' he ain't skyaid,
'Jes' what mought be de meanin'
Of de moon in blood?' . . . "
When de saints go ma'chin' home. . . . (28)

In the third and fourth sections, Davis continues playing but now wonders who might be excluded from his line of marching saints. He initially assumes that "*Whuffolks*" could have no place in heaven; but then remembers a few specific kindnesses, and allows that there "*Mought be another mansion fo' white saints, / A smaller one than his'n . . . not so gran'*" (28). Some blacks ("guzzlin', cuttin' shines") will not be among Davis's saints, including the lovely and loving Sophie, for fear that they might cause a commotion there. The final person Davis imagines marching into heaven is his loving, religious mother:

He sees her ma'chin' home, ma'chin' along,
Her perky joy shining in her furrowed face,

Her weak and quavering voice singing her song—
The best chair set apart for her worn out body
In that restful place. . . .
  I pray to de Lawd I'll meet her
  When de saints go ma'chin' home. (29)

Brown's Big Boy Davis makes the traditional spiritual a personal statement. The saints he sees marching into heaven are his saints—people he would remember, people whose prayers he would answer, and people he would rejoin if at all possible. The poem illustrates how the traditional spiritual can acquire personal significance and power as performers adapt its images to their own lives. Behind the performer Davis is Brown himself, whose representation of Davis is as striking and loving as Davis's personalizations of his saints. Davis is among Brown's saints; that is, he is, like Sporting Beasley, among those whom Brown would save, were he in a position to do so, by means other than poetic representation. The example of Davis enables Brown to appreciate the resources available to the poet in the traditional folk forms that both draw upon in their art, and Brown uses these resources to celebrate the humble, resourceful people who initially created and used them.

VII

By the time Brown's first collection, *Southern Roads,* was published in 1932 the Harlem Renaissance was effectively over—a victim, like so many other hopeful projections for the future, of the Depression.[8] The Harlem Renaissance was from the beginning fueled primarily by a hopeful attitude or mood, and that mood was impossible to sustain on a broad scale once the consequences of the Depression—for Harlem specifically, and for African Americans more generally—became unmistakable. Living conditions in Harlem had actually been deteriorating throughout the twenties. The once ample stock of modern housing became increasingly overcrowded because of the twin pressures caused by the continuing migration of African Americans to the famed city-within-a-city and by the high rents, which forced many residents to take in boarders. According to Wintz, "by 1925 nearly half of the black households contained a boarder or lodger" (25). Harlem's celebrated rent parties might have been an enjoyable novelty in the twenties, but it should not require much reflection to recognize the economic hardship that gave rise to them, or the fact that they could sustain only a small minority of households. "Largely within the space of a single decade," summarizes Gilbert Osofsky, "Harlem was transformed from a potentially ideal community to a neighborhood with manifold social and economic problems called 'deplorable,' 'unspeakable,' and 'incredible'" (135). The Depression made these already serious economic and social problems worse, and made it more difficult to sustain confidence that circumstances would improve in the imaginable future.

The Depression also made it clear that literary or artistic recognition could do little to assure for African Americans the realization of their broader aspirations. Writing in the January 1933 issue of *Opportunity*, Arthur Huff Fauset, Jessie's brother, ridiculed the belief that "social and economic recognition will be inevitable when once the race has produced a sufficiently large number of persons who have properly qualified themselves in the arts" (20). Even Alain Locke, who had earlier supposed that artistic recognition could win broader respect, would eventually concede that his prior confidence had been misplaced. Writing in the August 1936 *Survey Graphic*, the very journal in which he had launched the Harlem Renaissance eleven years earlier, Locke declares:

> Today, with . . . Harlem prostrate in the grip of the depression and throes of social unrest, we confront the sobering facts of serious relapse and premature setback; indeed, find it hard to believe that the rosy enthusiasms and hopes of 1925 were more than bright illusions or a cruelly deceptive mirage. . . . For there is no cure or saving magic in poetry and art, an enlarging generation of talent, or in international prestige and interracial recognition, for unemployment or precarious marginal employment, for high rents, high mortality rates, civic neglect, capitalistic exploitation on the one hand and radical exploitation on the other. ("Harlem" 457)

When Locke concedes that literary gains cannot redress economic losses, he implicitly acknowledges that the former were from the first doubly dependent: first, on the social and economic conditions that gave rise to Harlem, and second, on the hope for further improvements that these conditions inspired broadly among African Americans. Harlem was, in these years, the repository and representation of these hopes, and when conditions there deteriorated more was compromised than the lives of its residents. By the early thirties, it was already too clear that for some years yet the patrons in Maude's would have need of the "iron and blood" that Fauset's Angela Murray came belatedly to admire, and that the strength and dignity that Sterling Brown heard among the folk would continue to be tried.

I am arguing, in short, that the Harlem Renaissance was a failure on its own terms, that it did not sustain itself in the changed social and economic environment of the thirties, that it did not and could not make good on the promise for better lives it seemed to hold for African Americans. My reading of this important cultural episode thus more nearly resembles those of Nathan Huggins and David Levering Lewis than that of Houston Baker. The latter seems to resist terming the Harlem Renaissance a failure largely because modernism is otherwise generally taken to be so triumphant. In *Modernism and the Harlem Renaissance,* Baker strains to create terms that allow the literary efforts of African Americans in the twenties to be considered as successful as those by their white contemporaries. However, Baker understands modernism to be at once more monolithic and less socially engaged than it was. I am attempting to demonstrate the inadequacy of such definitions of modernism generally, and of American literary modernism more specifically. Within the terms I am developing, no special stigma is assigned the Harlem Renaissance if it is acknowledged that its broader program for social renewal ultimately falls short. The same must finally be said about the corresponding programs developed by T. S. Eliot, by the Southern Agrarians, and by other American literary modernists, as previous chapters demonstrate. Literary figures are not social engineers, and there is no reason to believe that they can supply the remedies for our social failings. Nor is there any reason why the respect won by individual writers will necessarily extend to others, whatever their relationship to these writers. And in the case of the Harlem Renaissance, that respect is precisely what was at issue: Locke's aspirations for racial betterment were predicated on the potential respect to be won by African-American writers among the broader reading public for their literary contributions to the store of common culture. It seems too much to ask, however, to expect

even the most accomplished writers to erase long-standing preju-
dices that serve other than literary ends.

In the euphoria of the early twenties, however, so much was
imaginable. After all, Harlem itself would have been unimaginable
a scant twenty years earlier, and its bustle seemed to testify on behalf of even bolder possibilities for the years ahead. We have already
seen the astonishment felt by Ellison's narrator and Fisher's King
Solomon Gillis when, upon their arrival in Harlem, they witness
white drivers accepting without question the authority of African-
American policemen directing traffic. This sight was beyond anything in their previous experience and seemed to confirm all that
they had heard about the new world to be glimpsed in the city-
within-a-city. "Harlem is wonderful," the sight seemed to say, "and
so too is the future there for African Americans." Both *Invisible
Man* and Rudolph Fisher's "City of Refuge" continue well beyond
these scenes, and in both Harlem's initial promise seems finally more
ambiguous. Harlem seemed at least to be the promised land.

This brief moment of general euphoria empowered writers as diverse as Jessie Fauset, Langston Hughes, and Sterling Brown to identify with segments of the African-American community and to take
them for the community as such. Fauset imagined African Americans who were in no essential way any different from their white
contemporaries. If their lives were different, it was only because
it was their mixed fate to live in a nation that made too much of
race and so enforced artificial distinctions. Like her character Angela
Murray, Fauset could eventually admire the special resilience displayed by people like those Angela encounters at Maude's; but her
abiding loyalties were to people like Angela herself, whose deepest
desires are as indistinguishable from those of the white people
among whom she passes as she is bodily. Angela's passing, in these
terms, is not so much an act of deception as it is the unveiling of
the deceptions enforced by the notion of race. When Angela em-
braces her racial heritage at the conclusion of the novel, she does so
for reasons of fellow feeling that are identical to those that might
be felt by individuals of any family, ethnic group, or race. There
is nothing distinctively African American about her decision; it is
simply the decision of a woman who happens to be African American. In a late article that looks back on the twenties, Langston

Hughes declares, "I was in love with Harlem long before I got there" ("Early Days" 312). In his poetry of the twenties Hughes would identify more with the common people of Harlem—those who, like him, had heard stories about opportunities available there and who journeyed to Harlem to experience it themselves. The excitement and exuberance evident in *The Weary Blues* represent new notes in African-American writings. Hughes's identification with the residents of Harlem led him back to their cultural resources, which became increasingly prominent features of his own poetry in *Fine Clothes for the Jews*. It was no doubt Hughes's identification with the common folk that led him for a time in the thirties to associate himself with the Left, and more particularly with the Communist Party, as the political force most likely to address dire economic conditions. In these years, he was as likely to identify with and speak as the generic worker as to create a distinctively black persona. By the time he turns again to distinctively African-American voices and concerns, Harlem would be represented as standing "on the edge of hell" (*Collected Poems* 363), not as the promised land. Sterling Brown has never been especially associated with Harlem, and for good reason. I would argue, however, that the same circumstances that made Harlem a particularly powerful image for African Americans in the twenties also inspired and enabled Brown's own research into the folkways of his people. In Brown's poetry, the New Negro discovers and celebrates the power of the Old Negro. Brown is the antithesis of Ralph Ellison's nameless narrator and his classmates, who were embarrassed by the earthy power of the spirituals. The cultural resources that Brown's poetry draws upon had been in place for many years, but his poetry could not have been written earlier, since it requires a measure of self-confidence and confidence in one's heritage for a poet to assume such voices. Brown began writing in the late twenties, and his confidence was produced by the same broad social forces that, for a time, made Harlem a powerful and positive image for African Americans. Brown's relative silence as a poet after the publication of *Southern Roads* no doubt has many sources, including the later loss of interest in African-American writing among commercial publishers; but it is at least suggestive that the temporal trajectory of his career as a poet so closely tracks the rapid emergence and decline of Harlem as possible and positive future for African Americans.

By the time Langston Hughes wrote the sequence *Montage for a Dream Deferred* in 1948 (it was not published until 1951), he had settled permanently in Harlem after years of wandering (Rampersad 2: 151). If Hughes had earlier when assembling *The Weary Blues* featured the music and nightclubs of Harlem in the twenties, *Montage* is structurally informed by more recent music, especially boogie-woogie and bebop. The Harlem of the forties is as well known as it had been two decades earlier, but the specific reasons for its fame are less sanguine—it is now known as a ghetto and slum more than as the promised land. Hughes clearly identifies as intensely with Harlem as he ever has, but it is now "a community in transition" (*Collected Poems* 387) and the poet cannot help but worry about the direction of this transition. The dream that Hughes and so many others had shared during the twenties, a dream seemingly at the time being made material in Harlem, has not come to fruition, and the sequence repeatedly asks, "What happens to a dream deferred?" (426). This is not a question that Hughes or other participants in the New Negro movement thought to ask twenty years earlier. It is a question, however, that African Americans had long asked in various ways prior to the twenties. The New Negro moment is precisely the moment in our literary and social history when that question seemed to many unnecessary because the realization of the dream seemed to be at hand.

5

WALLACE STEVENS AND THE LIMITS OF IMAGINATION

There must be in the world about us things that solace us quite
as fully as any heavenly visitation could.

      Stevens, *Letters* 661

IN THE SPRING of 1954 the publisher Alfred Knopf approached
Wallace Stevens, and not for the first time, about the possibility of
a collected edition of his poetry. The poet was diffident and agreed
to the undertaking with some reluctance. A few days after agreeing
to the project, Stevens expressed his continuing reservations about
it in a letter to Norman Holmes Pearson. "A collection," he wrote,
"is very much like sweeping under the rug" (*Letters* 829). A few
weeks later, this time in a letter to Barbara Church, Stevens suggested another reservation: "I have held off from a collection for
a number of years because, in a way, it puts an end to things. But
I am reaching an age where I don't have much choice: it is good
housekeeping for me to do what I am doing" (832). In doing his
housekeeping Stevens chose to sweep little under the rug; he excluded few poems from his earlier volumes, with the result that
the published volume contains poems that no longer pleased him.
"A book that contains everything that one has done in a lifetime,"
he wrote to Leonard van Geyzal, "does not reassure one" (839).
Stevens's misgivings about his cumulative achievement seem to have
been shared by few others; the *Collected Poems* appeared that fall, in
time to mark his seventy-fifth birthday, and the following year it
received both the National Book Award and the Pulitzer Prize. As
it turns out, Stevens agreed to the collected edition of his poetry
none too soon, for he died the following summer.

    Shortly after agreeing to the collected edition, Stevens suggested that the volume be entitled "The Whole of Harmonium: Collected Poems of Wallace Stevens" (*Letters* 831), but he readily agreed the following month to the eventual one, despite his sense that it is "a machine-made title if there ever was one" (834). By alluding to the title of his first volume, published in 1924, a full thirty years earlier, Stevens's proposed title for his collected poems would have claimed an essential continuity and coherence for his life's work. The proposed title would imply that the poems collected in subsequent volumes such as *Ideas of Order* (1936) and *Transports of Summer* (1947), as well as the most recent poems being published in book form for the first time, were part of a single, large project that had its effective beginning with *Harmonium* and was only now reaching completion. If Stevens feared that a collected edition implied an "end to things," as he had written to Barbara Church, his proposed title would have made that implication more definitive. The reiterations within these poems would have made that claim plausible. "Poetry is the supreme fiction, madame" (59), declares the confident speaker of Stevens's early "A High-Toned Old Christian Woman."[1] This notion would later occur elsewhere, throughout the "Adagia" and the occasional prose collected in *The Necessary Angel,* and most famously in the title of his celebrated poem written in the forties, "Notes toward a Supreme Fiction."

At the same time that Stevens's work is informed by a set of continuing preoccupations that would have lent credence to his proposed title for the collected poems, his life and work are simultaneously crossed by several equally compelling anomalies. Throughout most of his productive life Stevens was at once a poet and a lawyer who ultimately became a vice president of the Hartford Accident and Indemnity Company. Although there were no subscriptions undertaken to rescue him from the workaday world, such as those Ezra Pound undertook on behalf of Eliot, there can be no doubt that Stevens would have rebuffed such assistance, and not simply for fear that others might think the entire project unseemly. Less than a year before his death, when already well beyond the Hartford's mandatory retirement age, Stevens declined an invitation to be the Charles Eliot Norton professor at Harvard for 1955–56, as he explained in a letter to Archibald MacLeish, for fear that accepting this honor "would be only too likely to precipitate the retirement that I want so much to put off" (*Letters* 853). Similarly, both in his writing and in other areas of his life Stevens displayed an obvious affection for things French and for exotic words, objects, and foods from many cultures; yet at a time when other writers seemingly considered a trip to Paris a necessary pilgrimage, he never went to Europe. Instead, he would indulge these pleasures nearer to home by visiting galleries and shopping during his visits to New York City; he also relied upon a network of friends to provide him with objects from distant places and with postcards that would provide him almost his only visual impressions of these distant places. His letters contain many expressions of gratitude for postcards he had received, such as the following to Barbara Church: "The postcards from Ville d'Avray came the other day. They did me a lot of good. In fact, I survive on postcards from Europe" (797). As many critics have observed, his poetry too seems to fall into distinct categories. Some distinguish between early and later Stevens, calling attention to the way his interests evolved and his demeanor darkened; others distinguish among his characteristic forms, especially the brief, intense lyrics and the longer, looser meditative poems that seem predominant in the later Stevens. It is almost as though Stevens's proposed title for his collected poems is a last effort to pull these anomalies into alignment, to wrest at last a coherence for the otherwise puzzling contradictions in his life and work.

In this chapter I shall have little novel to say about particular Stevens poems. He has had many able commentators, and my own sense of these poems is in most respects heavily indebted to them. Instead, I shall try to demonstrate that Stevens represents a unique variant within American literary modernism, that his persistent wrestling with the relations between reality and the imagination constitutes a response, however abstract, to the same cultural conditions that inspired other American literary modernists, from Willa Cather through John Steinbeck. In the following pages I attend especially to Stevens's developing sense of the cultural work his poems need to perform, and thus pay more attention to the emerging structure of his thought than Helen Vendler, for one, deems appropriate (*Extended Wings* 8–10). I am primarily interested, in other words, in the Stevens who was only too eager to make pronouncements, whose poems and notebooks are replete with propositions about what he took to be important matters, and who felt, as Hugh

Kenner has derisively put it, that "he had Something to Say" (57). As it happens, Stevens's efforts have after the fact become among the most revered and influential, so that one understands why Fredric Jameson once proposed to begin a book about the sixties with a chapter on this poet who died in 1955. The special reverence that has come to be considered Stevens's due has made it less likely that his poetry and prose will now be considered critically. As William Pritchard wryly observes about the esteem with which Stevens is now usually regarded, "it is all a bit like going to church, but presumably much more exhilarating and free-breathing than going to church with T. S. Eliot" (205). Thus it seems to me important to suggest just what I think is wrong or misguided about so much in Stevens, especially as it constitutes a response to life in modern America. There is something undeniably grand and brave about this poetry—the *Collected Poems* is one of the singular accomplishments of American literary modernism—but we do it and ourselves no service if we make it a new gospel.

I

Stevens was a connoisseur. Frank Lentricchia has called our attention to the pleasure Stevens took from contemplating and collecting the objects and commodities that become available to those with sufficient means within an expanding market economy (*Ariel* 136–76; *Quartet* 164–73). A reader's initial impression upon picking up *Harmonium* or the *Collected Poems* must include amazement at the profusion of vocabulary and objects that could become either the occasion or the means for celebrating the riches available to citizens of the modern world. The foppish titles, the phrases from French and German, the lines of nonsense sounds—

Tum-ti-tum,
Ti-tum-tum-tum!
The turkey-cock's tail
Spreads to the sun. (20)

are all provocations against decorum and solemnity. These same resources might have been used, as they sometimes are by Eliot, primarily to indict a way of life that has become excessively refined and thus lost its way. However, Stevens is able to indulge pleasures that were seemingly lost upon Eliot, who seemed in contrast rather to enjoy appearing long-suffering. Especially in the early Stevens, the natural and cultural worlds seem to provide ample opportunities for enjoyment, and the poet is seemingly intent upon seizing and experiencing each, even the least consequential. Many of Stevens's most famous lines, such as "Chieftain Iffucan of Azcun in caftan / Of tan with henna hackles, halt!" (75), at once instance the pleasures available in the sounds of words and celebrate the poet's capacity to bring such pleasures to an intense pitch.

Stevens's capacity and willingness to celebrate what others might take to be trivial or passing pleasures lend credence to Yvor Winters's early characterization of him as a hedonist. Elsewhere, even in *Harmonium*, Stevens demonstrates that the pleasures he seeks out are in themselves neither simple-minded nor produced by refusing to recognize other and less satisfying moments. These typically brief lyrics are like the tails of peacocks in "Domination of Black," arresting swirls of color against a background of darkness. "The Worms at Heaven's Gate," "The Emperor of Ice-Cream," and "The Death of a Soldier" are each in their own way aggressive in their insistence upon the inevitability and finality of death. The first is deliberately grotesque; it is presumably spoken by one of the worms, who extends toward readers parts of Badroulbadour's decomposing body:

> Out of the tomb, we bring Badroulbadour,
> Within our bellies, we her chariot.
> Here is an eye. And here are, one by one,
> The lashes of that eye and its white lid. (49)

"The Death of a Soldier" initially compares the soldier's death to the coming of autumn, but concludes by denying any possibility that his life will revive with spring or that its loss will even be registered in the natural world:

> Death is absolute and without memorial,
> As in a season of autumn,
> When the wind stops,
> When the wind stops and, over the heavens,
> The clouds go, nevertheless,
> In their direction. (97)

In "Sunday Morning" and elsewhere, Stevens connects pleasure with an awareness of death. This poem, perhaps Stevens's best-known, has received many able and admiring readings, dating back at least to those by Yvor Winters and J. V. Cunningham. It purports to be a dialogue of sorts between the speaker and a woman, who is distracted from her pleasurable surroundings one Sunday morning by religious (specifically Christian) yearnings. It is not much of a dialogue; Stevens clearly reserves the best lines for the speaker, who is intent upon disabusing the woman of her traditional religious sentiments. Whereas she feels dissatisfied with passing pleasures and a need for some "imperishible bliss," the speaker argues that it is precisely the recognition that certain objects are transient that makes them so enjoyable, declaring:

> Death is the mother of beauty; hence from her,
> Alone, shall come fulfillment to our dreams
> And our desires. (68–69)

In other words, we would in time become indifferent to fruit that was forever ripe, and it in consequence would shortly lose its ability to satisfy our desires. If she could but set aside her inappropriate need for permanence, the speaker argues, the woman he addresses would be able to take more enjoyment from her current surroundings than she ever could from some unchanging paradise:

> The sky will be much friendlier then than now,
> A part of labor and a part of pain,
> And next in glory to enduring love,
> Not this dividing and indifferent blue. (68)

The Stevens who knows, as the title of another poem has it, that "Life Is Motion," and who is able to celebrate the opportunities for satisfaction available in a turning world, was apparently himself at other times in need of the hectoring directed at the uneasy woman in "Sunday Morning." It is not that the natural and social worlds at other times seemed to him too bare, as though a long winter had set in; it is more that he recognized that the satisfactions he sought required something beyond material opportunities, which he at such times understands as the necessary but not sufficient conditions for realizing these satisfactions. The achievement of these satisfactions requires as well the exercise of the imagination. Stevens's description of what the imagination contributes varies. It must, in the first place, be able to identify in the world about it circumstances that might yield the satisfactions the poet desires; as he puts it in the "Adagia," "The real is only the base. But it is the base" (*Opus Posthumous* 187). These circumstances might consist of little more than the opportunity to bring together particular words and sounds in ways that might be merely diverting, or they might be suggestive of other and less immediate conjunctions. The imagination must also and most critically be able to invest these circumstances with human meanings. In the long term, in other words, Stevens would not settle for a series of pleasurable moments, whatever the quality of frisson they individually and collectively afford; more than the appeasement of appetite was at issue, and thus Stevens was rarely the simple hedonist that Winters describes. On the other hand, Winters was right to recognize that Stevens's conception of "reality remains incurably nominalistic" (459), one dumb thing after another. Stevens believed, however, that the imagination could invest our experience of this realm with sufficient meaning to make our passage through it bearable and even cause for celebration.

"The Idea of Order at Key West" is perhaps Stevens's best-known illustration of the necessary physical conditions for satisfaction, and their realization through the workings of the imagination. The speaker recalls an occasion in the indefinite past, when he and a companion were moved by overhearing a woman singing while walking along a beach. The setting is propitious in a conventionally romantic way: it is evening, on a tropic beach, and a solitary woman sings as she walks along the shore. In the poem itself the speaker is attempting in retrospect to understand why he and his companion were so moved and to puzzle out the relationship among the woman, her song, and the simultaneous sound of the surf she walks beside. He rejects the notion that the woman has intuited something about the sea, so that her song gives word to it. Instead, he keeps the natural and human orders strictly distinct:

> The sea was not a mask. No more was she.
> The song and water were not medleyed sound
> Even if what she sang was what she heard,
> Since what she sang was uttered word by word. (128)

Since it is composed of words, the woman's song is humanly meaningful in a way that the sound of the surf cannot be; the latter is "sound alone" (129). The speaker eventually realizes that the woman's song somehow both creates and organizes her entire world:

> It was her voice that made
> The sky acutest at its vanishing.
> She measured to the hour its solitude.
> She was the single artificer of the world
> In which she sang. And when she sang, the sea,
> Whatever self it had, became the self
> That was her song, for she was the maker. (129)

The woman in her song has not articulated something essential about the sea; instead, the sea, indeed the entire natural scene, within the context of her song, has been made fit for human habitation. "The Idea of Order at Key West" is thus also a celebration, but it celebrates not the pleasure available in ripe plums so much as the capacity of the imagination to render the whole physical world inhabitable by those of us who find ourselves within it.

In poems like "Idea of Order at Key West" the physical world seems starker and less promising than it does in "Sunday Morning," even though the latter acknowledges that in the end we and the sources of our pleasure alike "sink, / Downward to darkness, on extended wings" (70).[2] The meaningless roar of the surf has taken the place of nature's bounty. In the earlier poem Stevens wants to counter the woman's disquiet by insisting upon the availability and sufficiency of transient pleasures, pleasures that are all the more intense precisely because they are transient. The later poem, however, suggests that Stevens himself at least partially shares the woman's reservations about the final adequacy of such temporary satisfactions. The pleasure felt by the speaker as he overhears the woman singing is intellectual, not visceral; it derives from his conviction that her song has in some sense articulated her location within the world. The speaker's admiration and gratitude for her achievement suggest that he (and, by implication, others, including the woman singing) feels a need for such an order, a need that could not be satisfied by eating the ripest plum. This need is analogous to that felt by the woman in "Sunday Morning." She, of course, yearns for an "imperishible bliss," and to acquire it is tempted to subject herself to the authority of traditional beliefs and divinities. The woman in "Idea of Order at Key West," in contrast, is prepared to exercise the

"Divinity [that] must live within herself" (67), and the order that she thereby creates is both contingent upon her immediate surroundings and presumably temporary. Without minimizing these differences, I want to observe that the kind of argument the speaker mounts in "Sunday Morning" against the woman's disquiet seems at best partial from the perspective of the concerns addressed in the latter poem. If the physical world in the latter poem seems less bountiful, it might be because its possible richness is beside the point; Stevens now recognizes that satisfying our appetites does nothing to quench our equally strong desire for order, that is to say, for beliefs that make our lives and our worlds as a whole meaningful as well as sporadically enjoyable.

II

Stevens believed that it was the office of the imagination to provide us with such beliefs. At other times and places, people found such beliefs ready to hand, as part of the legacy available to them as members of particular cultures. They acquired them easily, from a culture only too eager to have them perpetuated. However, Stevens, like many in the early decades of this century, thought that his own era was distinctive for the way people were discarding traditional beliefs. We have already seen how T. S. Eliot and Allen Tate at different stages of their careers agreed with this characterization of the period. They responded by attempting to revive various traditional institutions and beliefs. Stevens would have none of that; he usually felt that we were in fact well rid of such beliefs, which were being set aside precisely because they squared so poorly with other things people knew or believed. We already saw him in "Sunday Morning" trying to dispatch the woman's lingering religious convictions by arguing that they served chiefly to impoverish her and the pleasure she might otherwise take from her seemingly comfortable surroundings. In Stevens the reverence for tradition so common among other American literary modernists is seemingly narrowed to a fascination with family genealogy (Bates "Study"). In 1945, after the annual dinner of the New York Saint Nicholas Society, he recited a poem written for the occasion; initially entitled "Tradition," it appears somewhat revised in *Opus Posthumous* as "Recitation after Dinner." The poem surveys possible figures for tradition, rejecting in turn a code of laws, a bronze statue, and memory before setting upon "That of the son who bears upon his back / The father that he loves, and bears him from / The ruins of the past" (115). The son's act of reverence is praised for its preservation of the past. However, the poem is conspicuously silent about any benefits the son might derive from his labors; they do not, for instance, explicitly provide either guidance or opportunities for restful contemplation, as they might in Eliot and Cather, respectively. The poem concludes by dissolving such "survivals out of time and place" into "the general fiction of the mind: / Survivals of a good that we have loved, / Made eminent in a reflected seeming-so" (116). Whatever eminence tradition possesses, in other words, it has by means of reflection, as a consequence of past love, and as a constituent of the fictions by which we choose to live.

In "Two or Three Ideas," a lecture delivered at Mount Holyoke in 1951, Stevens explores a possible outcome of the loss of traditional beliefs. The exploration takes the form of a parable about the disappearance of the gods. He imagines that people initially feel abandoned: "It left us feeling dispossessed and alone in a solitude, like children without parents, in a home that seemed deserted, in which the amical rooms and halls had taken on a look of hardness and emptiness" (*Opus Posthumous* 260). Stevens imagines that people, despite their feelings of abandonment, did not hanker for the gods' return: "At the same time, no man ever muttered a petition in his heart for the restoration of those unreal shapes. There was always in every man the increasingly human self, which instead of remaining the observer, the non-participant, the delinquent, became constantly more and more all there was or so it seemed; and whether it was so or merely seemed so left it for him to resolve life and the world in his own terms" (260). The example of Eliot and Tate, among others, makes it clear that Stevens's contemporaries were not as consistently sanguine about the gods' disappearance as the abandoned people in his parable. The latter, however, clearly evidence Stevens's own usual conviction that life can thrive after the loss of traditional beliefs; more, that their absence is perhaps a precondition for our recognition of our own powers and for our full appreciation of the transient yet substantial satisfactions that the natural world provides.

Stevens's confidence that life can thrive after the loss of traditional beliefs does not mean that we can do without any beliefs. We have already seen that the speaker of "Idea of Order at Key West" is moved by the way the woman, through her song, becomes "the single artificer of the world / In which she sang" (129). Her song is a substitute for discarded traditional beliefs. Stevens believes that the traditional beliefs being set aside by his contemporaries were themselves the products of the imagination, products whose imaginative origins had over time been lost as they were increasingly accorded the status of accepted truths. In "The Noble Rider and the Sound of Words," an important essay collected in *The Necessary Angel*, Stevens uses a series of historical examples to suggest the devolution in our conception of nobility. We can draw upon that sketch to suggest how, on his account, traditional beliefs lose their authority. Stevens begins with Plato's figure in the *Phaedrus* of the soul as a pair of winged horses drawing a chariot. Stevens suggests that Plato "could yield himself, was free to yield himself, to this gorgeous nonsense" (4), but that we cannot. We might initially be moved by this figure, and put ourselves in the place of the charioteer, but finally "the reason checks us" (6). In this essay Stevens is primarily concerned to demonstrate the shifting proportions between imagination and reality necessary in different eras for images to be successful. It is at least plausible to suggest, however, that Stevens and his contemporaries were losing their traditional beliefs in the same way. These beliefs increasingly seemed to be "gorgeous nonsense," like Plato's winged horses and chariot, because they were incompatible with the contemporary dictates of the reason, which accordingly prohibited belief in them.

Stevens usually assumed that traditional beliefs were projections onto the gods and the physical world of abilities that were properly human. He thus assumed that at least some people, and especially poets, would grow more confident of their own abilities once they recognized the inadequacies of their inherited beliefs. They could not live without holding some beliefs. They might, however, find the courage to call again upon "the faculties of the past" (*Necessary Angel* 267), the faculties that produced these now discarded beliefs in the first place, to produce others that might better meet contemporary needs. These new beliefs would differ in several important respects from those they would replace; namely, we would now acknowledge our authorship of them and thus not forget again their fictive status. These are the considerations that inform the first stanza of "Asides on the Oboe":

> The prologues are over. It is a question, now,
> Of final belief. So, say that the final belief
> Must be in a fiction. It is time to choose. (250)

I shall have more to say later about the possibility of belief in fictions; in the present context, it is sufficient to observe that Stevens proposes that these imaginative fictions can fill the place in human life previously occupied by the traditional beliefs that were seemingly losing their authority.

Since Stevens assumed that these fictions should, like the woman's song in "Key West," engage their immediate surroundings, he also assumed that the most adequate would necessarily be local and contingent. As the first line of a late poem puts it, "A mythology reflects its region" (*Opus Posthumous* 141); it must lend meaning even to an ordinary evening in New Haven. A poem of winter would differ from a poem of summer, and one set in Pennsylvania would have a different coloration than another set in Florida. The demand for immediacy of reference keeps these fictions from becoming very encompassing and assures their inadequacy for other seasons and places. A fiction that is too insistent and insensitive to its surroundings, like the jar in "Anecdote of the Jar," will perhaps provide the requisite order, but at excessive cost. Thus these fictions need to be composed or revised continuously as a person over time moves from place to place.

It occasionally seems as though Stevens assumes each person must rely upon his or her own imagination to provide this essential orientation. In "Tea at the Palaz of Hoon," Hoon, one of Stevens's figures for the poet, certainly celebrates his own imaginative achievement in terms that leave little room for imagining that his beliefs derive from others:

> I was the world in which I walked, and what I saw
> Or heard or felt came not but from myself;
> And there I found myself more truly and more strange. (65)

Just as often, however, Stevens claims that it is the function of the poet, especially in an age of disbelief such as his own, to provide others with beliefs that can take the place of those that are losing their authority. In "The Noble Rider and the Sound of Words," he writes about the poet's social function: "I think that his function is to make his imagination theirs and that he fulfills himself only as he sees his imagination become the light in the minds of others. His role, in short, is to help people to live their lives" (*Necessary Angel* 29). As J. Hillis Miller observes in *Poets of Reality* in regard to Stevens's conception of the poet's role, "the fact that one man's fictions can be accepted by others makes society possible" (224). Or as Stevens writes about the poet in "Asides on the Oboe," "He is the transparence of the place in which / He is and in his poems we find peace" (251).

Stevens illustrates this received peace in "Idea of Order at Key West." After the speaker and his companion have overheard the woman's song, they turn to gaze back over the town:

> Ramon Fernandez, tell me, if you know,
> Why, when the singing ended and we turned
> Toward the town, tell why the glassy lights,
> The lights in the fishing boats at anchor there,
> As the night descended, tilting in the air,
> Mastered the night and portioned out the sea,
> Fixing emblazoned zones and fiery poles,
> Arranging, deepening, enchanting night. (130)

Until this stanza, the next to last, the speaker has primarily been concerned with the woman's song and the way it apparently makes her, like Hoon, the "single artificer of the world / In which she sang." When, after listening to her, the speaker and his companion turn their gaze to the harbor, they immediately perceive the lights as forming patterns in the evening sky. The order is now visual, not aural, but the pattern of lights is clearly comparable to the woman's song. It also establishes a similar relationship to the night that the woman's song does to the surf, since in itself the night is no more meaningful than the "meaningless plungings of water and the wind" (129). The ability of the speaker and his companion to see such patterns has clearly been inspired by the example of the woman's song. Since her song thus becomes a "light in the minds of others," the woman is an exemplary poet, who both makes her own world and makes it possible for others to do the same.

Stevens often uses the figure of a dance to illustrate the social harmony produced by shared fictions (Kessler 136–40). One of the better-known instances of this image occurs in the seventh stanza of "Sunday Morning," where the speaker is providing the uneasy woman with an illustration of how people might rejoice in their temporal existence:

> Supple and turbulent, a ring of men
> Shall chant in orgy on a summer morn
> Their boisterous devotion to the sun,
> Not as a god, but as a god might be,
> Naked among them, like a savage source.
> Their chant shall be a chant of paradise,
> Out of their blood, returning to the sky;
> And in their chant shall enter, voice by voice,
> The windy lake wherein their lord delights,
> The trees, like serafin, and echoing hills,
> That choir among themselves long afterward.
> They shall know well the heavenly fellowship
> Of men that perish and of summer morn.
> And whence they came and whither they shall go
> The dew upon their feet shall manifest. (69–70)

Unlike the cultivated woman, whose yearning for some permanence keeps her from enjoying her comfortable surroundings, these men have committed themselves to the pleasures of the temporal world. As a result, the landscape enters into their chant, as it does in a different way in "Idea of Order at Key West." Since they share a common vision or fiction, they can dance and chant together, enjoying among themselves a fellowship that is as "heavenly" as any could or should be. The speaker encourages the woman to join them figuratively in their chant, and thus to find, like them, her own pleasures within the transient physical world. He does not suggest that this vision of salvation is in any sense as fictive as the one she would be setting aside, and thus would allow her or the poem's initial readers to mistake the status of the vision being offered. Readers who are able to place "Sunday Morning" within the context of Stevens's evolving canon recognize that it articulates with great force one of Stevens's earliest imaginative efforts to provide himself and his contemporaries with one of the "supreme fictions without which we are unable to conceive of [life]" (*Necessary Angel* 31).

The ring of chanting men in "Sunday Morning" is one among

Stevens's anticipations of a possible future, a future in which people have been imaginatively reconciled to their place within existence. In other times and places such reconciliations had been unnecessary, since traditional beliefs had provided people with a sense of their place within the scheme of life. Stevens might have argued that the vision embodied in "Sunday Morning" is inherently superior to that available within the Christian tradition, but it would have won little assent as long as the authority of the latter was secure. The woman in "Sunday Morning" is no longer devout, otherwise she would have taken herself to church, but neither can she altogether shake free from her previous religious beliefs. She is initially prepared to indulge herself this fine Sunday morning, but then she finds her pleasure compromised by old doubts and desires. Her uncertainty makes the woman especially susceptible to the alternative proposed by the poem's speaker. Her situation is also for Stevens representative of the plight of his contemporaries—people who in the main can no longer assent to traditional beliefs but who are not yet in possession of adequate substitutes.

Stevens's poetry and prose return again and again to the urgency of providing substitutes for fading traditional beliefs, but he rarely locates that necessity in any very specific historical moment. Stevens's sense of a cultural crisis is wholly derivative; it could be—and has been—used by others to characterize almost any era in the history of the West at least since the time of Descartes. Moreover, the terms Stevens characteristically uses to describe this cultural necessity—terms such as "imagination," "reality," "fiction," and "tradition"—are themselves so abstract and so widely applicable that readers must be excused if they are typically unable to identify any particular historical exigency that Stevens would redress. "Sad Strains of a Gay Waltz," for instance, is clearly about the diminishing authority of both traditional forms and institutionalized postures of opposition to them. If dance elsewhere in Stevens is typically a figure for the celebration of life, the waltz in "Sad Strains" represents traditional forms that are losing their authority: "There comes a time when the waltz / Is no longer a mode of desire" (121). At the same time, Hoon, who until now has made his life "in solitude" and has not participated in culturally authorized activities such as the waltz, finds that the terms previously available for his own separate peace are likewise no longer adequate. Both the stately and inherently social waltz and the romantic opposition are about to be overwhelmed:

There are these sudden mobs of men,

These sudden clouds of faces and arms,
An immense suppression, freed,
These voices crying without knowing for what,

Except to be happy, without knowing how,
Imposing forms they cannot describe,
Requiring order beyond their speech. (122)

When this poem was initially published in a May 1935 number of the *New Republic,* readers might have readily assumed that it was addressing contemporary conditions—perhaps the riot that erupted in Harlem two months earlier—and thus that these mobs are representations of those dispossessed as a result of the current economic and social crisis. Although the poem's diction and procedures are clearly those of the twentieth century, there is no internal reason to make this identification; the mobs could as well be allusions to Europe in 1848, to the Paris Commune in 1870, to the social strife in the United States in the 1890s, or to any other modern instance of social turmoil, as well as to contemporary dislocations like the Harlem riot. Whenever Stevens seemingly gestures toward topical issues, he typically does so in such vague and abstract ways.[3]

In "The Irrational Element in Poetry," a lecture delivered at Harvard in 1936, Stevens provides one of his rare specific identifications of the cultural impasse that his career as a whole would address:

The pressure of the contemporaneous from the time of the beginning of the [First] World War to the present time has been constant and extreme. No one can have lived apart in a happy oblivion. For a long time before the war nothing was more common. In those days the sea was full of yachts and the yachts were full of millionaires. It was a time when only maniacs had disturbing things to say. The period was like a stage-setting that since then has been taken down and trucked away. It had been taken down by the end of the war, even though it took ten years of struggle with the consequences of the peace to bring about a realization of that fact. (*Opus Posthumous* 229)

The image of the "stage-setting" connects this passage with the first stanza of "Of Modern Poetry," and the passage as a whole provides a specific historical context for necessities described in the poem:

> The poem of the mind in the act of finding
> What will suffice. It has not always had
> To find: the scene was set; it repeated what
> Was in the script.
>   Then the theatre was changed
> To something else. Its past was a souvenir. (239)

The poem implies that in an earlier era traditional beliefs had enabled people to make sense of their worlds; they simply "repeated what / Was in the script." What Stevens in "The Irrational Element in Poetry" terms "the pressure of the contemporaneous" has subsequently rendered such beliefs useless, so that they are now little more than "souvenirs," reminders of earlier and easier times. The rest of the poem specifies the conditions that the mind must meet if it is to find what will suffice in this new social world. It must construct fictions that are living, that are consistent with contemporary diction, that acknowledge the possibility for catacylsmic wars, and that address the needs of people who can no longer rely upon traditional beliefs in making their way through life. Despite the trauma of recent losses, and notwithstanding the enormity of the task he was setting himself and poetry in general, Stevens was confident that the imagination could indeed meet the exigencies of the situation. After invoking the disturbing presence of the mobs in "Sad Strains of a Gay Waltz," Stevens concludes with a prediction:

>   The epic of disbelief
> Blares oftener and soon, will soon be constant.
> Some harmonious skeptic soon in a skeptical music
>
> Will unite these figures of men and their shapes
> Will glisten again with motion, the music
> Will be motion and full of shadows. (122)

Stevens offers himself to become this "harmonious skeptic" whose fictions can take the place of traditional beliefs and thus enable men (and, presumably, women) to join together in an energetic and joyous communal dance.

III

If Stevens saw his poetry as addressing contemporary social and cultural necessities, as providing substitutes for what was otherwise being lost, it must be conceded that its form of address was unusual. It is largely abstract, and this abstractness has several sources. First, Stevens usually declines to date or otherwise specify with any precision the cultural crisis he would redress; as a result, his characterizations of it frequently seem equally applicable to many cultural episodes in American and European history. Second, he usually declines to describe the direct social manifestations of the crisis—the wars, the dashed hopes, the lost faiths, the economic hardships, the breadlines, the shifts among political parties, the whole panorama of societies in the midst of wrenching changes in the ways they have sought to define and to provide the good life. To some extent, in this respect Stevens's poetry resembles the work of most other American literary modernists, who, with the exception of those to be considered in the following chapter, were typically preoccupied with the intellectual and affective dimensions of this cultural crisis. But Hoon is no Prufrock, and it would take many years for readers to recognize that the Crispin in "The Comedian as the Letter C" might occupy a place comparable to Prufrock's in Stevens's canon, which is to say that the jaunty irreverence of Stevens's early poetry seems to have obscured its fundamental, if oblique, seriousness of purpose. In retrospect, it is easier to appreciate that Stevens was no less concerned than T. S. Eliot or Allen Tate about the erosion of traditional beliefs in his era.

Stevens's response to this loss differed in several respects from those of other American literary modernists, and it is the shape of his response that makes his work a unique variant within American literary modernism. As we saw in the third chapter, Eliot initially responded to the apparent erosion of traditional beliefs and institutions by attempting to make the literary tradition do the cultural work earlier done by a whole array of traditional schemes. In short, Eliot initially attempted to address the contemporary crisis solely at the level of ideas. His conversion represents his acknowledgment of the inadequacy of this effort, and he subsequently worked to restore the authority of traditional institutions. Eliot's conversion, in other words, also represents his recognition that the authority of beliefs depends in large part upon the availability of institutional supports that at once embody them and keep them in general circulation. Allen Tate recognized the dependence of ideas upon institutional supports, and from the outset of his Agrarian activities he sought explicitly to restore legitimacy to traditional southern ways of life. Throughout this phase of his long career, Tate's efforts were at least as much political as they were narrowly literary; from his biographies of Stonewall Jackson and Jefferson Davis through essays like "Notes on Liberty and Property," he sought to provide an analysis of social and cultural developments that would lend credence to his call for the preservation of an agrarian social order. As we saw, Tate implicitly conceded the futility of this effort in 1938, with the publication of *The Fathers.* Like the other Agrarians, he appreciated the political dimension of their undertaking; but by the late thirties, after almost a decade of effort, it was no longer possible to imagine that their cause was politically viable. Tate remained in later years a cultural conservative and still regretted the continuing erosion of traditional institutions and beliefs, but he could no longer enlist himself in causes so clearly lost. By the time he converted to Catholicism in 1950, religion had become for him a personal allegiance rather than a social or political cause.

Like Eliot and Tate, Stevens was concerned about the consequences following upon the erosion of traditional beliefs; but unlike them, he held no brief for these beliefs and felt no urge to secure their restoration. Indeed, much of the time he seemed to feel that his contemporaries were well rid of them.[4] At the same time, he recognized that people could not operate without any beliefs, and so he set himself the task of imagining others that might better meet the exigencies of the emerging social order. He would replace rather than restore traditional beliefs. Since he believed that traditional beliefs were themselves the products of the imagination, it was a small additional step for him to believe that it could produce others that could now take their place. And since the poet was by vocation intimate with the workings of the imagination, it seemed reasonable for Stevens to assign the poet the culturally imperative task of supplying his or her contemporaries with fictions that would help them live their lives.

There is nothing in Stevens's canon that resembles Eliot's late *The Idea of a Christian Society* or Tate's early biographies of Stonewall Jackson and Jefferson Davis. Some might applaud this absence, either because they deplore the specific social and political agendas animating these works or because of a broader conviction that literary figures should confine their attention to properly literary concerns. I call attention to this absence because it provides another demonstration of the degree to which Stevens would address what he himself took to be a pervasive social and cultural crisis exclusively on the level of ideas. Eliot and Tate were also obviously concerned about ideas, but they came to recognize that ideas have their lives within institutions, and thus that taking them seriously could commit one to working on behalf of compatible and supportive institutional forms. Stevens apparently never made this connection between ideas and the institutional context that either hinders or assures their survival. Or at least he never felt compelled to take any steps—other than publishing his poems—that might propagate his own views as to how the contemporary crisis of belief might be resolved. He formed no alliances, joined no parties; instead, he simply continued to write and publish poems about the need and prospects for fictions in which people could now believe.

Stevens's relative neglect of the institutional context within which people hold beliefs makes his proposal to provide new beliefs more like Eliot's early effort to make a particular conception of the literary tradition serve the same ends than the latter's subsequent beliefs and activities. It also provides an initial point of comparison with Willa Cather's implicit cultural program. Cather, as we saw in the second chapter, was similarly concerned about the erosion of cultural mores. However, unlike either Eliot or Stevens, she had no confidence that the social changes she regretted could be themselves redressed. Instead, she would withdraw from a social world she increasingly regretted and seek consolation in the lonely company of her memories of what she took to be a better era, the era of her own childhood among the early settlers on the Nebraska plains. As we saw, there is reason to consider Cather's reconstructions of that life as constituted as much by fantasy as by memory, which brings them closer in kind than initial impressions might suggest to Stevens's necessary fictions. Both Cather's memories and Stevens's fictions are finally personal remedies to what both recognized as problems caused by fundamental changes in the social order. Memories qua memories cannot in principle be shared, whereas Stevens at least hoped that others might adopt and thus profit from the poet's new fictions. As we have seen, however, Stevens paid scant attention to the institutional context in which these fictions would be held, thereby both emphasizing the personal bias of his proposed remedy and making it seem as though they would, like Cather's memories, exist within an institutional environment that was at best indifferent to their survival.

If Cather's and Stevens's cultural programs are alike in taking the individual as their point of origin, they differ markedly in the degree of confidence with which they anticipated the future. Cather was pessimistic. She believed that the social order was now firmly in the hands of the Ivy Peters of the world, and she had few illusions that they would soon relinquish their authority. The ascendancy of these grasping individuals entailed for Cather the loss of certain traditional social niceties. Stevens, by way of contrast, conceived this same social transformation as fundamentally the loss of certain traditional beliefs. Thus in his efforts to imagine remedies to this situation, he did not need to reckon with the tenacity of these newly vested interests. Instead, he could think it sufficient to provide himself and his contemporaries with substitutes for their lost beliefs. Thus the sole resistance he anticipated derived from the lack of imagination among his contemporaries, not from whatever material stakes some had in maintaining the status quo. His relative optimism, in other words, is partially predicated on his conviction that the difficulties he would redress existed primarily at the level of ideas.

Finally, it is also instructive to note that Cather and Stevens located alternatives to regrettable contemporary conditions in quite different temporal directions. For Cather, these alternatives existed in the past—most immediately her own past, but also the historical past—in cultural moments like those reconstructed in *Death Comes for the Archbishop* and *Shadows on the Rock*. Cather had no hope that the cultural conditions she admired could be restored, but she was nonetheless comforted by recalling them. When Stevens looked to the past, he saw only beliefs that were no longer serviceable in his own time and place. However, he remained confident that the imagination could produce beliefs that would suffice; he looked for relief, as the tense of the final stanza of "Sad Strains of a Gay Waltz" attests, to the future products of the imagination: "Some harmonious skeptic *soon* in a skeptical music / *Will* unite these figures of men and their shapes" (122; my emphasis). Stevens often wrote as though this future were imminent or even already at hand; as a result, it is not always possible to appreciate the temporal orientation of his commitment to fictional beliefs. "Everything is dead / Except the future," he declares (*Opus Posthumous* 78). I call attention to the confidence with which Stevens typically contemplated the future for two reasons. First, it serves to differentiate his work from that of many other American literary modernists such as Eliot, Tate, and Cather, who, whatever their other differences, typically looked to the past for solutions to current social and cultural difficulties. Second, it also demonstrates a perhaps surprising affinity between Stevens's work and that produced by other contemporaries who primarily drew inspiration from the future, both by those associated with the Harlem or New Negro Renaissance and by those who placed their trust in the promise of a social rather than an imaginative or fictive revolution. The latter writers, of course, did not propose to settle for "ideas" about imaginable communities but were insistent upon constructing institutional arrangements compatible with them.

IV

Stevens's celebration of the renovating power of the imagination has in the end proven to be contagious. There might be any number of reasons for his belated prominence in the years following his death: a felt need for new cultural confidence, an emerging compatibility between his early emphasis on the imagination and continuing changes in the social order, or simply the recognition that his poetic was flattering to the literary sensibility. Whatever the reason or reasons for his eventual authority, Stevens has emerged in the years since his death as among the most prominent of the great American literary modernists. Signs of his prominence can be found in several quarters. The influential sociologist Robert Bellah, for instance, drew upon the final line of Stevens's "Flyer's Fall" for the title of a collection of his essays on contemporary religion, *Beyond Belief: Essays on Religion in a Post-Traditional World*. One of Stevens's earlier commentators, Ronald Sukenick, has subsequently become an experimental novelist of some note, and his fiction and occasional prose are clearly based upon Stevens's conceptions of the imagination (Chabot, "Fiction" 835–38). The respect with which Stevens is now received has perhaps discouraged most readers from subjecting his work to careful and dispassionate scrutiny. I want to demonstrate, however, that Stevens's celebration of the imagination is inherently faulty, that on his own terms it is both unequal to the tasks he sets it and unnecessary to them.

One of the most concise articulations of Stevens's position is a by now familiar entry in the "Adagia": "The final belief is to believe in a fiction, which you know to be a fiction, there being nothing else. The exquisite truth is to know that it is a fiction and that you believe in it willingly" (*Opus Posthumous* 189). There is something admirably austere about this formulation. I sense that Stevens wished the situation were otherwise, that his culture was able to provide him and others with more substantial beliefs. It cannot; but people must believe something, so the "final belief," after all others have been set aside, must be placed in an acknowledged fiction. As if in compensation for this necessity, Stevens is prepared to find a special psychological pleasure (the "exquisite truth") in knowingly and willingly placing one's belief in a fiction. This last point is crucial, for otherwise it might seem that Stevens is recommending a form of self-deception, that in the interest of expediency we forget that our final beliefs are no different in kind from those we discarded as inadequate on the way to them. The pleasure he anticipates from such feats of mind resembles that which he extols in "Sunday Morning" and elsewhere, where the recognition of an object's transiency intensifies the pleasures one can derive from it. A "true belief," were such possible, would be analogous to ripe fruit in paradise that never falls: since it is always available, we would finally become indifferent to its succulence. It is finally the intellectual risk that Stevens would relish in both situations, however odd it might seem to see such risks celebrated by a person who was for most of his professional life engaged in the insurance business.

When Stevens urges belief in fictions, he is being deliberately provocative, and the provocation is achieved by using the words *believe* and *belief* in unusual ways. In common usage, to say that one believes something is precisely to say that one takes it to be true. When we are unsure about the truth of a proposition or description, we typically say that we are "entertaining" or "toying with" it; we reserve the word *believe* until the question of its validity has been at least temporarily settled in its favor. Fictions, accordingly, are in common usage by definition things that we do not believe; we can be amused by them, can entertain them, can perhaps even, in Coleridge's phrase, temporarily "suspend disbelief" in them, but we cannot in common usage believe them. It is only by making something different and less than usual of the mental state of belief that Stevens can urge belief in fictions. Actually, the rhetorical force of such manifestly paradoxical proposals depends upon the simultaneous availability of both senses of the word: to make sense of the proposal, we must grant Stevens his new usage; but the proposal's force depends upon the continuing availability of our usual sense of the word. It is the discontinuity between common usage and Stevens's own that captures our attention and makes us puzzle out his likely meaning. The latter, then, is clearly parasitic upon common usage, and would have little rhetorical force if Stevens's own usage became commonplace.

Even if we grant Stevens the usage to which he puts the word *belief*, we must nonetheless recognize that what he urges is psychologically impossible. We cannot willingly believe in fictions. Of course we continually discover that certain of our beliefs are mistaken; as William James writes in "The Will to Believe," "Biologically considered, our minds are as ready to grind out falsehood as veracity" (25). Whenever we subsequently discover that our confidence in particular beliefs has been misplaced, we drop them in favor of others that strike us at the time as being more adequate. We must, in fact, revise our beliefs with distressing frequency, but our susceptibility to mistaken beliefs does not count as evidence that we can knowingly, in the full sense of the word, believe in fictions. It only demonstrates that we are fallible. The frequency with which we must revise our beliefs might over time incline some of us to become cautious about what we believe and modest in the tenacity with which we cling to any belief, but every belief is at bottom a commitment to the truth of a proposition or description, as the case might be.

To demonstrate this point, I ask that you attempt a small experiment in thought. Try to convince yourself that we now live in the best of all possible worlds.[5] Convince yourself, for instance, that medical science and practice have already been perfected, so that all maladies and their treatment are now so well known that no person in a lifetime suffers needlessly; that each enjoys such health as can be had, given his or her own constitution; that the full measure of relief is readily available whenever any person becomes ill; and that all people can be confident that in the course of treatment their dignity will suffer no more needless harm than their bodies. Convince yourself, too, that our economic, social, and political arrangements have achieved such efficiency and fairness that as many citizens are assured of the basic necessities as is conceivable; that as many citizens possess opportunities to share in the available rewards as is consistent with assuring economic health; that the interests of as many are consulted in establishing policies as is consistent with effective government; and that no needless barriers exist that might deprive some of a hearing in the institutions dedicated to the distribution of justice. Finally, convince yourself too that the actions of current nation-states are as rational and sensitive as one could imagine them ever being; that each carefully arranges its priorities in ways that maximize the benefits to its citizens; that none needlessly jeopardizes the well-being of its own or others' citizens; and that each, within the limits of economic necessity, wisely husbands its own natural resources and environment in order to preserve them for future generations. I could continue, but I trust that I have already strained your credulity, and that at some point in this exercise you found it impossible to believe this description of our current estate. I asked that you engage in this exercise to demonstrate a simple point—namely, that we cannot believe just anything, any more than Stevens could place credence in Plato's figure of a chariot drawn by winged horses. We withhold belief from statements, like those above, that we cannot imagine being true; to say that we believe something is the same as saying we believe it to be true. We cannot believe the above characterization of our world because we are aware of too many ways in which our world might be improved and are thus aware of too many ways in which this characterization of it is false to our sense of things. Stevens proposes to break this link between a mental state (belief) and the status of its object (truth). He proposes that we come to assume this mental state in other circumstances, when we no longer take its object to be necessarily true, when in fact we know that it cannot possibly be true. While it is certainly the case that we often enough discover that one or another of our settled beliefs is not true, and while we can also consider and even believe ideas whose truth or falsity we cannot establish with any confidence, we cannot in any meaningful sense of the word believe in fictions: the belief *that* something is fictive precludes belief *in* it.

On at least one occasion Stevens was personally confronted by this objection. In a letter to Henry Church he recounts an encounter with an otherwise admiring student: "One evening, a week or so ago, a student at Trinity College came to the office and walked home with me. We talked about this book [*Notes toward a Supreme Fiction*]. I said that I thought that we had reached a point at which we could no longer really believe in anything unless we recognized that it is a fiction. The student said that that was an impossibility, that there was no such thing as believing in something that one knew was not true" (*Letters* 430). In his letter, Stevens responds to the student's objection by observing that people do so continuously. In particular, he invokes Coleridge's notion of the willing suspension of disbelief, writing that "if there is a will to believe, . . . it seems to me that we can suspend disbelief with reference to a fiction as easily as we can suspend it with reference to anything else" (430). But this is to beg the question. Coleridge developed the notion of a willing suspension of disbelief in order to account for aesthetic experiences, in which individuals seemingly accept propositions or descriptions that are at odds with their usual beliefs. Coleridge assumed that these were special experiences, and that they occurred within the context of others in which disbelief was not suspended. Stevens's proposed generalization of this experience would collapse the distinction Coleridge wished to preserve between aesthetic and other experiences; it would in fact aestheticize all aspects of life. Even Coleridge's phrasing suggests that he understood the suspension of disbelief to be a special state, and he nowhere suggests that it is either possible or desirable to carry it over, as Stevens proposes, into our daily lives. Stevens concludes his account of the student's objection by observing that many people believe in heaven, as though the prevalence of that belief illustrates his contention that people can and do believe in fictions. Many now might be ready to consider the belief in heaven to be a belief in a fiction; but the example demonstrates at most that our beliefs are corrigible. I suspect that few if any people who believe or believed in heaven simultaneously thought that they are or were thereby believing in a fiction; to the contrary, they most likely thought of it as an actual estate, with its own geography and flora, to which they aspired. The fact that we can in retrospect identify in ourselves and others beliefs that have been shown to be mistaken does nothing to establish the possibility that we can believe propositions or descriptions we know from the outset to be fictive.[6]

I suspect that Stevens came to this finally untenable position regarding the possibilities of belief in fictions out of a sense that alternatives were unavailable. We seem to be the kind of creatures that require beliefs, and Stevens was eager to supply that need. At the same time, he was convinced that we could not find anything very definitive in which to believe. Since we cannot attain reliable knowledge, he proposes to fill this human need with fictions, the pure products of the imagination. Since on his account all earlier beliefs were themselves fictions, even though few contemporary believers recognized their status as such, he proposed that we continue to believe in fictions, but with this crucial difference: that we henceforth acknowledge their fictive status even as we believe in them. There is something incoherent about this desperate remedy. How do we *know* that all our beliefs are and must be fictive? Is this belief, too, fictive? If so, why not simply abandon it in favor of another that would require fewer mental contortions? And how do we *know* that the imagination is able to produce fictive beliefs? The imagination exists in the world as part of our mental equipment; if we can know about its capabilities, we should be able by the same means to learn about other aspects of our worlds and thus should not need to trust exclusively to fictive beliefs. Stevens's skepticism about the possibility of true beliefs, in other words, rarely extends to include his conception of the imagination, which remains singularly immune, the only reality that can be reliably known. In his poetry Stevens usually struggles to create an interplay between imagination and its physical surroundings; occasionally, however, a telling slippage occurs, so that the former seems completely to override the latter, as in the third stanza of "Another Weeping Woman":

> The magnificent cause of being,
> The imagination, the only reality
> In this imagined world (25)

It says something about the presumed redemptive power of the imagination that Stevens, among its most ardent celebrants, clings tenaciously to the belief that, at a bare minimum, it and its capabilities are true and not fictive. It says, first, that fictive consolations must not in the end prove to be as reassuring as he otherwise implies; it also says, and by way of compensation, that they might not after all be as necessary, since we can presumably learn about other facets of life by the same means that we learn about the imagination.

V

I have tried to demonstrate that Stevens's celebrated notion of belief in fictions is both psychologically impossible and conceptually incoherent. As Stevens himself knew, people have held all manner of beliefs; they need not allow conceptual incoherence to undermine their beliefs when the felt need is strong enough. Many of Stevens's readers have clearly been willing to follow him in placing trust for the future in the resources of the imagination. I have come to believe, however, that Stevens himself finally was not. In the years since the publication of Peter Brazeau's oral biography there has been a controversy surrounding Father Arthur Hanley's claim that Stevens converted to Catholicism in the course of his final illness.[7] I suspect that the resistance to this claim derives in part from concern about what it implies about Stevens's own final assessment of the redemptive powers of the imagination. If Stevens himself finally accepted the authority of the Catholic Church, was he also prepared to jettison his faith in supreme fictions, a faith that had been in the making at least since "A High-Toned Old Christian Woman" and "To the One of Fictive Music," poems that date from the early twenties?

Aside from the available confirmations of Father Hanley's reliability, I find his report plausible for two reasons. First, I can imagine that Stevens himself would eventually be forced to acknowledge, if only at the end and only to himself, the psychological impossibility of knowingly vesting belief in fictions. We have in the testimony of the *Collected Poems* ample evidence that Stevens made a long and determined effort to create fictions that could serve as his beliefs. It seems at least plausible that the same integrity that kept him from deceiving himself about their fictive status would eventually compel him to acknowledge the futility of this entire endeavor. My second reason derives from a reading of the poetry and prose in which Stevens appears most determined to work out the implications of his notion of imaginative redemption. This is a remarkable and often moving body of work, not least for the way it returns again and again to Stevens's fundamental working terms, as if attempting to convince himself and others of their adequacy. Even in "Notes toward a Supreme Fiction" he must seemingly struggle to reassure himself about the feasibility of his undertaking:

> It is possible, possible, possible. It must
> Be possible. It must be that in time
> The real will from its crude compoundings come,
>
> Seeming, at first, a beast disgorged, unlike,
> Warmed by a desperate milk. (404)

The repetition in these first lines can represent the repetitions throughout Stevens's canon, the way in which in poem after poem he keeps returning to a few animating issues. It also obviously represents an effort to assuage his own doubts; when he writes, "It must / Be possible," the verb expresses less a conviction than a felt necessity (Vendler, *Extended Wings* 21).

In the same letter in which Stevens reports his encounter with the skeptical student from nearby Trinity College, a letter written after the initial publication of "Notes," Stevens makes the following concession: "I have no idea of the form that a supreme fiction would take" (*Letters* 430). The poem itself, like many written in Stevens's later years, is an extended meditation on the necessary requirements ("*It Must Be Abstract*" [380], etc.) that any candidate for consideration as a supreme fiction would need to meet. The poem is addressed to an aspiring poet and purports to follow a train of thought that might lead to the composition of supreme fictions. At several points the train of thought is broken by more fully imagined episodes or fables, including those introducing MacCullough (386–87), the deserted plantation (393), and Canon Aspirin (401–03). Each of these episodes might be conceived as a tentative approximation of such a fiction, but each is inevitably abandoned, to be followed by others, in the same manner that Stevens's other poems on this theme from "The Comedian as the Letter C" on appear to be provisional resolutions, satisfactory for the moment but then in need of revision.

The number of and variety among these poems testify to Stevens's powers of invention, but they also and less obviously suggest that he was never able to articulate a supreme fiction that compelled his own assent. The problem was not simply, as Stevens conceded to Henry Church, that he did not know what form such a fiction should take, but also that he could imagine little about its substance other than his great need for something.[8]

What I finally find most remarkable about Stevens's many poems about the necessity of supreme fictions is the absence in them of anything that could conceivably now take the place of the beliefs that Stevens thought no longer viable. As we know from "Sunday Morning" and other poems, traditional Western religious beliefs are among those Stevens long aspired to supplant. He felt that these beliefs enjoyed an institutional sanction that increasingly exceeded their authority over individual believers, and that they in any event unduly limited the pleasures people might derive from the temporal world. If Stevens thought of himself primarily as providing his contemporaries with substitutes for these fading beliefs, it must at last be conceded that his endeavor came to little. Like many other intellectuals then and now, he grossly underestimated the continuing authority that these seemingly discredited beliefs would possess for others (and in the end, apparently, for himself); at the same time, he was clearly unduly optimistic about his capacity to imagine more adequate substitutes that could win wide assent. The only plausible candidates in Stevens's large canon for being supreme fictions are his notion of the supreme fiction itself and his confidence in the redemptive powers of the imagination. But taking these notions as themselves substitutes for traditional religion would be rather like taking the discipline of religious studies as itself being a religion. That is, one might have anticipated that these notions were developed as intellectual tools that would help us account for and understand instances of such fictions instead of themselves being the only available examples of the phenomenon they purport to describe.

Saying that Stevens finally failed in his efforts to renovate the beliefs of his contemporaries is less an assessment of his accomplishment as a poet than a comment on the magnitude of his aspirations. His long, repeated, and even obsessive efforts to fulfill his own and his contemporaries' apparent need for more satisfying beliefs produced an unusually large and varied canon, one perhaps containing a greater number of memorable poems than were written by any other American literary modernist. If he somehow exaggerated both his contemporaries' needs and their ability to believe in fictions, it is difficult not to admire his persistence and resourcefulness. He explicitly refused to acknowledge any social obligation for the poet. "He has none" (*Necessary Angel* 27), he said with finality in "The Noble Rider and the Sound of Words." Nonetheless, his entire career can best be understood as being dedicated to fulfilling a need he recognized among his contemporaries and felt within himself. He would deliver new beliefs to a populace whose old ones were apparently wearing thin. These new beliefs would transform the "sudden mobs of men" evoked in "Sad Strains of a Gay Waltz" into a community of shared belief. The fact that Stevens understood this social necessity exclusively as a question of belief often makes it seem as if he was indifferent to the fate of an increasingly troubled world. It also renders his imaginative remedies improbable, more so even than Eliot's and Tate's efforts to revive fading social institutions and practices. The latter at least recognized the dependence of beliefs upon institutional supports, however futile and ill-advised their efforts to revive residual institutions might largely seem to us now. If Stevens lacked their appreciation of the tangible way beliefs exist and exert their influence within the social world, he was at least able and willing to relinquish the past in his own quest for solutions to contemporary difficulties, producing in the process his own distinctive variant of American literary modernism. And if he in the final days of his life converted to Catholicism, we need not consider his conversion so much as his abandonment of his long commitment to the imagination as a belated acknowledgment that it too takes its life in the midst of social institutions.

6

THE THIRTIES AND THE FAILURE
OF THE FUTURE

In the thirties, I wanted to be ravished by a community.
  Waldo Frank, *Memoirs* 196

IN 1936 Allen Tate and Herbert Agar edited *Who Owns America?*
The published symposium represented the temporary alignment
of two conservative movements. It included essays by Donald
Davidson, John Crowe Ransom, and others who had earlier contributed to the Agrarian *I'll Take My Stand,* as well as by Hilaire Belloc
and other English Distributivists, who shared the Agrarian's belief
in the cultural significance of the independent small farmer.[1] Both
its title and the transatlantic list of contributors indicate that the
volume represents a late phase of Agrarianism, when the Agrarians
were not so much directly defending the South per se as reaching
out to other social conservatives with whom they might make common cause, as Tate himself did that same year in "What Is a Traditional Society?" Despite its provocative title, *Who Owns America?*
excited little of the interest stirred by *I'll Take My Stand,* and it
remains largely neglected.

However, Robert Penn Warren's contribution to the volume, an
essay entitled "Literature as a Symptom," remains of interest because of the comparison he draws between two contemporary literary tendencies. "The 'regional movement' and the 'proletarian
movement' are the two rationalizations in greatest vogue at this
moment" (271), writes Warren. Whereas the regional writer, according to Warren, establishes a special tie with a particular geo-
graphical area and its traditions, the proletarian writer forms corresponding relations with a particular class and its future. Warren

claims that these writers, whatever their other differences, share a common animus:

> But there is one important aspect which these two movements, as literary movements, share in common: both are revolutionary. Both the proletarian and the regional writer are dissatisfied with the present relation of the writer to society. The destructive criticism, the negative side of the argument, which is leveled against the present condition, may frequently be presented in terms of either the regional or the proletarian movement; both may be said to be opposed to finance-capitalism and to resent the indignity heaped by that system of society upon the creative impulse, indignity which has succeeded in estranging the artist from society and from the proper exercise of his function as "a man speaking to men." To heal that rupture, to come to accord with self and with society, may be taken, in so far as the writers are concerned, as the underlying motivation of both movements. (275–76)

Warren makes regional and proletarian writers seem chiefly concerned with the diminished status accorded them within the existing social and economic order. To be sure, these writers did "resent the indignity heaped by [finance-capitalism] upon the creative impulse," and so on, but their rancor was fueled as much by their sense that such indignities were heaped upon many of their fellow citizens. By confining their grievances to the literary plane, Warren risks making these literary movements appear more self-interested and less revolutionary than they were. Neither the regionalists nor the proletarian writers would be satisfied by improvements solely in the circumstances of writers; both sought changes in social life such that all citizens could better exist, in the words Warren quotes, as "men speaking to men."

Such misgivings aside, Warren early recognized that he and his fellow Agrarians shared a common animus and similar ends with writers who were otherwise markedly different. Similarly opposed to what Warren here terms "finance-capitalism," the regional and proletarian literary movements formed around alternative images of more satisfying ways of life and correspondingly different programs of action. The agrarian South functions in the Agrarians' work in the same manner that some new social order functions in the work of writers on the Left. One group looked to the past for relief from contemporary exigencies, and the other looked to the future, but they were united in their opposition to the terms of life then available in industrial America. Whether they looked back or forward, these writers, like many of their fellow citizens at the time, were trying to imagine social forms that would enable all citizens to overcome their isolation and to establish anew viable, humane communities.

The Agrarians typically combined their reactionary social program with an aggressive and unmistakable adherence to literary modernism. Few would question the Agrarians'—especially Tate's and Warren's—credentials as modernist writers. For all their political radicalism, on the other hand, the writers of the thirties, those who participated in what Warren terms the "proletarian movement," can seem committed to literary practices that predate modernism. A Jack Conroy, Farrell, or Steinbeck initially seems to have more in common with Dreiser, Crane, or even Howells than with contemporaries such as Eliot, Tate, or Warren. As a result, the proletarian writers of the thirties are typically taken to be an interruption of literary modernism in the United States. The literary realism or naturalism that they apparently espoused is commonly thought to put these writers out of phase with their modernist contemporaries. The writers affiliated with *Partisan Review,* first issued in 1934 under the sponsorship of the New York City John Reed Club, seem unique in the degree to which they were initially committed equally to political radicalism and obvious versions of literary modernism.

In this chapter I want to argue that the self-consciously proletarian writers produced a variant within American literary modernism, not an alternative to it. As we saw in the first chapter, an emergent American literary modernism was often accompanied by and occasionally informed by an equally insistent call for radical political action. The cultural revival called for by Van Wyck Brooks in *America's Coming-of-Age* was to be complemented by the establishment of socialism in the social and economic realms. During the twenties the literary portions of this program were initially more successful than the political, but the advent of the Depression convinced many Americans that nothing short of a fundamental change in the economic and social system could provide an adequate remedy. The Agrarian program announced in *I'll Take My Stand* had been formulated prior to the Depression, in response to the increasing in-

dustrialization of the southern economy and way of life. The subsequent collapse of American industry during the thirties seemed
to validate the Agrarians' argument, and throughout the early thirties they continued to press their case in essays published in Seward
Collins's *American Review* and elsewhere. As we saw in the third
chapter, however, Agrarianism soon exhausted itself, as Tate and
others drifted away to pursue other issues later in the decade. Writers on the Left produced the more substantial and characteristic
body of literature during the period. Their work, like that of other
American literary modernists, was animated by an abiding dissatis-
faction with the terms of contemporary life; they believed that the
economic dislocations of the thirties revealed the decisive nature of
American capitalism, thereby demonstrating the need to replace it
with a more humane economic and social system.

If Warren's linkage of regional and proletarian impulses in the
thirties is suggestive, the literary work produced by leftist writers in
some ways resembles as closely that written by participants in the
Harlem or New Negro Renaissance, especially in seeming to be in
most accounts outside the ambit of literary modernism. The proletarian fiction of the thirties evolved some characteristic forms
(Foley), but it was little more formally experimental than the novels
of Jessie Fauset. It is their shared preoccupation with the fates of
peoples who are not necessarily white and middle class that unites
them, as does the ambition that companionable lives and other
benefits of full citizenship be available to such peoples. Writers animated by both impulses wanted to quicken the consciousness and
pride of a new social entity—in the one case a race, in the other a
class—so that it might claim for itself a more ample future. Langston Hughes participated in both literary impulses and provides a
direct link between them. For a time in the thirties he wrote more
about and on behalf of "workers" not identified by race than
specifically about and for African Americans, and in these years he
more often identified capitalism as his primary antagonist than ra-
cism. Hughes's proletarian poems are typically free verse and do not
draw extensively upon blues forms, as he had especially in his second
collection, *Fine Clothes for the Jews*. Some proletarian poetry drew
upon ballad and other oral forms, but none turned, as Sterling
Brown did, to a rich folk tradition, perhaps because such writers
were more impatient to create a new class and better future than

concerned with preserving and dignifying any cultural past. If the Depression brought the Harlem Renaissance to an untimely end by demonstrating the limits to the economic and social progress made to date by African Americans, it gave the broader political ambitions already evident in American literary modernism in the teens a new legitimacy and urgency.

Writers who identified themselves with the dispossessed typically looked to the future in the search for alternatives to the status quo, especially as it seemed to be figured by the Soviet Union. The following stanza from H. H. Lewis's "The Sweeter Our Fruits . . . " illustrates the rhetorical place occupied in the early thirties for those on the political Left by the Soviet Union:

> Before 1918 we were "visionaries,"
> Socialism "against human nature,"
> But now
> We point
>   To Red Russia.[2]

Enough writers joined the Communist Party during these years that Warren, in his contribution to *Who Owns America?*, could quote an American publisher saying "It's smart to be a communist" (276); others let their sympathy with the communists be known by participating in organizations and conferences sponsored by the party, such as the League of American Writers. It is understandable how the desire for fundamental revisions in American life came to be intimately linked with the Communist Party. For some years, both here and abroad, the party had been decrying the evils of capitalism and offering itself as a vehicle for bringing about a more benign and just future. Early reports from travelers to the Soviet Union intimated that the new social system worked, as people during the Depression were beginning to believe that capitalism no longer could. Furthermore, the party provided the political apparatus not available to the Agrarians, making it conceivable that its aspirations could be fulfilled. In the end, however, the close identification of the party of the future with the Communist Party proved to be the former's undoing. When in the course of international events the latter was discredited, so too were the goals of the former; and with the vehicle for meaningful change seemingly off the tracks, many lost faith in the very possibility of change. Because this disillusionment has proven to be even more consequential to the subsequent course of American literature than the body of work produced during the thirties, this chapter, after considering some characteristic work produced in these years, will largely focus on several writers then coming of age and in whose work this ironic legacy of the thirties becomes clear.

I

John Steinbeck did not participate actively in the literary politics of the thirties and was never affiliated with the Communist Party. Indeed, when his publisher initially rejected *In Dubious Battle,* Steinbeck suspected that editors sympathetic to communism were responsible. "Between you and me," he wrote in a letter to his agent, Elizabeth Otis, "I suspect a strong communist bias in that office, since the reasons given against the book are all those I have heard from communists of the intellectual bent and of the Jewish race" (109–10). His sympathetic treatment of the poor, however, made his work similar to that of more explicitly political writers. After his commercial successes in the latter half of the decade, and especially after the inauguration of the Popular Front in 1935, Steinbeck was courted by the Left and eventually lent his name to some of its causes, including the League of American Writers. Granville Hicks, writing in *New Masses,* claimed that the long struggle to invent an indigenous proletarian literature had finally culminated with the 1939 publication of *The Grapes of Wrath,* declaring that the novel possessed "all the qualities proletarian literature has to have" (139). I shall follow Hicks's suggestion and use Steinbeck's work as representative of American literary modernism during the thirties.

Steinbeck's earlier *Of Mice and Men,* on the other hand, is not a political novel. The ranch hands are lowly enough, but nowhere in the novel does Steinbeck suggest that their condition is caused or worsened by the machinations of owners, the introduction of new technology, or other commonly cited causes of working-class hardship. Although written during the thirties, the novel does not directly allude to conditions peculiar to the Depression. Unencumbered by such specific issues, *Of Mice and Men* offers a particularly concentrated and forceful vision of what ails its characters.

George and Lennie's arrival together at the ranch is the occasion for comment by the other hands. The boss assumes that George must somehow be taking advantage of his companion, and even Slim is surprised by their friendship. " 'Ain't many guys travel around together,' he muses. 'I don't know why. Maybe ever'body in the whole damn world is scared of each other' " (64). George later partially explains to Slim why he travels with Lennie: " 'I ain't got no people,' George said. 'I seen the guys that go around on the ranches alone. That ain't no good. They don't have no fun. After a long time they get mean. They get wantin' to fight all the time' " (73–74). Curly's wife, the lone woman on the ranch, can find no one to talk with, and she accuses the hands of being afraid of one another: "You're all scared of each other, that's what. Ever' one of you's scared the rest is going to get something on you" (135). It soon appears that loneliness and a consequent distrust of others is the common condition of the ranch's inhabitants.

The hands in the bunkhouse typically find mundane ways to re-dress their loneliness. Candy finds companionship with his aged dog until he agrees to have it put out of its misery. The others play cards, throw horseshoes, and regularly visit the local whores. Crooks, the only black man on the ranch, lives alone in the harness room and generally cannot participate in the small comforts available to the other hands. His loneliness might be more extreme, but his comments to Lennie, when the latter visits his room, typify the conditions of all the hands. When Lennie first appears in Crooks's door-way, the latter insists that he leave. He soon realizes, however, that Lennie cannot understand much that is said to him, and with this realization he invites Lennie into his room for further conversation:

> "A guy can talk to you an' be sure yu won't go blabbin'. . . . " He leaned forward excitedly. "This is just a nigger talkin', an' a busted-back nigger. So it don't mean nothing, see? You couldn't remember it anyways. I seen it over an' over—a guy talkin' to another guy and it don't make no difference if he don't hear or understand. The thing is, they're talkin', or they're sittin' still not talkin'. It don't make no difference, no difference." His excitement had increased until he pounded his knee with his hand. "George can tell you screwy things, and it don't matter. It's just the talking. It's just being with another guy. . . . You got George. You *know* he's goin' to come back. S'pose you didn't have nobody. S'pose you couldn't go into the bunkhouse and play rummy 'cause you was black.

> How'd you like that? S'pose yo had to sit out here an' read books.
> . . . Books ain't no good. A guy needs somebody—to be near him."
> He whined, "a guy goes nuts if he ain't got nobody. Don't make
> no difference who the guy is, long's he's with you. I tell ya," he
> cried, "I tell ya a guy gets too lonely an' he gets sick." (123–27)

Crooks needs companionship of a very fundamental sort. A companion need not particularly love or care for him, as George cares for Lennie, nor even understand his needs and desires. Crooks craves the simple presence of another person, someone to talk to, someone simply "to be near him."

Candy and Curly's wife soon join Lennie in Crooks's room, each looking for companionship on a Saturday night when the other hands have gone to town. When Curly's wife verbally abuses them, Crooks initially retires "into the terrible protective dignity of the Negro" (137), and later asks them all to leave. "I ain't sure I want you in here no more. A colored man got to have some rights even if he don't like 'em" (143). Crooks's rights in this case are merely defensive, yet he insists upon them even though doing so increases the isolation he otherwise regrets. He lacks the means to secure at once companionship and his sense of dignity. Crooks's loneliness might be more extreme than that of the other hands, but his lament to Lennie serves to illustrate their common plight. The characters in *Of Mice and Men* suffer an initial isolation that in turn makes them touchy, and so less likely to overcome their common estrangement from one another.

The companionship enjoyed by George and Lennie, despite the latter's condition, serves as a counterpoint to the loneliness of the others. Each has in the other the companion that Crooks so desires. They also have a dream for the future—the purchase of their own farm, with rabbits for Lennie to tend, where they would, in a phrase Lennie enjoys repeating, "live on the fatta the lan'." Candy and even Crooks are for a time drawn by this dream, and it temporarily seems within reach. In the end, of course, it comes to nothing, as George mercifully shoots Lennie as the latter looks out over the river and visualizes what might have been.

The power of *Of Mice and Men* derives from Steinbeck's depiction of loneliness and its consequences. Whatever their hardships and misfortunes, their companionship saves George and Lennie from this otherwise common affliction. It also provides the basis for the dream of owning their own farm. The rabbits that Lennie wants to tend, and that the reader knows he will pet, represent for Lennie the same need for physical closeness that the more articulate Crooks can put into words. *Of Mice and Men,* in other words, turns on questions of loneliness and companionship, and other issues, such as ownership of one's own land, are strictly subsidiary. If many of the hands yearn for a piece of land, that land turns out to be a place where they can imagine enjoying companionable lives. In this novel Steinbeck does not imply that isolation is either caused or aggravated by particular social arrangements; rancher owners are obviously not responsible for Lennie's condition, and Steinbeck does not suggest that they conspire in the continuing poverty of the hands. Accordingly, he does not suggest social programs that might address the needs of such people. Their problems seem irremediable, and it is difficult to imagine how the tone of the novel could be other than grim.

Steinbeck returns to these issues two years later in *The Grapes of Wrath,* this time placing them in a larger social context. A series of bad crops, which had already driven farmers into dire straits, is used by banks as an occasion to foreclose mortgages and by owners to release tenant farmers, thereby dispossessing families of their means of livelihood. At the same time, these developments provide the opportunity to introduce modern farming techniques. "The tenant system won't work any more," explain the owners. "One man on a tractor can take the place of twelve or fourteen families. Pay him a wage and take all the crop" (44). Thus the land is made profitable to some at the cost of impoverishing the many; and Steinbeck suggests, following Marx on this point, that in the end the process will condemn many who think initially to profit by it, until both capital and tillable land are concentrated in very few hands (324–26).

In *The Grapes of Wrath* Steinbeck emphasizes two effects of this process. First, introducing modern technology not only deprives most of their means of securing livelihoods, but rends as well the fructifying ties to the land even of the few who do remain. Grampa Joad dies almost as soon as he is uprooted from the family plot, as if his life were somehow part and parcel of the land he had worked; but even those who remain behind now find machinery interposed between themselves and the land they work:

> The man sitting in the iron seat did not look like a man; gloved, goggled, rubber dust mask over nose and mouth, he was part of the monster, a robot in the seat. . . . The driver could not control it—straight across the country it went, cutting through a dozen farms and straight back. . . . He could not see the land as it was, he could not smell the land as it smelled; his feet did not stamp the clods or feel the warmth and power of the earth. He sat in an iron seat and stepped on iron pedals. He could not cheer or beat or curse or encourage the extension of his power, and because of this he could not cheer or whip or curse or encourage himself. He did not know or own or trust or beseech the land. . . . He loved the land no more than the bank loved the land. (48)

One villain of the piece, then, is modern technology, which Steinbeck perceives as destructive of some organic bond between humans and the land they work. He depicts it as inherently destructive of the quality of life. Second, those now forced like the Joads to wander westward in search of wages find themselves cruelly manipulated into a Hobbesian competition of all against all for what jobs remain. In these circumstances, other families become competitors in a shrinking marketplace, and under the pressure of the competition, and with the contrivance of employers, wages sink to the level of barest subsistence. If other authors allude to the new abrasiveness of social relations during the thirties, few manage to present it with Steinbeck's intensity, for social intercourse here is reduced to fighting it out for a chance at survival.

In *The Grapes of Wrath*, the barbarity of the Okies' lives is clearly attributed to determinate historical developments. Steinbeck's remedy for it is equally straightforward. "This is the beginning—from 'I' to 'we'" (206). As the migrants congregate at evening in roadside camps, they build up folkways that parcel out rights and obligations; they learn that their plights are shared; and they come, finally, to extend to one another small acts of charity. "If you're in trouble or hurt or need—go to the poor people," says Ma Joad. "They're the only ones that'll help—the only ones" (513–14). Throughout the novel Ma Joad fights to keep her family intact, seeing it as a bulwark against an otherwise heartless world. In the end she recognizes that their world can only be made more livable on the condition that the small charities, ties, and continuities of the family be extended outward so as to incorporate one's neighbors.

When, in the famous final scene, Rose of Sharon nurses a starving stranger at her breast, she is doing her mother's bidding and thereby illustrating the presumed willingness of these displaced people to assume familial responsibilities for one another.

Ma Joad had already endorsed a similar if more conventional action by another of her children when she acceded to Tom's determination to leave the family and become a labor organizer. Tom decides to continue the work of Casy, the former preacher who was killed for leading a strike. "I know now a fella ain't no good alone" (570), he declares when expressing his resolve. Neither Tom nor his mother can completely understand his motivation; Tom's explanation is an uneasy mixture of union slogans and religious sentiments. Tom's final recognition of the need for the migrants to organize, however, places *The Grapes of Wrath* squarely in the tradition of revolutionary fiction as it emerged during the thirties. Many of these novels conclude with similar scenes. For instance, in the final lines of Mike Gold's *Jews without Money* the confused adolescent boy is converted to communism by a soapbox orator; and Jack Conroy's *The Disinherited* concludes with Larry's decision to organize farmers after he spontaneously participates in resistance to a farm auction. Such conversions enable these novels, which otherwise concentrate on the drab lives available to the great majority of people, to conclude on a hopeful note by suggesting that a means of redress has at last been located.

Tom Joad's decision to become a labor organizer and Rose of Sharon's more graphic willingness to meet an other's needs gesture toward the sense of solidarity typically evoked as revolutionary texts from the thirties conclude. In the final scene of Clifford Odets's *Waiting for Lefty*, the actors address the audience:

> *To audience:* Well, what's the answer?
> All: STRIKE!
> Agate: LOUDER!
> All: STRIKE!
> Agate and others on stage: AGAIN!
> All: STRIKE, STRIKE, STRIKE!!! (52)

The audience here is meant to be swept up and to share in the sense of solidarity achieved by the cab drivers as they resolve to strike. The sense of solidarity or revolutionary élan serves as an antidote to the despair and helplessness that previously typified the characters' attitude. Characters and readers in these texts are instructed time and again that "a fella ain't no good alone," that they must overcome their individual predicaments by seeking relief in one another. These works often conclude precisely in the full flush of that recognition, with characters seemingly swooning with gratitude that relief is now at hand. I have been arguing that American literary modernism as a whole was motivated by a sense that the lives of all citizens were increasingly being impoverished by the lack of any sense of community. By placing such emphasis on the experience of solidarity, these revolutionary texts foreground the way they would repair that absence. Paula Rabinowitz has convincingly demonstrated that women writers working in this genre typically figured this solidarity in maternal terms (97–136), but none ventured a more directly maternal image of solidarity than that used by Steinbeck to conclude *The Grapes of Wrath*.

At the same time, such conclusions raise several questions. "If the communist spirit is really a New Beginning," asks Amy Godine, "why does one writer after another choose to *end* his novel with it? Isn't there anything more to say?" (206). Such endings obviously relieve the writer of the need to imagine and render either what life might be like in any new social order or the grim process by which that order might be brought into existence. As *The Grapes of Wrath* concludes, Tom is about to embark upon a life similar to Mac's in Steinbeck's earlier *In Dubious Battle*, and he too will no doubt manipulate particular workers in the service of larger ends. By sending him upon such errands only as the novel concludes, Steinbeck obviates the need to depict again in the latter novel the compromises, deceptions, and frustrations common to the organizer's life, thereby managing to preserve the affirmation implicit in Tom's conversion from the qualifications that shadow Mac's activities. One cannot know what success Tom or other late converts in such novels will have in their new lives, and most of these novels provide readers with little sense of what "success" would mean in terms of the general populace. Few do more than gesture toward the glow of some new but unimagined life. In the folkways that develop in the roadside camps as the migrants head west, and especially in the life the Joads find temporarily in the government camp, Steinbeck in *The Grapes of Wrath* does at least sketch the outlines of a better world.

"Why, I feel like people again" (420), says Ma Joad after the family lives for a time in the government camp, suggesting that life there has restored a sense of dignity lost with the family farm. To the degree that Steinbeck is thus able to imagine and render in such scenes the contours of an alternative social order, *The Grapes of Wrath* advances beyond the typical proletarian novel of the period.

If Tom's rhetoric and life in the government camp separately imply some form of socialism, it is a socialism with a peculiarly American cast. Like other products of the late thirties, the period of the Popular Front, when "Communism is Americanism" was a party slogan, *The Grapes of Wrath* glorifies the American past at the same time that it struggles to imagine a future equally worthy of celebrating. Tom Joad, for instance, sounds more like Emerson than Marx. The Joads and the other Okies were farmers, and throughout the novel they never relinquish their ties to the land to search for work in the industrial sector.[3] *The Grapes of Wrath* clearly celebrates aspects of the American past, and clearly its remarkable commercial success was due in large part to that celebration. Nonetheless, the novel also evokes a new America, one built upon the native tradition, perhaps, but one that will restore to the populace all that was now unavailable on the contemporary scene.

Like the proletarian writers generally, Steinbeck in *The Grapes of Wrath* espoused socialism as he understood it in order to rectify the social injustices that the novel otherwise documents. In *Of Mice and Men* he had earlier explored the apparent human need for companionship. With the possible exception of Crooks, the lives of Steinbeck's characters in the earlier novel do not lend themselves to social remedies. In *The Grapes of Wrath,* Steinbeck works with a variant of this same need, but this time he suggests that its fulfillment is thwarted by contemporary economic practices. Like Cather, Eliot, Tate, and other American literary modernists, he set himself in opposition to these practices. Steinbeck and others in the thirties differ from their fellow American literary modernists in believing that socialism, not the imagination or the past in any of their manifestations, represents the most efficacious means for restoring viable forms of community to the nation as a whole. He looked to the future, albeit a future he occasionally grasped in received terms, for solutions, whereas the majority of his contemporaries looked to the past. A socialist future, in other words, fulfilled for a time the same functions in Steinbeck's work that the feudal past fulfilled in the work of several canonical American literary modernists. When we recognize this substitution, we are better able to appreciate the nature of Steinbeck's own contribution to the development of American literary modernism.

II

As it turns out, *The Grapes of Wrath* was not only among the most fully realized revolutionary novels of the period, it was also among the last. By late 1939 the American Left was disheartened and in disarray. The persistence of the Depression and the impending war surely contributed to this condition, but I would here like to emphasize another cause. For a time during the thirties the Communist Party appeared to be a viable alternative to the ills then besetting the United States and other industrial nations. Marxism offered an explanation of the economic collapse, and it promised to relieve the suffering of the common man once and for all through the introduction of socialism. When Hitler assumed power in Germany, international communism led the way in calling attention to the menace of fascism and in resisting its encroachments. The party initiated the Popular Front in 1935 and thereafter seemingly welcomed all to make common cause against the dangers of fascism. Many people were decrying current conditions; but, as a political entity, the party itself seemed to offer the organization that was needed if such conditions were to be addressed effectively. For many intellectuals, then, the Communist Party became the vehicle most likely to bring the nation through the Depression and into a better future. Even Waldo Frank, who studiously kept his distance from the party, nonetheless concedes in his *Memoirs* that for many years he believed that "the Communists were the sole organized instrument for the transformation of the capitalist into a socialist society" (185).

In the end, however, the close identification of the Communist Party with the promise for a better future proved to be the latter's undoing. Beginning in the late twenties with Trotsky's banishment from the Soviet Union and extending through the thirties to the Soviet-German nonaggression pact and beyond, a long series of controversies severely tried the credibility of the Communist Party as an agent for beneficial change. The years during and shortly after World War II saw the publication of several works by chastened writers who had formerly been sympathetic to leftist causes. These works draw upon the experience of the thirties for their characters and situations, but they draw distinctively different conclusions. If many novels of the thirties concluded with an inspiring invocation to political activism (Godine), these later works typically begin with characters either currently involved in some political organization or already disenchanted. The plots of these novels show how the characters' aspirations miscarry in the political fray. These are works of disillusionment, and I would argue that they ironically constitute the most important and influential legacy of the thirties for subsequent American fiction. American writers did not at midcentury abandon activist notions, as Malcolm Cowley suggests in — *And I Worked at the Writer's Trade,* simply in reaction to the excesses of the thirties (95–97). Their own experience during the thirties caused a number of American writers who came of age during the decade to set a tone that would decisively influence the literary climate in later years. That tone was gloomy, it derived from the seemingly irreducible isolation of the individual, and it was forged in the political turmoil of the late thirties. One reason that later American writers seemingly abandoned political ambitions and turned instead to a more existential fiction, in other words, is that their formative experience during the thirties suggested to them the necessary futility of such ambitions.

Mark Shechner has already convincingly argued that for a generation of Jewish-American intellectuals, including the three considered below, an early disillusionment with the Left during the thirties constituted a fortunate fall, providing them, in the form of anticommunism, terms with which they "could join the American intelligentsia as full partners for the first time" (9). Their early and passionate engagement with the Left thus becomes, in retrospect, a temporary stopping-place in their journey to the mainstream. In what follows, I propose to adapt Shechner's analysis in two ways: first, by including Richard Wright and Ralph Ellison, thereby demonstrating that writers with other backgrounds underwent this crucial formative experience, albeit with somewhat different results; and second, by concentrating on the moment of disillusionment, before their anticommunism hardens into a new dogma, when they are still in search of new convictions. I shall begin with Lionel Trilling's *The*

Middle of the Journey, since it illustrates so well the hegemony the Communist Party enjoyed among certain intellectuals during the thirties. I shall then turn to Richard Wright's *American Hunger,* Ralph Ellison's *Invisible Man,* Norman Mailer's *Barbary Shore,* and Saul Bellow's *Dangling Man* to demonstrate the rout of political hope and the consequences of that loss.

III

Lionel Trilling believed that American intellectuals' experiences during the thirties proved decisive for them. He states this conviction most clearly in an afterword he provided for the 1966 reissue of Tess Slesinger's *The Unpossessed:* "In any view of the American cultural situation, the importance of the radical movement of the Thirties cannot be overestimated. It may be said to have created the American intellectual class as we now know it in its size and influence. It fixed the character of this class as being, through all mutations of opinion, predominantly of the Left" (15). Trilling's own *The Middle of the Journey,* published in 1947, represents another attempt to weigh in fiction the consequences upon intellectuals of this formative experience. In the new introduction he provided in 1975, he retrospectively identifies his purposes when composing his only novel: "So far as *The Middle of the Journey* had a polemical end in view, it was that of bringing to light the clandestine negation of the political life which Stalinist Communism had fostered among the intellectuals of the West. This negation was one aspect of an ever more impervious and bitter refusal to consent to the conditioned nature of human existence" (xx–xxi). Trilling's qualifications for this task include his own affiliation during the early and mid-thirties with various organizations on the Left, including the small circle of cultural and political radicals satirized in Slesinger's roman à clef. He had participated in the activities of the National Committee for the Defense of Political Prisoners, signed an open letter published in the *New Masses* protesting the communists' disruption of a rally sponsored by the Socialist Party, and otherwise played a marginal role in the political turmoil of the time (Krupnick 35–46; Wald 56–64). In his introduction, Trilling concedes that his circle, "for a short time in 1932 and even into 1933, had been in a tenuous relation with the Communist Party through some of its fringe activities" (xv); but Mark Krupnick persuasively argues that Trilling's involvement with such causes lasted longer than he was later prepared to acknowledge.

The Middle of the Journey is a novel of ideas. It is more concerned with the place the Communist Party occupies in the imagination of a segment of the middle class than with the party's activities. The novel traces John Laskell's gradual disillusionment with the party. Trilling provides two explanations for this change. First, Gifford Maxim, a friend and party member, interrupts Laskell's recuperation from a nearly fatal illness. Maxim explains that he has broken from the party and asks Laskell's assistance in establishing a new life, since he fears reprisal, including perhaps an attempt on his life. Laskell is initially incredulous, but during the course of the novel he comes reluctantly to believe that Maxim's fears are plausible. This change occurs because of Laskell's new sense of his friends, the Crooms. Arthur and Nancy Croom are the favored children of the middle class; much of the novel is set at their summer home in rural Connecticut. Although not party members, they are ardent sympathizers, who would like nothing better than to share their own good fortune with the less fortunate. As he continues his recuperation as their guest, Laskell becomes appreciative of the Crooms' limitations: they are sentimental in their view of the lower class; they are unwilling to countenance the idea of death—Nancy cannot quite bring herself to utter the word; and they are willful in their allegiance to sentiments of the Left. When Laskell recognizes that Nancy possesses "a passion of the mind and will so pure that, as it swept through her, she could not believe that anything that opposed it required consideration" (233), he reluctantly concedes that, insofar as Nancy's passion is representative of attitudes on the Left, Maxim's fears for his life might be creditable.

Maxim's charges against the party are particularly disturbing to the other characters because of the place he had come to occupy in their minds. In a crucial passage, Trilling describes the unspoken agreement with Laskell that Maxim now disrupts: "Certain things were clear between Laskell and Maxim. It was established that Laskell accepted Maxim's extreme commitment to the future. It was understood between them that Laskell did not accept all of Maxim's ideas. At the same time, Laskell did not oppose Maxim's ideas. One could not oppose them without being illiberal, even reactionary.

One would have to have something better to offer and Laskell had nothing better. He could not even imagine what the better ideas would be" (115). Maxim's membership in the party and his willingness to devote himself to its secret activities had given him, in the minds of his friends, a special intellectual and moral authority. Maxim possesses this authority because of his intimacy with the Communist Party. Laskell, the Crooms, and other sympathizers are not only sympathetic to the party's ends, but they also concede it a monopoly on defining these ends and on determining how they might best be achieved. Whatever reservations such sympathizers might have about the party or its activities are not debatable, since they would thereby be exposed to the accusation of being reactionary. One could only oppose the party in the name of more desirable ends; but it had already laid claim to the decisive terms, and what could be more desirable than a free, just, and peaceful social order? Thus Maxim receives from his friends the respect and reverence that the faithful have for clerics, whose dedication exceeds their own and whose relations to the institutions of reverence are correspondingly more intimate.

When Maxim thrusts himself back into his friends' lives with news that he has broken from the party and now fears for his life, he challenges their settled convictions. These are people who had, as Trilling writes in the introduction, "an impassioned longing to believe" (xviii). If Maxim's fears are justified, what then are they to make of their fondest hopes for the future? The Crooms resolve this dilemma simply by refusing to credit his fears. Maxim himself becomes deeply religious. When Laskell accuses him of having lost his community with men, Maxim replies, "My community with men is that we are children of God" (221). Laskell loses his intellectual and moral bearings once he overcomes his reluctance and accepts that Maxim's fears are plausible. He "was aware of a large vacancy in his thought—it was the place where the Party and the Movement had been. It was also the place where Nancy and Arthur had been. The Party represented what he would reach if he ever really developed in intelligence, virtue, and courage, and the Crooms had pointed out the way he must travel to reach this high estate" (234).

The Middle of the Journey concludes before Laskell can identify any other party or body of thought that might serve the intellectual and moral purposes once served by his allegiance to the party. Thus it is difficult to characterize a positive political resolution for the novel. The organized Left has been discredited both by Maxim's revelations and by what Laskell learns about the Crooms. At the same time, Laskell never seriously entertains adopting Maxim's new religious beliefs; they seem excessive, little more than another manifestation of Maxim's "impassioned longing to believe." The wealthy liberal Kermit Simpson, who provides Maxim with a new life, is likable and well meaning but finally too immune to the strains of life, "too bland" (208). Laskell himself remains subject to the party's monopoly on ideas and unable to imagine alternatives with which to oppose its vision of the future. The direction of his thoughts is entirely negative, almost ascetic. The pressure of events, including his own illness, has made him newly appreciative of the contingent character of so much in life, but it is difficult to translate this appreciation into a political program. In the end, the disillusionment set in motion by Maxim's disturbing charges seemingly ends by placing Laskell altogether beyond politics. It might be said that he thereby acquires instead a sensibility by which all political programs will subsequently be judged.

Trilling implies that the unique authority initially vested in Maxim and the Communist Party by Laskell and other sympathizers subsequently causes their disillusionment to be especially severe. If at the time the Communist Party had simply been one voice among others in a general debate about a better future, viable alternatives would have been available should it have become discredited. However, Trilling represents the choices available to those concerned about a better future as being very narrow: one could simply be either for the party or against it. One could be for the party without accepting its every pronouncement—such, indeed, would be the position of most sympathizers like Laskell or the Crooms—but such reservations could not be voiced and debated, for one could not oppose the party without being termed "illiberal, even reactionary." Given the antipathy that such people felt toward the current social and political order, the mere threat of these charges was often sufficient to silence their reservations. Thus the party's prestige among some intellectuals at once limited debate about its policies and retarded the exploration of the full range of possible solutions to the nation's obvious economic and social difficulties. In this situation, people were understandably reluctant to accept information that might discredit the party, for fear that its vision of the future would thereby be jeopardized as well.

Trilling's novel can be usefully compared with Allen Tate's *The Fathers,* which Trilling had favorably reviewed in *Partisan Review.* Both are the only novels published by writers whose reputations depend upon other work. Central to both novels are certain willful characters (Tate's George Posey and Trilling's the Crooms) who are also curiously unable to contemplate the thought of death. As we have seen, Posey could not participate in Mrs. Buchan's funeral, and the Crooms annoy Laskell by refusing him an opportunity to discuss his serious recent illness. These willful characters have aligned themselves stubbornly and fatefully with certain ideas. Posey is Tate's figure of the modern man who would find shelter in the idea of the South, and the Crooms are Trilling's fellow travelers who would redress contemporary conditions by following the party's line. Posey is not sentimental like the Crooms; he can only too well see the deficiencies in the Buchans' way of life, but for lack of a viable alternative he aligns himself with them nonetheless. His allegiance is born of desperation. In *The Fathers,* Tate dramatizes the destructiveness occasioned by the willful Posey, whereas Trilling simply alludes ominously to its possibility in *The Middle of the Journey.* It is Nancy Croom's fierce refusal to credit Maxim's fears that finally compels Laskell to believe that the latter are plausible. This violence causes both Tate and Trilling to recoil and makes both *The Fathers* and *The Middle of the Journey* finally novels of disillusionment: Tate thereafter abandons Agrarianism, and Trilling thereafter becomes increasingly skeptical that the Communist Party would lead the way to a better future.

Alan Wald and others have demonstrated that the hegemony enjoyed by the Communist Party during the thirties was not as complete as Trilling suggests in *The Middle of the Journey.* There were other options on the Left—socialists and Trotskyites, for example—but these movements were typically forced to define themselves in opposition to the communists as well as to the mainstream political parties. These movements never enjoyed the mass following or developed the political machinery possessed by the Communist Party; they could never point in the same way to developments in the Soviet Union to illustrate their platforms or to inspire confidence in their political efficacy. These parties spent their energies as much in sectarian disputes on the Left as in formulating policies that would address current economic and social conditions. These movements were responsible for bringing small numbers of people to the Left during the thirties and for sheltering them during the turmoil of the period, but in the end they were collectively unable to sustain a viable independent Left. In a 1932 symposium published in the leftist *Modern Quarterly,* John Dos Passos dismissed the efficacy of socialists and others on the Left with these words: "I personally think the socialists, and all other radicals have their usefulness, but I should think that becoming a socialist right now would have just about the same effect on anybody as drinking a bottle of near-beer" (11). In short, I do not believe that Trilling's failure to acknowledge these alternatives in *The Middle of the Journey* damages his assessment of the place occupied for a time in the thirties by the Communist Party in the thought of a significant number of American intellectuals. He also does not refer specifically to the Moscow trials, the Spanish Civil War, the Soviet-German pact, or any of the other events that caused many to become disenchanted with communism; the novel nonetheless convincingly explains why these revelations proved so disturbing to so many.

IV

Throughout the thirties, Richard Wright was much more intimately involved in the affairs of the Communist Party than Lionel Trilling had been. He apparently joined the party in 1932, in order to retain an administrative position in the Chicago John Reed Club. His growing status as a writer and advocate for racial justice gave credibility to the party's claims to be a vehicle for improving the lot of the dispossessed. Wright and his wife apparently broke with the party in early 1942, their final departure precipitated by their belief that it was deemphasizing its campaign for racial justice for fear of compromising the war effort.[4]

Shortly thereafter Wright began writing what would become *Black Boy.* When first submitted to his agent, that manuscript was entitled "American Hunger," and its final section contained Wright's account of his long involvement with the Communist Party. Somewhere in the production process the title was changed; it was also decided that *Black Boy* should conclude with Wright's departure from the South for Chicago, and that a subsequent volume would cover his experiences in the North. Wright never returned to this project, and thus he never wrote the anticipated companion volume to *Black Boy*. Portions of the material deleted from the autobiography were published later, most famously in his contribution to Richard Crossman's *The God That Failed,* but the complete text was not generally available until 1977, when it was posthumously published under Wright's original title for the entire autobiography.

Although *American Hunger* was conceived and written as the final section of *Black Boy,* the published version possesses a shape and integrity of its own. It begins with Wright's arrival in Chicago in 1927. He is worried about his future, about his ability to survive in a social order so different from what he had known in the South. He is nervous as he takes a seat beside a white man on a streetcar. As much as anything, however, he is disconcerted by the isolation and anonymity he feels and sees: "People got on and off the car, but they never glanced at one another. Each person seemed to regard the other as a part of the city landscape" (2). *American Hunger* ends with Wright again being ignored and isolated by people on the streets of Chicago. On this occasion, however, which he puts on May Day of 1936, Wright is being forcibly excluded from a May Day parade by his erstwhile comrades. "They're blind, I said to myself. Their enemies have blinded them with too much oppression" (133). Thus *American Hunger* concludes with Wright seemingly as isolated as he had been ten years earlier, upon his arrival in Chicago.

Wright depicts himself as first venturing to the Chicago John Reed Club with few expectations. The aspiring writer was welcomed and given copies of *Masses, International Literature,* and the club's own journal, *Left Front.* He reports being inspired as he read this literature by the "possibility of uniting scattered but kindred peoples into a whole" (63). He also believed that the communists, for all their goodwill, failed to understand the dispossessed and mistook the meaning of their lives. That failure did not dissuade Wright; instead it provided him with a vocation within the party: "I would make voyages, discoveries, explorations with words and try to put some of that meaning back. I would address my words to two groups: I would tell Communists how common people felt, and I would tell common people of the self-sacrifice of Communists who strove for unity among them" (66). In retrospect, *Native Son* seems to have been calculated to address in turn each of these audiences.

Wright was elected executive secretary of the Reed Club less than two months after becoming a member, and was subsequently told that his office required him to become a member of the Communist Party. As a party member and delegate to a 1934 national congress, Wright unsuccessfully opposed the decision to close the Reed Clubs because they were not in keeping with Popular Front policies. The decision made the party seem no more sensitive to the needs of the writers Wright had recruited for the Chicago Reed Club than it was aware of the feelings of common people. Wright recounts many similar incidents in *American Hunger,* making a reader wonder how and why he maintained his affiliation with the party for so long. But he did, accepting assignment in 1937 as Harlem editor of the *Daily Worker,* submitting reviews and articles to *New Masses,* and standing for election to the board of the League of American Writers.

When writing *American Hunger* in 1943 and 1944, Wright seemingly wants to place his defection from the Communist Party in 1936; the text concludes with his exclusion from the May Day parade that year. We know from other sources, however, that Wright remained an active member for another six years. When other members, including Granville Hicks, resigned in 1939 after the Soviet-German pact, Wright remained in the fold and commented on his former comrades in an unpublished piece:

> It takes a more integral order of feeling to accept what is happening in Europe from the angle of the USSR than the Hicks, Sheeans, and Bateses possess. They are rebels against capitalism; the ones who stick [such as Wright himself], who are contemptuously referred to as the "faithful," are rebels against the limits of life, the limits of experience as they know it. They are (and not in a mystical or religious sense) striving against the world. For work of that caliber there is no right and no wrong; words and theory are but faint reflections of their struggle. Just as Lenin turned from the men who went mystic after the failure of 1905, . . . so the men who today stay do so because they are living more meaningfully (as they *must!*). They tense themselves for another push. Those who left make it easier. (qtd. in Webb 150)[5]

Even as late as 1939, then, Wright, despite his own misgivings, remained a party member who could watch the seemingly faint of heart fall away with equanimity. His own break came several years later, in response to the repeated failure of the party to pursue racial justice during World War II. However, after his defection, when writing *American Hunger* the following year, he dates his defection earlier: there is little honor in being among the last to recognize misplaced loyalties.

Wright's disillusionment with the Communist Party seemingly made it impossible for him to acknowledge the place it earlier held in his life. In *American Hunger* he claims that he was never comfortable with the party:

> At no time had I felt at home in the Communist Party. I had always felt that the possibility was there, but always I was not quite sure of the motives of the people with whom I worked and they never seemed quite sure of mine. My comrades had known me, my family, my friends; they, God knows, had known my aching poverty. But they had never been able to conquer their fear of the individual way in which I acted and lived, an individuality which life had seared into my blood and bones. (112)

In other words, Wright would have us believe that party members were no more able to understand him than their fictional counterparts in *Native Son* were able to understand Bigger Thomas. Elsewhere in *American Hunger*, however, he acknowledges that the Reed Club introduced him to "men and women whom I would know for decades to come, who were to form the first sustained relationships in my life" (62), including his two wives. As if to protect these friends from the charges leveled against the party, Wright does not identify them by name; he even uses pseudonyms when recounting incidents involving party functionaries who most clearly doubted his loyalty. *American Hunger* also minimizes the degree to which the party contributed to Wright's development as a writer; it introduced him to other aspiring writers and provided him, through its various publications, with his initial readership. If in time Wright would not need such assistance, his later success was in some measure owing to the party's support during a formative period in his career. Written shortly after Wright's apostasy from the party, when its failure to steadfastly support racial justice was still fresh, *American Hunger* does not provide a balanced or especially trustworthy account of Wright's involvement with the Communist Party.

After Wright resigned from the party, his work continued to address questions of racial justice, but he seemingly lost faith in all political solutions. From the outset Wright was interested in giving voice to the experience of the dispossessed—doing so was to have been his special contribution to the communist cause. In his later work, the potentially political dimensions of this undertaking drop away; in their stead, Wright concentrates on the anguish and fury of his isolated characters. There is little sense that these isolated individuals can come together and their fury be put to political ends. Their potential for violence lacks a properly political meaning, unless as a warning to the powers that be about some possible consequences of their policies. If Wright was always most interested in giving voice to the dispossessed, in making their suffering visible to their privileged fellows, his later writings are of a piece with his earlier ones. Early in his career, Wright tries to balance these existential concerns with an explicit political commitment; later, after he abandons the Communist Party, Dostoyevsky becomes a more important influence upon Wright than Marx or Lenin. In short, the existentialism characteristic of Wright's later writings derives in part from his disillusionment in the early forties with the Communist Party.

V

In 1937, when Richard Wright was serving as Harlem editor of the *Daily Worker*, he was introduced by Langston Hughes to a young black man who had recently arrived in New York (Webb 145–46). Ralph Ellison was on leave from Tuskegee Institute, where he had been studying music, and was in New York to earn money needed to continue his education. The younger Ellison would in time and with Wright's assistance come to share the latter's literary ambitions. When they met, Wright was an active member of the American Communist Party; how completely the younger Ellison also adopted Wright's politics in the years immediately ahead remains unclear. In the introduction to *Shadow and Act*, Ellison acknowledges a brief attraction to Marxist political theory (xxi). And beginning in 1938, Ellison published more than twenty pieces in *New Masses*; thus he was obviously at least acquainted with the activities and workings of the Communist Party during the late thirties and early forties. The last of Ellison's contributions to *New Masses* appeared in 1942, the same year in which Wright withdrew from the party. Ellison subsequently enlisted in the Merchant

Marine, since, in his own words, he "wanted to contribute to the war, but didn't want to be in a Jim Crow army" (qtd. in Kostelanetz, *Master Minds* 42). Michel Fabre quotes a letter to Wright dated 18 August 1945, in which Ellison describes the literary benefits that have accrued from his "break" with the Communist Party (208). Nothing known about Ellison's life after the war suggests that he remained close to the Communist Party and its policies upon his return to New York.

Ellison obviously drew upon his earlier association with left-ist causes and parties when writing the Brotherhood portion of *Invisible Man*. I am not suggesting that *Invisible Man* is in any simple sense autobiographical—that, for instance, Ellison, like his narrator, had been a paid party functionary. On the other hand, I am sug-gesting that the course of the narrator's involvement with the Brotherhood probably resembles, in perhaps exaggerated form, the trajectory of Ellison's own involvement with the Communist Party. I suspect that the affectionate irony that Ellison directs against his narrator's initial enthusiasm for the Brotherhood is, among other things, a comment upon himself some ten years earlier, as a young contributor to *New Masses*. Once the narrator finally breaks with the Brotherhood, however, there is nothing in the novel or elsewhere in his work to suggest that Ellison does not share his narrator's thor-ough disillusionment with political activities like those undertaken by the Brotherhood. To the contrary, in the epilogue the narrator seems to have appropriated a discourse with affirmations motivated elsewhere primarily by aversion to Stalin's Soviet Union. At the same time, the final chapters of *Invisible Man* offer little by way of a spe-cific alternative, leaving his novel with a final optimism that seems more a wish than a reasoned position.

Ellison's use of his own experience in *Invisible Man* is part of the novel's complicated relation to history. Russell Fischer and others have demonstrated that in writing *Invisible Man* Ellison made ex-tensive and imaginative use of the historical record. The characters and roles of the Founder and Ras, for instance, are clearly based upon those of Booker T. Washington and Marcus Garvey, respec-tively.[6] On the other hand, Ellison does not give the novel a very particular temporal setting. In the prologue and epilogue the nar-rator addresses the reader in the present tense; however, he does not refer to either the Depression or World War II, curious omissions for a novel otherwise presumably set in midcentury America. These omissions make clear that *Invisible Man* is not a historical novel in the usual sense; it is less interested in re-creating a particular historical period than in assessing the political and social options that have historically been available to African Americans. Thus Ellison collapses historical time in order to allow the narrator to experience the alternatives advocated by Booker T. Washington, Marcus Garvey, and the Communist Party as though they were completely contemporary and competing for the support of African Americans. The novel imaginatively tests these alternatives and finds that all fail to provide African Americans with an acceptable means to a better future (J. Frank 233; Kostelanetz, "Politics" 90).

The narrator initially encounters the Brotherhood at a vulnerable time. From the beginning he wants to be of service to his people, but his earlier misadventures have made it clear that he cannot rely upon more common and socially sanctioned ways to be of use. In particular, he has become wary of the offices of influential patrons, whether white or black. After overhearing his spontaneous speech against a Harlem eviction, the Brotherhood approaches the narrator with the opportunity to become another Booker T. Washington. The narrator soon recognizes that the potential beneficiaries of his new responsibilities are more numerous than he had anticipated: "As a Brotherhood spokesman I would represent not only my own group but one that was much larger. The audience was mixed, their claims broader than race. I would do whatever was necessary to serve them well. . . . For the first time . . . I could glimpse the possibility of being more than a member of a race" (345–46). The narrator seizes this possibility and devotes himself to the party's work. He would later look back at this period of his life: "I was dominated by the all-embracing idea of Brotherhood. The organization had given the world a new shape, and me a vital role. We recognized no loose ends, everything could be controlled by our science. Life was all pattern and discipline; and the beauty of discipline is when it works" (373). The scope of the Brotherhood's vision, in other words, was part of its initial appeal. It enables the narrator to understand the similarities between African Americans and similarly dispossessed people of other races; it seemingly provides explanations for social injustices; it displays a willingness to agitate on behalf of the otherwise ignored; and it offers the narrator a seemingly central role in its activities.

Eventually, however, these same qualities contribute to the narrator's estrangement from and final break with the Brotherhood. His initial successes in Harlem lead to jealousies and charges that he is an opportunist. He is told that he must either take a leave or accept an assignment elsewhere until the charges are properly investigated. When he later complains about deteriorating conditions in Harlem, he is told that the community is being sacrificed for the greater good: "It's unfortunate, Brother, but your members will have to be sacrificed. . . . We are making temporary alliances with other political groups and the interests of one group of brothers must be sacrificed to that of the whole" (490).[7] The larger political ambitions of the Brotherhood thus represent limits to the immediate aspirations of its members; its support for local causes is always conditional. If the narrator was initially taken by the way the Brotherhood placed racial issues within a larger informing context, he later recognized that the demand for racial justice would be and was sacrificed whenever it apparently conflicted with other goals.

The narrator suspects that the Brotherhood was prepared to exploit the Harlem riot that closes *Invisible Man*. He recognizes that, when their fury is spent, Harlem residents will need to contend with the devastation produced by their outburst. In the aftermath of the riot, the narrator himself must contend with a largely conceptual devastation. He comes to see the world in very different terms from those sanctioned by the Brotherhood. Although the latter was obviously pleased to recruit an African-American spokesman, it characteristically minimizes the causal importance of race. "Why do you fellows always talk in terms of race" (286), Brother Jack asks the narrator. The Brotherhood instead talks in terms of class. The narrator is initially pleased by this change, since it enables him to see himself as "more than a member of a race." When he learns, however, that the Brotherhood is sacrificing its Harlem activities in order to preserve its standing elsewhere, he suspects that he and Harlem have again become the victims of white hypocrisy. It seems that Ras had been right to question the Brotherhood's commitment to Harlem and its residents. After his break with the Brotherhood, the narrator reverts to understanding himself and his experience in largely racial terms.

The Brotherhood also insists upon the importance of discipline and the inevitably progressive nature of history. In his random encounters on subway platforms and then the streets of Harlem, however, the narrator begins to recognize that history as conceived by the Brotherhood has an outside and that numberless people live there, untouched by its tendencies and unknown by the Brotherhood. Whereas the Brotherhood emphasizes historical necessity, Rinehart makes the narrator appreciate the degree of possibility available to everyone, an appreciation that increases later, during his time underground: "I believed in hard work and progress and action, but now, after first being 'for' society and then 'against' it, I assign myself no rank or any limit, and such an attitude is very much against the trend of the times. But my world has become one of infinite possibilities. What a phrase—still it's a good phrase and a good view of life, and a man shouldn't accept any other; that much I've learned underground. Until some gang succeeds in putting the world in a strait jacket, its definition is possibility" (563). When the narrator withdraws from the Brotherhood, in other words, he rejects more than its moral duplicity; he sets aside as well its conceptions of history and social life in favor of others that seem more accurate and encompassing.

The narrator might now believe that the world's "definition is possibility," which seems a positive and engaging creed, but his isolated life underground is the possibility he has temporarily chosen for himself. He has gone from being a spokesman and organizer for the Brotherhood to being withdrawn almost completely from social life. Life in the basement is a deliberate attempt to get "away from it all" (560) and thereby secure a measure of peace. He obviously ventures out of his basement to secure necessities; otherwise, however, he apparently devotes himself to trying to understand the series of misadventures that led to his current meager estate. The narrative is itself the fruit of his efforts. The difference in tone between the prologue and epilogue suggests that his efforts have been successful; the edgy, hyperactive voice of the former largely gives way to the more assured and contemplative voice of the latter. Somewhat to his own surprise, an exercise that began simply as an effort "to throw [his] anger into the world's face" (566) rekindles his fascination with social life. In the end, of course, he declares his intention to emerge from his underground retreat: "The hibernation is over. I must shake off the old skin and come up for breath" (567).

The reader has been prepared for this change. In the midst of his several traumas before the narrator takes up residence underground, he encounters Rinehart and increasingly appreciates the implications of the latter's way of life. Most immediately, the narrator learns to avoid Ras's followers by donning a disguise. The emphasis on "possibility" allows the reader, if not always the narrator, to imagine that in the longer term alternatives to the larger, social difficulties at hand might be found. It also suggests that the world and future are open and thus that we need not accept any particular stance, including the narrator's withdrawal, as final. Indeed, the narrator's peculiarly closed underground life could be thought inconsistent with his growing appreciation of life's openness. Despite this thematic preparation, however, I agree with Irving Howe, Marcus Klein, and Lawrence Hogue in finding something unconvincing or hollow about this final narrative turn; it feels as though Ellison is willing an affirmative conclusion to his novel.

Although the narrator's final decision is not inconsistent with the developing thematic emphasis on possibility, that thematic development has taken place exclusively on a conceptual level. As the narrator fumbles toward his decision, he refers at one point to "the principle on which the country was built" (561) and concludes that he must affirm that and similar principles. These affirmations are apparently meant as steps toward the narrator's final emergence from underground; and they are obviously important to Ellison himself, who repeatedly makes them in the essays collected in *Shadow and Act* and *Going to the Territory.* However, these principles have been known and presumably operative for two hundred years. They might be, on the level of ideas, inconsistent with the invidious social practices depicted in *Invisible Man,* but social life has demonstrated a remarkable tolerance for such conceptual inconsistencies. The difficulty has always been to imagine forms of life that will abide fully by such principles and then to secure their adoption by the entire nation. The principles themselves provide no guarantees, as Ellison and his narrator by this time should know. When the narrator affirms them, accordingly, he is affirming ideas about, or ideals for, social life, but not any particular form of social life. When he emerges from his basement, however, he will be returning to the very social world he earlier fled, a world where social relations remain those illuminated by the battle royal, a world still populated by school superintendents and Tadlocks; and it is unclear how his new appreciation for the principles articulated by the Founding

Fathers will reconcile him to or guide him in his new life there. By choosing to conclude *Invisible Man* with the narrator's ringing declaration to end his hibernation, Ellison achieves a final affirmation for the novel as a whole without needing to imagine how the narrator's life will be different.

We know how Rinehart takes advantage of the world's apparent openness, but we do not know what particular uses Ellison's narrator will make of it. Will he, for instance, stay in New York, or will he return to the South? Could he stay at Mary's while resuming his social life?[8] Clearly he will not return to the Brotherhood; might he, however, agitate for social reforms inspired by the principles he now affirms, say as a spokesman for the NAACP? The narrator will encounter familiar people, attitudes, and practices when he emerges from his basement; what changes in him will enable him now to live with greater equanimity? How will he now react to a Bledsoe or Tadlock? Is he now able to understand and prepared to follow his grandfather's advice? What difference, in short, will his new recognitions and affirmations, won with such difficulty, make in the way he conducts himself? Nothing in the novel enables me to answer these questions. What is more worrisome, I believe that when concluding *Invisible Man* Ellison could not answer them either; and I occasionally suspect that his continuing inability to answer such questions to his own satisfaction contributed to the long and continuing wait for a second novel.

VI

Unlike Wright and the other writers under consideration, Norman Mailer was apparently not involved in the sectarian political controversies of the late thirties and early forties. He joined the Progressive Citizens of America in 1947, and the famous young author of *The Naked and the Dead* campaigned actively for Henry Wallace in 1948, after returning from a year in Paris. While abroad he had met Jean Malaquais, a novelist and independent intellectual on the Left. Malaquais believed that Wallace's candidacy represented a greater danger to world peace than either Dewey's or Truman's, but he was unable to dissuade his young friend (Mills 98–99). Mailer would later, for a few years in the late forties and early fifties, while struggling with *Barbary Shore*, adopt Malaquais's political position.

Published in 1951 and dedicated to Malaquais, *Barbary Shore* is Mailer's second and perhaps least-read novel. Mailer would later claim in an interview that he "started *Barbary Shore* as some sort of fellow-traveler, and finished with a political position which was a far-flung mutation of Trotskyism" (85). The novel lacks both the scope and immediate interest to readers in the late forties of *The Naked and the Dead* on the one hand, and on the other the vitality and self-promotion that would so characterize his later work. It is set in a shabby Brooklyn boardinghouse and rarely follows its characters outside, and then never farther than a neighborhood tavern and the nearby Brooklyn Bridge. Its characters enact a vaguely political allegory for the possession of Guinevere, who perhaps represents the debased contemporary condition of the working class. Mailer probably intends the atmosphere of troubled sexuality and shadowy intrigue to be ominous, but alas it is merely vague.

Barbary Shore is narrated by Mike Lovett, who is initially attracted to this rooming house by the inexpensive rent and the consequent possibility that he can here make a beginning on the novel he wants to write. Lovett suffers from amnesia. "Probably I was in the war" (3) is the novel's promising first sentence. As he works on this first novel, the isolated Lovett is gradually drawn into the affairs of other residents of the boardinghouse. The latter include the landlady, Guinevere, who has been thoroughly debauched by popular culture; Lannie Madison, who has been deranged by the assassination of Trotsky; Hollingsworth, a federal agent; and McLeod, Guinevere's husband and a longtime political activist. In his initial conversations with McLeod, Lovett expresses disdain for politics: "Out of the futilities with which man attempts to express himself, I find politics among the most pathetic" (35), he tells his neighbor. Under the pressure of his continuing association with McLeod, however, Lovett regains lost memories of his own ardent participation as a Trotskyite in the politics of the thirties:

> I was an adolescent again, and it was before the war, and I belonged to a small organization dedicated to a worker's revolution, although that dedication already tempered by a series of reverses was about to spawn its opposite and create a functionary for each large segment of the masses who had failed to arouse. I was young then, and no dedication could match mine. The revolution was tomorrow, and the inevitable crises of capitalism ticked away in my

mind with the certainty of a time bomb, and even then could never begin to match the ticking of my pulse. There was a great man who led us, and I read almost every word he had written, and listened with the passion of a novitiate to each message he sent from the magical center in Mexico. (125)

Mailer, of course, did not himself possess the political heritage he gives his narrator, but it nonetheless seems to have been his ambition when writing *Barbary Shore* to shake his readers in the early fifties out of their political torpor as effectively as McLeod revives Lovett's earlier political commitments.

McLeod was presumably to be the agent of the reader's transformation. Much of the tiresome second half of the novel consists of McLeod's explanations and justifications for his political life as he is interrogated by Hollingsworth. Mailer gives McLeod a largely representative political career. The latter was apparently born in 1900 and is thus a figure for the twentieth century; he tells Lovett that he was twenty-one when he joined the Communist Party and forty when he left it. For almost twenty years he had been a hardened and dedicated revolutionary. He does not demur when Hollingsworth, during his stagey and improbable interrogation, implies that McLeod had been instrumental in the assassinations of anarchists and other sympathizers during the Spanish Civil War. He implies that he finally broke with the party as a result of the Soviet-German pact: "I knew that if I remained in my old position any longer, I would be brought to trial, and it would be m'neck. There was a certain military pact completed at the time, which I found impossible to support" (221). Like Gifford Maxim in Trilling's *The Middle of the Journey*, McLeod fears reprisals after his defection; however, he goes further in establishing a new life, trading information about his former activities for a government position during the war. Thus far McLeod conforms to type as the former political radical who in the end recognizes that he and his principles have been betrayed from afar.

Barbary Shore is set in the late forties, almost ten years after McLeod's defection. In the meantime, he has again become uneasy about his current political allegiances. True, his life had been saved, but to what end? As he explains to Hollingsworth, "I had come to the conclusion that I was destroyed as a person" (222). McLeod can no more implicitly endorse the political positions of the West in the early days of the Cold War than he could unquestioningly follow those of the Communist Party in the months just prior to World War II. Thus he decamps again, this time becoming an independent pamphleteer determined to understand how the dream of a better world had gone so wrong. These pamphlets, which Hollingsworth cites during the interrogation, and McLeod's subsequent lectures are no doubt what Mailer had in mind when he claimed to have adapted "a far-flung mutation of Trotskyism" by the time he finished working on *Barbary Shore*. They suggest that West and East are now mirror images of one another, one driven by monopoly capitalism, the other by state capitalism. In order to survive, the inner dynamic of each system dictates that it feverishly prepare for war, which, when it comes, will be fought by "two virtually identical forms of exploitation" (278). McLeod believes that this coming war is inevitable; he writes his pamphlets in the faint hope that its survivors will find it possible to renew the earlier promise and to create genuine socialism amidst the rubble. In the end, Mailer would have McLeod be truer to the principles of freedom and equality than either of the rival claimants from East and West.

After Mailer has allowed McLeod only too much opportunity to articulate his current political convictions, the novel's final scenes are hurried and confusing. Hollingsworth apparently kills McLeod when the latter refuses to return a small object that he had presumably taken when leaving his government position.[9] Hollingsworth flees the boardinghouse with Guinevere; Lannie is arrested by other government agents who suddenly arrive; and Lovett embarks upon a life as a fugitive. "If I fled down the alley which led from that rooming house, it was only to enter another, and then another. I am obliged to live waiting for the signs which tell me I must move on again" (311). Before going to his final confrontation with Hollingsworth, McLeod leaves Lovett with his will: "To Michael Lovett to whom, at the end of my life and for the first time within it, I find myself capable of the rudiments of selfless friendship, I bequeath in heritage the remnants of my socialist culture. And may he be alive to see the rising of the Phoenix" (311). McLeod's rhetoric exceeds the events of the novel ("What 'selfless friendship'?" the reader wants to ask), just as the rhetoric of the novel repeatedly exceeds Mailer's ability here to provide it warrant.

In *Barbary Shore*, Mailer is characteristically defiant but also finally despairing. He refuses to reconcile himself to the terms of life available in midcentury America, but by this time the organized Left as embodied in the Communist Party cannot provide a viable alternative. Instead, he adopts a position from which both appear to be intellectually and morally bankrupt. He engages large issues, but then allows them to be reduced to debating points for the residents of a dingy boardinghouse. The novel was too much of a tract even to please Malaquais, Mailer's political mentor at the time (Mills 126). Lovett emerges from the novel a confirmed socialist, but few can sustain faith when it must be placed in possibilities that *might* emerge, and then only *after* a catastrophic war. It might be, of course, that Mailer could only conceive of socialism as a viable alternative in circumstances that prohibited it from becoming more than a party of one. Be that as it may, Mailer himself obviously did not long espouse such a view; despite his subsequent affiliation with Irving Howe and *Dissent,* Mailer would find little of use among the conventional political positions available in the fifties. Later in the decade, most notoriously in "The White Negro," he developed his famous stance as white hipster, with its existential politics. This would be essentially a politics of opposition, with little of the constructive vision available within the socialist tradition. At the end of the decade, in *Advertisements for Myself,* he would claim that *Barbary Shore* was the "first of the existential novels in America" (106). This is a curious claim. It might be more accurate to say that *Barbary Shore* dramatizes the bankruptcy of conventional and oppositional politics at midcentury, thereby suggesting the necessity for devising other terms for understanding and undertaking one's life.

VII

Saul Bellow was a schoolboy in Chicago during the early thirties when Richard Wright, elsewhere in the city, was working with the John Reed Club. Bellow was active in several Trotskyite political organizations while in high school and college (Wald 246), but he seems to have largely discarded these specific political convictions by 1940, when he left for New York and a literary career. In New York he became a part of the set associated with *Partisan Review,* many of whom had undergone a similar political devolution. Two of Bellow's early stories were subsequently published in *Partisan,* including "The Mexican General," which concerns the personal advantage the title character would take from having been among the first on the scene after Trotsky's assassination. Given the furor caused by this event only three years previously and Bellow's own earlier convictions, the story is remarkable for the emotional reserve with which it imagines an exploitation of Trotsky's death. Trotsky himself makes a cameo appearance in Bellow's *The Adventures of Augie March,* published in 1953. Augie is living in Mexico at the time and encounters Trotsky when the latter drives into town with his retinue in order to tour the local cathedral. Augie is momentarily stirred by this glimpse at greatness: "I was excited by this famous figure, and I believe what it was about him that stirred me up was the instant impression he gave . . . of navigation by the great stars, of the highest considerations, of being fit to speak the most important human words and universal terms" (374). It is Trotsky's celebrity and not his political convictions that engage Augie's imagination in this chance encounter. His enthusiasm is quickly qualified when Bellow has Augie recognize two acquaintances from Chicago in Trotsky's entourage. Sylvester and Frazer are broadly comic figures; by placing them among Trotsky's final loyalists, Bellow dramatizes how far Trotsky has fallen since the early years of the Russian Revolution and makes light of his own earlier political convictions.

Bellow published his first novel, *Dangling Man,* late in World War II. The novel takes the form of a journal kept during the winter and early spring of 1942–43 by the protagonist as he awaits induction into the military service. Joseph has quit his job, but his induction is repeatedly delayed by a series of bureaucratic mishaps. He initially thinks to take advantage of this temporary freedom to resume work on a series of articles on the philosophers of the Enlightenment. However, he cannot concentrate and the undertaking comes to nothing. Circumstances have conspired to make Joseph unusually free from the normal demands of life. His wife is willing to support him as he awaits induction, so he dangles, no longer faced by the demands of everyday social life, not yet faced by those of military life and combat. His freedom proves a burden to Joseph: "It is perfectly clear to me that I am deteriorating, storing bitterness and spite which eat like acids at my endowment of generosity and good will" (12).

Keeping a journal becomes for Joseph an occupation. He uses it primarily to record his few social engagements as he dangles and to think through the reasons that these engagements are so uniformly unsatisfying. When one recalls that the novel was written and published during World War II, and that Joseph himself awaits military service in it, the journal becomes remarkable for its lack of explicit concern about the course of larger events in which he will eventually be swept up. One might imagine that Joseph would be preoccupied by the general devastation and his own prospects for survival. Will he live or die, and how? One might also anticipate indictments of the people and system he must shortly fight, or outpourings of bravado and patriotism as he works himself up for the inevitable. Two consecutive entries do concern news about the death of a pilot he might have known, which produce in turn some thoughts about his own imminent involvement in the war; otherwise, the war is generally absent from the journal, its place taken by Joseph's more mundane activities and remembrances, and its existence acknowledged primarily in occasional images, as when Joseph writes, "I feel I am a sort of human grenade whose pin has been withdrawn" (147).

Despite his age and current disengagement from the great events of the day, Joseph, like Bellow, had earlier been politically engaged. We learn that he was already a communist at the age of seventeen when he is first introduced to his future in-laws. He does not relate the specific reasons for his subsequent break from the party. One of his longer journal entries concerns a chance encounter with Jimmy Burns, who has remained loyal to the party. Burns refuses to return Joseph's greeting. The snub enrages Joseph, as he explains to his companion: "I have a right to be spoken to. It's the most elementary thing in the world. Simply that. I insist on it. . . . And his party doesn't want him to think, but to follow its discipline. So there you are. Because it's supposed to be a revolutionary party. That's what's offending me. When a man obeys an order like that he's helping to abolish freedom and begin tyranny" (33–34). Joseph creates a scene in the restaurant, embarrassing his companion and retrospectively himself, until he at last forces Burns to acknowledge his greeting. This incident occurs early in the novel, when the reader is still perhaps prepared to grant the aptness of Joseph's outburst. He will go on to challenge the motives and behavior of almost everyone he encounters in the same manner, and as such incidents multiply his own moral authority will diminish. Joseph turns rancid in his freedom, and had this encounter with Jimmy Burns been placed later in the novel, the reader would have been correspondingly less willing to place credence in Joseph's explanation or to find Burns's behavior culpable.[10]

After a series of such incidents, Joseph eventually acknowledges that his unusual freedom is proving destructive. He goes to the draft board, asks to be taken at the earliest possible time, and shortly thereafter receives his notice. His final entry expresses sadness at leaving his wife, but otherwise expresses relief: "I am no longer to be held accountable for myself; I am grateful for that. I am in other hands, relieved of self-determination, freedom canceled. Hurray for regular hours! And for the supervision of the spirit! Long live regimentation!" (191) In his sarcastic relief at being released from his freedom, Joseph does not pause to notice that his new appreciation of discipline would equip him to reenlist in the Communist Party as well as for military life. That he doesn't tells us more about his eagerness to go at last to his fate than about the sturdiness of his current political convictions. Joseph has earlier acknowledged that he supports the war and that he is prepared to shoot and be shot at. It does not have for him, however, the character of a crusade; he disposes of his reasons by saying simply, "But between their imperialism and ours, if a full choice were possible, I would take ours" (84).

Dangling Man is thus a peculiarly dispirited novel. Its protagonist has seemingly been disabused of all saving beliefs. He cannot even muster much conviction from the need to preserve a way of life from the likely ravages of fascism. Indeed, the entries in Joseph's journal rarely concern the war directly, and then not in terms that lend themselves to taking sides. The war simply looms in his future like a fact of nature. I have come to understand the disquieting absence of positive terms in *Dangling Man* less as a result of the war than as the lingering consequence of Bellow's and Joseph's earlier disillusionment with the politics of the Left (Shechner 125). Joseph's passing reference to "our imperialism" is in this respect symptomatic; it bespeaks a residual antagonism toward capitalism, but one that is no longer part of a larger vision of an alternative way of life. Joseph and Bellow are thus dangling between convictions: they can no longer place faith in the vision and politics of the Left, but neither can they as yet muster genuine enthusiasm for the status quo, which is the only apparent alternative. In *The Adventures of Augie March* and later novels Bellow would subsequently complete this transition, but at the time he wrote *Dangling Man* he had set aside one vision of social life and not yet adapted another. As a result, terms such as "life," "death," and "freedom" possess little positive substance in *Dangling Man;* Joseph conjures with them, trying in vain to rub some saving vision from their too smooth surfaces.

VIII

Joseph's situation in *Dangling Man* in certain respects resembles in extreme form Laskell's in *The Middle of the Journey.* After the latter accepts that Maxim's fears are plausible, he becomes "aware of a large vacancy in his thought—it was the place where the Party and the Movement had been" (234). Trilling allows his readers to witness the creation of that vacancy as Laskell becomes gradually and reluctantly disabused of his settled political convictions. In *Dangling Man,* Joseph's break with the party occurs at some indeterminate time in the past. His break, like Laskell's, has left him with a similar "vacancy in his thought," one that the intervening years have done nothing to repair. It had been a part of Laskell's unspoken agreement with Maxim that he would not oppose the future envisioned by the Communist Party unless he were able to propose a better one. Although Laskell is unable to place trust in that future by the time the novel concludes, he remains unable to articulate an alternative. Joseph's situation seems similar. He has no positive alternative, and thus when contemplating his coming military service he seems reduced to choosing between "their imperialism and ours." Laskell and Joseph seem to inhabit worlds that provide only two political orientations: they must accede either to the vision of the party or to that embodied by the mainstream political parties. Neither in the end can accede to the former and thus must uncomfortably find some means to accommodate themselves to the latter. Trilling and Bellow do not focus much attention on this outcome, much as though they would prefer that it were not the necessary corollary of their rejection of the radical alternative.

Invisible Man was the last of these works to be composed, and in it Ellison goes further than the others in accommodating himself to contemporary conditions. Like *The Grapes of Wrath* and so many proletarian novels, *Invisible Man* concludes with an abrupt conversion, but this time the political implications are quite different. When the narrator announces his decision to emerge from his basement and reaffirms "the principle on which the country was built" (561), he finds something positive to replace his earlier commitment to the Brotherhood, unlike Trilling's Laskell and Bellow's Joseph, who are left only with a "vacancy" in the place of their previous ideals. He also echoes many of the participants in a 1952 symposium published by *Partisan Review*. Although *Partisan* was initially sponsored by the John Reed Club of New York, by the late thirties it was already establishing an independent political position, one sharply critical of the organized Left.[11] The symposium was entitled "Our Country and Our Culture" and was designed to examine an apparent shift in the attitudes of intellectuals toward the United States. The editors prefaced the symposium with the following observation: "Until little more than a decade ago, America was commonly thought to be hostile to art and culture. Since then, however, the tide has begun to turn, and many writers and intellectuals now feel closer to their country and its culture" (282). Norman Mailer and C. Wright Mills were sharply critical of the assumptions behind the symposium, but most contributors were prepared to find some virtue in American life and culture of the early 1950s. They were in general more concerned about potential threats posed by Stalin's Soviet Union than by indigenous formations. The "democratic values which America either embodies or promises are desirable in purely human terms," wrote the editors of *Partisan*. "We are certain that these values are necessary conditions for civilization and represent the only immediate alternative as long as Russian totalitarianism threatens world domination" (285).

Ellison himself did not contribute to this symposium. However, the evolving political convictions of *Partisan Review* and its editors were well known at the time, and Ellison's decision to publish his novel's prologue in *Partisan* in the same year as the symposium suggests his own willingness to align himself and his forthcoming novel with such beliefs. When, with the publication of the novel a few months later, his narrator ringingly affirms the principle upon which this country was founded, he demonstrates his and his creator's participation in this new discourse of political accommodation. I suspect that Ellison's new allegiances, like those of writers in *Parti-*

san generally, derive more from disillusionment with the apparent alternatives than from the identification of positive developments in American life at that time. It was seemingly a matter of settling for the lesser evil. Ellison had begun his apprenticeship as a writer at a time when the American economy was exhausted but there was an energetic debate about the best means for revitalizing it. By the time he completed *Invisible Man* in the early fifties, the nation was experiencing a new prosperity, and the search for alternatives was itself exhausted. Many Americans who had earlier looked to the Left for solutions felt that their trust had been betrayed. Stalin's Soviet Union became for many the most serious threat to freedom, rather than a plausible engine for its expansion. The pressure of this apparent threat made it expedient to reassess the possibilities for political justice inherent in our national tradition.

Wright and Mailer are characteristically more defiant in their refusal to accommodate themselves, more determined to imagine some other course. Neither particularly complies with Shechner's claim that former leftist intellectuals eventually came to terms with the status quo. Of these five writers, Wright, as a member of the Communist Party for nearly ten years, had obviously made the most substantial investment in its policies. His commitment to the party was based on his belief that it was uniquely prepared to address racial and other social inequities. It was perhaps his preoccupation with such domestic issues that enabled him to remain in the party when others were defecting in response to international events. He finally resigned in protest when, during the war, he came to believe that the party's commitment to victory was causing it to reduce its emphasis upon securing immediate justice for African Americans. He was for obvious reasons less prepared than the others to reach an accommodation with American culture, and so became an expatriate. Living in Paris obviously dramatized Wright's profound estrangement from American life, but that estrangement should not obscure his equally unequivocal rejection of communism. Mailer's radicalism came late and secondhand. The "far-flung mutation of Trotskyism" he adopts in *Barbary Shore* seems more a matter of temperament than of political commitment. There is little sentiment in the novel that would incline a reader to believe that Mailer or his characters would soon reach an accommodation with mainstream politics. But the novel is no less severe in its characterization of the

Soviet Union and the Communist Party; the former is stigmatized as "state capitalism," hardly the herald of a better world. McLeod and then Lovett in *Barbary Shore* are able to avoid the "vacancy" that troubles Trilling's Laskell by transferring their allegiance to a distant and improbable future. The novel concludes with Lovett a confirmed radical, but one deprived of both party and state. He is a figure of defiance directed at both mainstream America and what remained of the organized Left. Mailer is the only one of these writers who did not participate directly in the shifting politics of the thirties, and it might be that this relative lack of experience made his final gesture both possible and necessary.

Had radical alternatives during the course of the thirties not come to be exclusively identified with the Communist Party, the latter could have been discredited without thereby creating the "vacancy" troubling Laskell and others. These writers and their characters might have been able to switch their allegiance to other parties and other visions of a better future, thereby sustaining their aspirations for a better world. However, the Communist Party did manage to crowd out such options during the thirties and to establish itself as the only credible party on the Left. Its success was partially due to its ability to gesture toward the example of the Soviet Union and its international apparatus. In the end, precisely these characteristics made the party uniquely answerable for questionable practices elsewhere, and thus its credibility was from the first especially vulnerable. A few committed radicals were able to sustain their convictions by switching their allegiance to one or another of the small splinter groups that survived; but after the flush of optimism surrounding what had seemed about to become a mass party, the sectarian disputes and empty meeting halls could only have seemed a setback to those who managed to sustain their convictions. In the main, however, former party members and sympathizers were left either to register their continuing dismay about social and cultural life by other, less overtly political means or to resign themselves to lending their qualified support to mainstream political parties.[12] In the cultural realm, as we have seen, this loss of radical convictions typically took one of two forms: a renewed willingness to accommodate oneself, however uncomfortably, to contemporary conditions, as in Bellow, Ellison, and Trilling; or a defiant refusal of those conditions, as in Wright and Mailer, even though better were not at hand, even though they were now scarcely imaginable.

AFTERWORD

> For the first time in the history of the modern American
> intellectual, America is not conceived of as *a priori* the vulgarest
> and stupidest nation in the world.
>
> Trilling, "Our Country" 319

I

IN 1951 THE young critic John Aldridge published *After the Lost
Generation*. It is a study of the fiction being written by writers of
his own generation who had participated in or otherwise felt the
pressures of World War II. Aldridge focuses his study by measuring
the emerging vision and accomplishments of his own generation
against those of an older generation that had been marked by what
was now known as World War I. Aldridge and his friends were college students when their own war began, as some of the writers they
admired had been during the teens. "We had read a great deal about
the Lost Generation," writes Aldridge in his preface, "and we were
sure that our age would be like theirs—a time of discovery, transition, and revolt" (xi). In *After the Lost Generation*, Aldridge sets
out to assess whether young writers after World War II were meeting these expectations for themselves and their age. His judgments
are not flattering; no reader can mistake his sense that in decades
to come his own generation is unlikely to stir the imaginations of
younger readers in the way that their imaginations had been stirred
by reading *In Our Time, The Great Gatsby*, and even *Exile's Return*.

The book begins by setting out the standards for measurement
in several chapters devoted to the earlier generation. Aldridge believes that the first war represented the final dissolution of a world
characterized by shared values, however attenuated those values had
already become and however long their attenuation had already been

247

under way. The young American writers who were drawn to Europe by the war and its aftermath went eager to free themselves from conventions and beliefs that felt outmoded, but they could not be prepared for the harsh terms of existence available in a world without them. Some of the writers of this earlier generation, according to Aldridge, retreated in terror from social life by creating a private symbolism; others tried to provide themselves and others with some substitute for what had been lost, whether "in the worship of old gods or a simple primitivism" (85). It is a third possibility that especially interests Aldridge: "In the modern world it has been possible for a short time under peculiarly fortunate circumstances for writers to discover dramatic material in the process and residue of the value breakdown itself; and it is this possibility which a few of them have until recently exploited admirably" (85–86).

Although Aldridge consistently writes about values, and thus could seem to be addressing American literary modernism in terms quite different from those I have been using, I believe that our analyses are complementary. Aldridge is concerned with "shared values," values held in common by most citizens or by writers and contemporary readers. He believes that World War I represents a final collapse of shared values, and that it was uniquely incumbent upon the generation that experienced that collapse to create some viable substitute for the lost consensus. The literature produced by that generation that Aldridge most admires addresses the loss of shared values directly, dramatizing the resulting struggle to create life on new terms. This is the literature that Aldridge and his friends were reading in the late 1930s. They might have envied the opportunity to display heroism along the western front, and been enchanted by the literary life described by Malcolm Cowley in *Exile's Return,* but Aldridge implies that his contemporaries were also taken by the moral heroism displayed by those willfully living beyond the collapse of shared values, creating lives and literature in a stark new world.

When world events conspired to put Aldridge's own generation to a seemingly similar ordeal, the results were surprisingly different. Aldridge accounts for the difference in these terms:

> In the years since Hemingway, Dos Passos, and Fitzgerald began to write, the forces that gave impetus to their development—particularly the forces of disillusionment and denial released by the

broken promises of the first war—have declined. The young novelists of the present generation are consequently deprived of that
impetus at the same time that their own age and experience offer
them nothing comparable. They have come through a war even
more profoundly disturbing than the first; but the illusions and
causes of war, having once been lost, cannot be relost. Their world,
ironically enough, is almost the same world their predecessors discovered; but the fundamental discoveries of modern life can be
made but once. (86–87)

When these younger writers went off to war they were armed in
part by their reading of their predecessors. They knew what to expect. Accordingly, the war itself, however personally harrowing it
might have been, did not disorient them in the same way or to the
same extent that it had participants in World War I, since they went
to it with fewer illusions. As a result, concludes Aldridge, when this
generation began to represent its experience in fiction, it typically
exhibited little of the technical venturesomeness of the earlier novels and instead worked within what were by then predictable forms:

> One explanation is that the experience of war is no longer new and,
> consequently, does not require a new method of presentation. An-
> other is that the Lost Generation writers were engaged in a revo-
> lution designed to purge language of the old restraints of the time.
> . . . Today that revolution is over. . . . The unique has become the
> ordinary; young writers using the effects of their predecessors are
> often not even aware that those effects did not belong to our lit-
> erature until years after many of them were born. (88)

Aldridge's analysis of this generational difference resembles my
own earlier discussion of Willa Cather. Cather, you will recall, came
to believe that she had been uniquely fortunate to have directly experienced the settling of the West. At least as she recalled it, people
like Alexandra Bergson, Captain Forrester, and the other settlers established new lives that were nonetheless thoroughly and satisfyingly
informed by mutual regard. When that regard was broken by the
subsequent emergence of individuals like Ivy Peters, Cather drew
comfort from her memories of this earlier, more generous era, even
though it now seemed otherwise lost forever. Aldridge places the
initial American literary modernists in a comparable historical moment; if they chafed at existing values, left at the first opportunity,

and gladly participated in those values' dissolution, they seem in retrospect to recognize the social and personal functions those lost values had fulfilled. Their careers were spent in dramatizing their loss and imagining viable substitutes. Aldridge's own generation, by way of contrast, never knew at first hand social worlds bound by shared values and respected institutions. "The generation of the Forties could never be lost because the safe and ordered world had never been theirs" (118). They had lived from the first in the world discovered by their predecessors in midlife, and they understood it largely in those received terms. They did not share in the excitement aroused among the earlier generation by the need to invent those terms. As Aldridge writes, "the fundamental discoveries of modern life can be made but once," and all reiterations are necessarily a matter of routine (87–88). At the same time, those terms could not reverberate for the younger writers in the same way, since they lacked the direct comparisons only too available to writers earlier in the century. According to Aldridge, in short, his generation has been doubly deprived by the lateness of its arrival on the scene: it was too late to recall a world of shared values, too late even to participate in the nervous excitement attendant upon initial efforts to repair its loss. Much of the time he writes as though their failings are the product of their historical location, but he occasionally lapses into a chiding tone that implies that their failures have more personal sources.

Reading *After the Lost Generation* now, more than forty years after its publication, can be an odd experience. It suggests how quickly and decisively the first generation of American literary modernists captured the imaginations of at least some readers. Aldridge the critic can be measured in his praise of their achievement, but he also reports that he and his college classmates had been eager to see their own lives in terms learned from reading Hemingway, Fitzgerald, and their contemporaries. It also demonstrates how early some readers were prepared to mark a terminus to American literary modernism, or at least to its period of achievement. In recent years critics have typically used some notion of the "postmodern" to mark this closure, but they typically locate it later, well after World War II, and prefer to understand the transition in positive terms. Finally, the personal and autobiographical voice is crucial to *After the Lost Generation;* it establishes the terms for Aldridge's under-

standing of this fiction and the reasons its measure of success matters to him and presumably others of his generation. It has become
commonplace for critics now to assume that academic discourse in
these years strove to be impersonal, and thus that we can signal our
own allegiance to different goals by "locating" ourselves within our
own discourse. Aldridge's example should demonstrate both the inadequacy of our usual understanding of criticism during the decade
after World War II and that our strategies of self-presentation in
themselves are neither inherently radical nor especially innovative.[1]

One of the most striking features of *After the Lost Generation*
for readers now, however, is surely Aldridge's selection of representative figures among the younger generation of writers. He includes
a generally favorable discussion of Norman Mailer, who would later
provide an introduction to a new edition of *After the Lost Generation*, but otherwise the writers taken to be indicative of the state of
fiction at midcentury hardly figure even in literary histories of the
era. Paul Bowles, Frederick Buechner, and Truman Capote might
each continue to possess a small appreciative readership, but I trust
I am not now alone in knowing nothing about the fiction of Merle
Miller, John Horne Burns, or Alfred Hayes. In his preface, Aldridge
justifies his choices. He omits some, including Lionel Trilling and
Robert Penn Warren, because "they are not young enough to belong
to the newest literary generation or to have been affected in the same
way by the experiences that generation endured" (x). He excludes
another and largely female group, including Jean Stafford, Mary
McCarthy, and Eudora Welty, by simply stating that they are "less
relevant to my purpose than those I have discussed in detail." In an
era sympathetic to the recovery of neglected writers, Aldridge's unusual sample might seem a strength, but I cannot help but suspect
that it also accounts for his judgment that he was living in an era
of literary decline.

Had Aldridge written *After the Lost Generation* later in the fifties,
both his literary sample and his assessment of its accomplishment
might have been quite different. It might have included, for instance, a discussion of James Jones's first novel about World War II,
From Here to Eternity, which was published later in 1951. Aldridge
has subsequently written dismissively about Jones, but the latter
would necessarily be included in any study like *After the Lost Generation* that focused on fiction produced by the war (*Devil in the*

Fire 241–48). He might also have discussed J. D. Salinger, whose *The Catcher in the Rye* appeared later in 1951; Bernard Malamud, whose *The Natural* appeared in 1952; Ralph Ellison, whose *Invisible Man* appeared in 1952; Flannery O'Connor, whose *Wise Blood* also appeared in 1952; or Saul Bellow, whose *The Adventures of Augie March* appeared in 1953. The omission of Bellow is particularly striking. *Dangling Man* (1944), after all, is about its narrator's disquiet as he awaits being drafted for service in the war. Be that as it may, all these writers belong roughly to the same generation that Aldridge writes about in *After the Lost Generation,* and even this abbreviated list arguably constitutes sufficient reason for us to reconsider—or at least to complicate—his negative assessment of this generation's accomplishment.

I agree that after World War II American writing feels like a different and generally lesser entity. However, I would identify the reasons for this in different terms. Aldridge argues that its experience of the final erosion of shared values proved decisive for the first generation of American literary modernists. If it at times participated gleefully in this process, it nonetheless came eventually to appreciate the stabilizing functions performed by such values and dedicated itself to the creation of viable substitutes. Both when it kicked free from existing values and later when it busied itself in creating values to stand in their place, in Aldridge's terms, this first generation constituted itself in opposition to contemporary social life. It felt, that is, as oppressed by a social world seemingly without shared values as it had been by a social world informed by genteel values. In Stevens's terms, it was a generation in search of "what will suffice." As we have seen, Aldridge seems to believe that later writers cannot hope to duplicate the accomplishments of the early American literary modernists. They are born into a world already lacking shared values and thus cannot experience the decisive erosion of an original consensus.

Aldridge's emphasis on values constitutes one of the virtues of *After the Lost Generation.* He appreciates the degree to which American literary modernists were from the first earnestly engaged in a conversation about the future of their culture, and he does not assume that American literary modernists were addressing exclusively aesthetic issues. The language of values captures the social dimension of their project, but it does not sufficiently differentiate the various strategies developed by these writers or adequately represent the nature of their dissent. It is not the erosion of values per se that troubled these writers about contemporary social and cultural conditions, nor even the absence of shared values. Instead, or so I have been arguing, they were troubled by the absence of specific values, in particular values that provided terms allowing citizens to understand their rights and obligations to one another. They believed that social life itself had been eroded, so that the United States no longer afforded its citizens with the sense that they were members of what Randolph Bourne in the teens called a "Beloved Community." American literary modernism is a response to that particular absence within contemporary life. As we have seen, it strove to repair that absence in various ways; the differences largely followed from different conceptions of the nature of and requirements for a cohesive community. A Cather, for instance, might believe that it required settled classes whose members respected their given places, whereas in the thirties others believed that it required an equitable distribution of social resources and rights; but in both cases, such writers were attempting to imagine a way to restore the possibility for mutual regard.

Some of these writers feared that shared values were precisely the problem. That is, they believed that values inspired by a market economy threatened to erode any prospect for understanding social life in other than commercial terms. Ivy Peters might be the chief representative of the burgeoning marketplace in Cather's *A Lost Lady*, but Cather knew well enough that others shared his values, and she believed that the values she represented by Captain Forrester had not been able to defend themselves against the logic of the market. It was just such a defeat that Allen Tate and the other Southern Agrarians sought to avert by preserving their native region against further encroachments by the market economy. Needless to say, they did not succeed, and for better and worse many in their region cast their lot with the market. Another of the Agrarians, Robert Penn Warren, as we saw, recognized a similarity between the Agrarians' conservative program and otherwise radically different ambitions. The latter opposed the market in the name of some future social order in which goods and privileges would be distributed equitably, whereas the former opposed it in the name of a traditional way of life. In each case, the conflict is between competing sets of shared values, not between shared values and their absence. The market has its values, and by the early decades of this century its values had obviously come to be widely shared. American literary modernists were among those who do not share those values, but it is not useful to conceive of their adversarial stance in terms that imply that only one side in the controversy was concerned about perpetuating values. The issue was what specific set of values would and should be perpetuated. Instead of writing about the loss of values, Aldridge would have done better to write about the conflict between specific sets of values and the ways in which some values were seemingly being replaced by others.

By casting his analysis in *After the Lost Generation* and elsewhere so largely in terms of values, Aldridge stays at the level of ideas. Some American literary modernists, however, recognized that ideas and values are sustained by social institutions. When T. S. Eliot converted to Anglo-Catholicism, he was not simply giving assent to its religious doctrines. Eliot was also assenting to an entire way of life, a way of life that would be informed by his participation in the rituals and institutions of his new church. The latter are crucial because ideas—values, beliefs, and so on—have their lives in particular institutional forms and cannot be sustained in their absence. Eliot's assent, in other words, was not to religion per se, nor to Christianity, nor even to Protestantism, but specifically to the way of life sustained by the doctrines and institutions of Anglo-Catholicism. The same recognition motivated the Agrarians to defend the various traditional institutions and practices of their native region, since they recognized that the values that way of life represented for them could not be perpetuated if the specific institutions that sustained it should erode. Progressive writers in the thirties agitated for the creation of new institutions for the same reason. They were not committed to the "idea" of an equitable society but to its realization, and thus to the creation of institutions that would perpetuate an unprecedented way of life. Their task was in one way more difficult than either Eliot's or the Agrarians', since they could not align themselves with existing institutions; instead, they needed to imagine and agitate on behalf of new ones, institutions that could sustain an unprecedented social order. This necessity no doubt largely accounts for the prominence of references to the Soviet Union in their writings, since there, at least, some plausible new institutions seemed already under construction. These writers' investments in various specific institutions are not incidental to their "ideas" or literary projects; to the contrary, they demonstrate their seriousness, once the link between specific ideas and their institutional embodiments came into view. Since Aldridge writes exclusively about ideas, he is unable to represent this dimension of cultural activity in the twenties and thirties, and thus in a way he unintentionally slights the seriousness with which these literary figures contributed to the broader cultural debate.

II

This debate was from the beginning about alternative possible futures for social life in the United States. When Van Wyck Brooks published *America's Coming-of-Age* in 1915, he used literary history to document his complaints, but it was clear that his concerns were as broadly social as those being articulated during these years in the *New Republic* and elsewhere. All the participants in the debate assumed that it was in fact possible to alter current social arrangements and thereby restore the possibility that citizens could share a sense of common purpose and mutual regard. Whenever that enabling assumption became questionable, participants were likely to withdraw their own proposals from the debate. Thus by the late thirties most of the Agrarians recognized that the preservation of traditional southern institutions was no longer plausible or perhaps even desirable, and they accordingly withdrew from the conversation. As we saw in the sixth chapter, in these same years, though for quite different reasons, many on the Left also lost faith in the efficacy of their proposals and found it necessary to reevaluate their allegiances. If the Soviet Union had once seemed an image for a better world, for many the Moscow trials, the Soviet-German nonaggression pact, and the invasion of Poland cumulatively diminished their confidence not just in that particular better future but also in the very possibility that any better future could be deliberately made. This disappointment, I would argue, has been even more consequential to the subsequent course of American culture than the initial enthusiasm.

It seems that many, like Joseph in Bellow's *Dangling Man* and John Laskell in Trilling's *The Middle of the Journey,* took this betrayal to mean that all efforts to alter the larger course of events had been discredited. This disappointment need not have had this consequence. In another world, writers and other concerned citizens might have transferred their aspirations to other, still plausible sources of possibility and continued agitating, now on behalf of other ends. A few, like the young Irving Howe, did manage to continue hoping against hope. However, the disappointment typically transcended its specific occasions; people lost interest in discriminating between the necessary and the contingent and were resigned to finding the former everywhere, as if by way of compensating for an earlier hubris. They seemed to tell themselves that it had been naive to ever believe otherwise, that to persist in the belief now would mark one as either foolish or evil. Instead of aspiring to transform the world, we should accommodate ourselves to its changing necessities as best we can and with as much grace as we can muster. An era characterized by raucous debates and revolutionary aspirations thus ironically produced an era in which quietly muddling through seemed the course of wisdom. If the fiction or poetry of the forties and fifties now seems tired, it bespeaks the exhaustion of failed expectations.

In the years just after World War II, the Soviet Union, which earlier had inspired such hopes, emerged as a real limit and potential threat to whatever contentment people could muster. I do not want to excuse or minimize the excesses of anticommunism in these years; lives were diminished and opportunities lost (Heale, Whitfield). At the same time, it seems important to acknowledge that apprehension about international communism had some basis in fact, as those who felt betrayed during the thirties knew only too well.[2] Indeed, it must have been especially galling to the disillusioned to discover the source of their earlier hope now revealed as a threat to even their diminished expectations. Many influential voices in the culture became preoccupied by the need to protect the nation against the potential encroachments of this external threat. Many contributors to the "Our Country and Our Culture" symposium published in 1952 by *Partisan Review* stressed this necessity. According to Newton Arvin, "the habit of rejection, or repudiation, of mere exacerbated alienation, has ceased to seem relevant or defensible—inevitably, since the culture we profoundly cherish is now disastrously threatened from without, and the truer this becomes, the intenser becomes the awareness of our necessary identification with it" (287).

The apparent necessity to defend these values transformed and narrowed the continuing conversation about the quality of American life. The need to defend the nation against an external threat often became the felt need to defend contemporary life in the United States. Writers had earlier assumed that the nation was relatively free to work out the terms of its own destiny. If something was amiss, we could propose remedies without worrying about interventions from abroad. That apparent freedom now seemed a luxury that could not be afforded. Much has been written about the international dimensions of modernism in all the arts; thus it is perhaps ironic that in these years international politics closed down the vigorous national debate about the quality of life. It also changed its terms. Whereas earlier commentators, including most American literary modernists, worried about the apparently increasing isolation endured by individuals and had proposed various ways to make a sense of collective life again available to their contemporaries, the very notion of collective life was now stigmatized by association with the collectivism practiced in the Soviet Union. Individualism was again considered definitive of American life; it was to be celebrated and protected against all threats. This renewed emphasis upon the individual legitimated a turning away from broader questions about the quality of national life in favor of questions about how each individual can work out terms for his or her contentment. The latter seemed difficult enough, so why try one's peace of mind by trying to imagine ways to improve the lot of whole classes and groups of people? In these years, wherever one looked elsewhere on the globe, in some obvious ways most people were less well off, so perhaps Americans should simply be thankful for their blessings and cease whining about unmet desires, desires that could not, perhaps by the very nature of things, ever be met.

These new terms of the cultural conversation were inimical to American literary modernism as it was initially constituted. It had been preoccupied from the first by certain perceived deficiencies in the quality of American life during the first decades of this century. In particular, it recognized that even the middle class, which otherwise seemed to benefit from new social and economic arrangements, was in a way being impoverished by the loss of mutual regard in social life. The strength of American literary modernism derived directly from the cogency of its criticisms of contemporary social formations and from the restlessness with which it pursued possible remedies. When the cultural agenda changed during the years after World War II, the change simply reflected new urgencies and did not indicate that earlier needs had by now been met. They were simply pushed lower on the agenda, where they were, unfortunately, lost. There are signs that the culture is again feeling the need to address the issues that had preoccupied so many earlier in this century, including those who produced American literary modernism. If so, I trust that we will become able to read this body of literature anew, and to restore to it at last the broad social and cultural concerns that animated its creation.

NOTES

Introduction

1. Genevieve Taggard observes that even *The Masses* was edited for an adventurous segment of the middle class: "Because this magazine of rebellion was edited, in spite of its title, for the bourgeois liberal, to give him the freedom he had grown needy of, and because, although it did talk in a very specific and realistic tone of voice about the proletariat, it did not talk *to* the proletariat, scoffers said, rightly enough:

> They draw nude women for the *Masses,*
> Thick, fat, ungainly lasses—
> How does that help the working classes. (354)

In *Rebels in Bohemia,* Leslie Fishbein makes the same observation, though often in the form of an accusation.

2. The literature proposing definitions of modernism is enormous; for representative attempts see Adams, Beebe, Bradbury, Peter Faulkner, Kermode, Levin, Nicholls, Singal ("Towards a Definition"), Spears, and Sultan. The collections edited by Bradbury and McFarlane, by Chefdor et al., and by Kiely contain interesting contributions; see also the special issues of *American Quarterly* (1987), *Journal of Modern Literature* (1974), and *New Literary History* (1971).

3. For some of the more interesting and influential efforts to trace the influence of other arts upon American literary modernism, see Costello, Djikstra, Perloff (*Futurist Moment*), and Tashjian; Altieri's *Painterly Abstraction in Modernist American Poetry: The Contemporaneity of Modernism* is an impressive sustained argument against my own position.

4. There is nothing in principle that restrains such works from being sensitive to the social function and ambitions of the arts; nonetheless, there is in practice a clear tendency for them to touch upon such considerations in at best a glancing manner.

5. See also Wilson's "An Imaginary Conversation." For an account of American dadaism, see Tashjian's *Skyscraper Primitive.*

Chapter 1. Van Wyck Brooks and the Varieties of American Literary Modernism

1. This passage is taken from a broadside entitled "Announcement to Authors" prepared by the editors of *Seven Arts;* it was initially distributed separately and later quoted in an editorial published in the first issue (52–53). In his *Autobiography,* Brooks credits Waldo Frank with being its primary author (269).

2. What Eliot does not acknowledge in this letter is that he had also reviewed Brooks's *The Wine of the Puritans* for the Harvard *Advocate*. The young
Eliot predicts that Brooks's dialogue will particularly interest Americans who
cannot indulge their yearnings for Europe:

> To these, double-dealers with themselves, people of divided allegiance ex-
> cept in times of emotional crisis, Mr. Brooks' treatise will come as a defini-
> tion of their discontent. But he should find a larger audience than this class
> alone. The reasons for the failure of American life (at present)—social, po-
> litical, in education and in art, are surgically exposed; with an unusual
> acuteness of distinction and refinement of taste; and the more sensitive
> of us may find ourselves shivering under the operation. For the book is a
> confession of national weakness; if one takes it rightly, a wholesome reve-
> lation. (80)

3. Although Brooks is perhaps responsible for giving these terms greater
circulation, he did not coin them. For a history of these terms and the attitudes
they embody, see Levine; given Brooks's acknowledged prominence during the
teens and twenties, it strikes me as odd that Levine pays him so little attention.
4. "Patria Mia" was initially serialized in *The New Age;* Pound revised it in
1913 for publication in the United States, but the revised text did not appear
here until 1950, when it was included in his *Selected Prose*. Keith Tuma has convincingly demonstrated the influence of progressive thought upon "Patria Mia."
5. Although they agreed in identifying individualism as a peculiar problem in American life, Croly and Brooks understood its causes differently. In *The
Promise of American Life,* Croly regrets the triumph of Jefferson over Hamilton
and attributes the subsequent weakness of social life in the United States to it;
see Levy. Brooks's writings in the teens do not allude to this controversy, but
Jefferson would later, in *The World of Washington Irving* (1944), emerge as a
central and positive figure in his cultural history. Brooks comments on Jefferson's role in a letter to Lewis Mumford: "As you say, Jefferson was rightly central
to my scheme and will remain so throughout the series; for I've found, what I
never *suspected* before and have never seen stated anywhere, that 'the left really
is the side of the American imagination.' It began with the clustering of minds
round Jefferson, setting the current that ran still stronger through our own
League of American Writers before the Communists took it over" (259–60).
6. At least social historians routinely pay it this compliment, often group-
ing it with *The Masses* and the *New Republic;* see Alexander, Bender, May, and
Wertheim. See Oppenheim and Frank's *Memoirs* (83–95) for recollections of
Seven Arts. I am especially indebted to Bender, Blake (*Beloved Community*), and
May for my own sense of this period.
7. The circumstances behind Rolland's contribution are described in
Frank's *Memoirs* (86). A few months later, *The Masses* also published an en-
dorsement by Rolland; see "From Romain Rolland," *The Masses* (Nov.–Dec.
1917): 24.
8. Hoopes demonstrates that Brooks did not share the antiwar sentiments
of the other editors (121–25). Brooks mentions his reservations about his colleagues' opposition to American entry into the war in his *Autobiography* (286)
and a late portrait of Bourne included in *Fenollosa and His Circle* ("Randolph
Bourne" 309–10).

9. Paul Bourke argues that the intellectual benefits of this friendship were reciprocal, since Brooks likely helped Bourne frame the terms of his celebrated attack on Dewey for supporting American participation in World War I.

10. For information about Coady and *The Soil*, see Tashjian (*Skyscraper* 71–84), Sanborn, and the two articles by Zilczer.

11. Stein's "Mrs. Th—y" appeared in the first issue of *The Soil*, Stevens's "Primordia" in the second. "Primordia" is a sequence with nine numbered sections and a titled epilogue; it is reprinted in *Opus Posthumous* (25–28). Although Stevens did not include the entire sequence in *Harmonium*, three poems in that collection—"In the Carolinas," "Indian River," and "To the Roaring Wind" (*Collected Poems* 4, 112, 113)—are drawn from it.

12. In his *Autobiography*, Brooks writes tellingly about his own and others' attitudes toward expatriation in this period:

> It seemed to me later, looking back, that all the young writers of my generation had been asking, What is wrong with American living?—not realizing that anyone else had been asking the same question,—seeking for answers in one form or another and whether they wrote poems or plays or novels or short stories or criticism. Some shared the typical Harvard feeling that Americans were born Philistines and could only become anything else through contact with Europe, and I actually supposed that the only chance an American had to succeed as a writer was to betake himself there with all possible speed. . . . For me, at that time, the American writer could neither successfully stay *nor go*,—he had only two alternatives, the frying-pan and the fire; and the question was therefore how to change the whole texture of life at home so that writers and artists might develop there. (150)

13. For an unusually concentrated example of Brooks's contempt for most modern writing, consider the following passage from *Opinions of Oliver Allston:*

> When I think what one's years of reading mean in youth, . . . then I feel a blind rage on behalf of younger sensitive minds who have had no other pabulum than these one-eyed writers, sickly adolescents, self-centered and neurotic, inexperienced persons, divorced from the soil, divorced from their country, often, and from parenthood and love, ignorant of the general life, with no horizon beyond their noses or the spiritual slums in which they live. They are besotted egoists, one and all, stewing in their vanity, throwing dust in the eyes of their readers, mystagogues and swindlers. When I think how easily the eyes of youth are dazzled, then I understand Jeremiah, who curses the false prophets. (248–49)

14. It is ironic that Brooks hardly seems to have been aware of the singular persistence of this constellation in the immediate postwar years represented by the Harlem or New Negro Renaissance, especially since, as I shall demonstrate in chapter four, Alain Locke's contributions to *The New Negro* provide the clearest evidence of Brooks's own continuing cultural influence at a time when it was otherwise waning.

15. Leslie Fishbein criticizes the writers associated with *The Masses* in these terms. A more generous and, I think, finally fairer assessment of the political implications of the Young Intellectuals' commitment to self-fulfillment is provided by Casey Blake in his "Young Intellectuals."

Chapter 2. Willa Cather and the Limits of Memory

1. A few pages later Niel encounters Peters on a train when returning to Sweet Water after an absence of two years. The latter replies as follows to Niel's question about whether he is practicing law: "Yes, along with a few other things. Have to keep more than one iron in the fire to make a living with us" (100). Peters's use of the latter phrase, earlier used by Judge Pommeroy in characterizing the Captain's Denver associates, demonstrates that Cather wants us to consider them all of the same ilk.

2. Compare the following passage from Ezra Pound's "Patria Mia," which was initially serialized in *The New Age* late in 1912:

> The type of man who built railways, cleared the forest, planned irrigation, is different from the type of man who can hold on to the profits of subsequent industry. Whereas this first man was a man of dreams, in a time when dreams paid, a man of adventure, careless—this latter is a close person, acquisitive, rapacious, tenacious. The first man had personality, and was, "god damn you" himself, Silas P. Hacker, or such like. The present type is primarily a mask, his ideal is the nickel-plated cash register, and toward the virtues thereof he doth continual strive and tend. (108)

Although by temperament and ambition two people could be scarcely more different than Pound and Cather, the sentiments—even the phrasing—in these passages are remarkably similar. I don't think there is an issue of influence here; instead, the similarities suggest to me the degree to which Cather and Pound shared a body of beliefs about recent American history, and thus should lend credence to my claim that she should be numbered among American literary modernists.

3. There is what I take to be an inadvertent irony about this advice, since architecture, of all the "artistic" professions, is precisely the one that requires practitioners to be most intimately involved in getting and spending: it costs money to turn blueprints into buildings. In Henry Fuller's *The Cliff-Dwellers* the successful architect Atwater offers this advice to those who aspire to his profession: "My dear boy, go in for mining or dredging, or build bridges, or put up railway sheds, if you must; but don't go on believing that architecture nowadays has any great place for the artist" (97).

4. By using Captain Forrester as a representative of pioneer values instead of another settler on the land, in *A Lost Lady* Cather makes it clear that in this novel at least the values at issue cannot simply be reduced to a choice between agrarian and urban ways of life. The Bergson brothers in *O Pioneers!* and Ambrosch Shimerda in *My Ántonia* should have already amply demonstrated that in Cather's fiction farm life in itself is no guarantee of character. Despite her admiration for people like Alexandra Bergson and Ántonia Shimerda, Cather was never an agrarian in the manner of other American literary modernists or of Wendell Berry today.

5. These implications were not lost upon Cather's early readers, especially as social conditions worsened in the thirties; see Hicks ("Case against Cather") and Kronenberger for criticisms of her reversions to the past. Cather uncharacteristically undertook a public defense in a letter published in a 1936 number of *Commonweal* under the title "Escapism." The piece is frankly not among

Cather's stronger critical efforts. In it, she argues that art is always an escape from more mundane concerns, thereby betraying the degree to which she remained loyal throughout her career to her earliest conceptions of art, conceptions that seem a throwback to the poetry collected in *April Twilights* and her earliest fiction. When she concludes the piece by mocking efforts to produce "pure poetry" (28), she confuses matters and demonstrates how unfamiliar she was with the debates being conducted by other literary modernists.

6. I am not claiming that fantasy is inherently incapable of providing an alternative, or that its appearance necessarily vitiates whatever alternative is under consideration. Indeed, Cather admires Alexandra Bergson and Captain Forrester partially for their capacity to imagine (a friendlier term for "fantasize") prosperous and comfortable lives on the initially unpromising prairie. However, Cather's claims for the efficacy of memory critically depend on the actual superiority of an earlier era; thus anything, such as the appearance of fantasy, that occasions doubts about that superiority weakens her position.

7. Archbishop Latour comes to a similar recognition: "The Bishop seldom questioned Jacinto about his thoughts or beliefs. He didn't think it polite, and believed it useless. There was no way in which he could transfer his own memories of European civilization into the Indian mind, and he was quite willing to believe that behind Jacinto there was a long tradition, a story of experience, which no language could translate to him" (92).

8. *Faulkner in the University* (84); I discuss Faulkner's fiction at greater length in "Faulkner's Rescued Patrimony."

9. One of the least pleasant scenes in *A Lost Lady* occurs during the Captain's final illness, when the women of Sweet Water invade the Forrester home under the pretense of providing assistance: "They went over the house like ants, the house where they had never before got past the parlour; and they found they had been fooled all these years. There was nothing remarkable about the place at all! The kitchen was inconvenient, the sink was smelly. . . . The creatures grew bolder and bolder,—and Mrs. Forrester, apparently, had no power of resistance" (134). In this passage Cather clearly shares Niel Herbert's antipathy for the townswomen, who express pleasure at the apparent unmasking of the Forresters' pretensions. If in her fiction Cather is often sympathetic to the situations of ordinary people, scenes like this one demonstrate that her sympathy depends upon their acknowledgment of their appointed place in the social order.

10. Edward A. and Lillian D. Bloom have written an admirable and comprehensive study of Cather's use of sources in writing *Death Comes for the Archbishop*. Sandra Gilbert and Susan Gubar find Cather's historical novels more problematic than either the Blooms or I.

Chapter 3. Eliot, Tate, and the Limits of Tradition

1. For information about Eliot's initiation into the Anglican Church, I am indebted to Ackroyd (149–77), Gordon (120–40) and Sencourt (128–39).

2. Eliot later refers to this review in "Thoughts after Lambeth":

When . . . I brought out a small book of essays, several years ago, called *For Lancelot Andrewes,* the anonymous reviewer in the *Times Literary Supplement* made it the occasion for what I can only describe as a flattering obituary notice. In words of great seriousness and manifest sincerity, he pointed out that I had suddenly arrested my progress—whither he had supposed me to be moving I do not know—and that to his distress I was unmistakably making off in the wrong direction. Somehow I had failed, and had admitted failure; if not a lost leader, at least a lost sheep; what is more, I was a kind of traitor; and those who were to find their way to the promised land beyond the waste, might drop a tear at my absence from the roll-call of the new saints. I suppose that the curiosity of this point of view will be apparent to only a few people. But its appearance in what is not only the best but the most respected and most respectable of our literary periodicals, came home to me as a hopeful sign of the times. For it meant that the orthodox faith of England is at last relieved from the burden of its respectability. (315)

3. Unless otherwise noted parenthetically, all quotations from Eliot's poetry are from the *Collected Poems*.

4. I am not claiming that the example of Noh theater or other remote literary practices are inherently less useful or effective because they are culturally remote. I am simply observing that they necessarily possess a *different* cultural authority and force. The same situation obtains when such practices are identified in the other arts, whether contemporary or past. In the latter case, the practices of their contemporaries in the other arts often have a particular force for writers, despite the obvious difficulties involved in translating among the mediums in which they work.

5. At a time when people like the lady portrayed in this poem might well be as effusive about Eliot and his poetry as she is about Chopin, readers must now guard against becoming unwittingly another object of its satire.

6. In a BBC broadcast Eliot made more than twenty years after writing "Prufrock," he makes some observations that pertain to the predicament of his most famous persona: "To have a passionate conviction about anything is like falling in love: it is not merely to risk being ridiculous (and such people are afraid of being ridiculous, though nothing makes a man more ridiculous really than the fear of ridicule); it is to surrender oneself to something, to surrender liberty, the liberty of thinking irresponsibly" ("Christianity and Communism" 383). This piece elsewhere deliberately evokes "Prufrock," suggesting that Eliot has his earlier persona in mind when writing it. Eliot claims that the problems of the age are ultimately religious in character; at one point he anticipates a possible trivializing response and writes, "that is not what I mean at all" (383).

7. Longenbach also attributes Eliot's increasing appreciation of the uses to which the literary tradition might be put to Pound, especially the example of the latter's "Near Perigord" and *Three Cantos* (156). I am less interested in tracing the derivation of this recognition than in understanding its utility in Eliot's poetry and prose of these years.

8. Eliot would later give this term a broader inflection, so as to include familiarity with cultural spheres beyond literature itself. Thus, for instance, in his essay on John Bramhall, written closer to his conversion, he claims that Bramhall "had also what Hobbes lacked, the historical sense, which is a gift not only of the historian, but of the efficient lawyer, statesman, or theologian" ("John Bramhall" 305).

9. Eliot had earlier, in "The Function of Criticism," criticized John Middleton Murry's similar notion of the "inner voice." The latter is part of Murry's advocacy of romanticism, and Eliot counters it by arguing for the advantages of what he is content to term classicism and a respect for fact. Thus in 1923, at a time when he was himself something of a humanist, Eliot does not resolve the issue as he would later by invoking the final authority of religious doctrine.

10. John Stewart (191), Rubin (323–24), and Law also make this observation.

11. Tate's phrasing suggests a possible indebtedness to John Middleton Murry's "The 'Classical' Revival," an assessment of the resurgence in England of classicism after World War I. Murry pays special attention to Eliot, whose classicism he considers uniquely serious and deeply conflicted—more an expression of yearning for classical order than a belief in its possibility. Murry writes: "To order such an experience on classical principles is almost beyond human powers. It might conceivably be done, by an act of violence, by joining the Catholic Church" (593). Murry was clearly prescient in sensing the logic of Eliot's subsequent conversion. Tate's interest in Eliot and wide familiarity with contemporary letters make it at least conceivable that he read Murry's piece.

12. Such stressful political involvements are not required of the genuinely traditional individual. The appropriate institutions are in place, and he accepts them as an inevitable part of his birthright. For Tate's traditional individual, in other words, political involvement is simply another aspect of a coherent way of life; it does not require extraordinary commitment or do violence to his inclinations.

13. Tate subsequently denied that he was ever very sanguine about the prospects for success. "I never expected it to have any political influence," he writes Davidson in 1942 (Fain and Young 328). However, we should not mistake his doubts about a successful outcome for lack of conviction or seriousness; if anything, indeed, his willingness to undertake the effort despite such doubts only underscores his commitment to the Agrarian project.

14. It goes without saying that Tate and the other Agrarians were exclusively concerned about the costs being imposed upon white southerners by an expanding market economy. The decades immediately prior to the publication of *I'll Take My Stand* had seen a massive emigration of southern African Americans drawn north precisely by the greater promise industrialization seemed to hold for them. The argument of *I'll Take My Stand* is clear to Sterling A. Brown, who reviewed the book in *Opportunity,* as are its racial implications (Brown, "Romantic Defense").

15. "A genuine tradition," Tate writes, "must on the whole be unconsciously operative" ("Regionalism" 159). In *The Fathers* Lacy explains Susan's disorientation at life in the Posey household in analogous terms: "To Susan the life around her in childhood had been final; there could be no other, there never had been any other way of life—which is, I suppose, a way of saying that people living in formal societies, lacking the historical imagination, can imagine for themselves only a timeless existence: they themselves never had any origin anywhere and they can have no end, but will go on forever" (183). In these passages Tate is obviously defining "tradition" in a way more in keeping with Eliot's latter definition than with his earlier and more restrictive one.

Chapter 4. Harlem and the Limits of a Time and Place

1. David Levering Lewis and Arnold Rampersad both describe an incident that occurred in 1932, when Langston Hughes was in Nashville to give a reading at Fisk University. A young member of the Vanderbilt English department arranged a small party to include James Weldon Johnson (by then on the faculty at Fisk), Hughes, and poets then at Vanderbilt, several of whom had recently contributed to *I'll Take My Stand*, the Agrarians' defense of the traditional South. Allen Tate publicly protested the idea of such a gathering of American literary figures across racial lines. In a public letter, Tate wrote that he might be willing to meet the two African-American poets in the North or elsewhere, but believed the idea of meeting them in the South was comparable "to meeting socially with his black cook. Southern custom was 'unfortunate,' but Tate was not willing 'to expend any effort' to change it" (Rampersad 1: 231; Lewis 269–70). The invitations to Johnson and Hughes were withdrawn. This incident is obviously among the minor indignities endured by African Americans living in the South. It nonetheless illustrates the social distances separating poets such as Tate and Hughes and demonstrates why whites and African Americans might value specific traditions differently. A specific custom or tradition is the bulwark making such social gatherings in the South unthinkable to Tate in the early thirties.

2. Writing in the early thirties, Nancy Cunard has a different impression of international awareness in Harlem: "The Harlem Public Library, with its good collection of books on Negro matters, and just a few pieces of African art, so few that the idea strikes one vexingly: why, in this capital of the Negro world, is there no centre, however small, of Africanology? The American Negroes—this is a generalisation with hardly any exceptions—are utterly uninterested in, callous to what Africa is, and to what it was. Many of them are fiercely 'racial,' as and when it applies to the States, but concerning their forefathers they have not even curiosity" (49).

3. Although he does not seem to be aware of the personal links between Brooks and Locke, S. P. Fullinwider is explicit about the similarity between their roles, writing: "Alain Locke was, by analogy, the Van Wyck Brooks of the black Americans. In announcing the 'new Negro' he was, in effect, proclaiming 'the Negro's coming of age' " (120). Nathan Huggins also calls attention to similarities between Locke and Brooks when writing about *The New Negro* (60).

4. As Ann Douglas observes, contemporary readers familiar with Harlem might recognize a quiet irony in the Murray sisters' New York living arrangements. Whereas the ambitious Angela lives among whites in a small Greenwich Village apartment, Virginia lives on Harlem's "Striver's Row," in a townhouse designed by Stanford White, where her neighbors would include many of Harlem's most distinguished residents, including Walter White, the NAACP official and novelist (Douglas 310).

5. My reading of the novel, in other words, is closer to Jacquelyn McLendon's than to Cheryl Wall's.

6. All quotations from Hughes's poetry are from the Rampersad and Roessel edition of the *Collected Poems*.

7. The apparatus provided by Rampersad and Roessel to Hughes's *Collected Poems* suggests that his commitment to the diction of particular poems was slight. After describing the way Hughes changed the diction of particular poems, usually by using standard forms rather than dialect ones (e.g., using "the" instead of "de"), they conclude, in their comment on changes in "Misery": "Hughes eliminated much of the dialect from the poems of *Fine Clothes for the Jews* he included in *Selected Poems*" (622). By way of comparison, it is difficult to imagine Sterling Brown revising his poems by reducing their reliance on dialect.

8. I use this date for convenience and have no interest in participating in any debate about the definitive beginning and ending of the Harlem Renaissance. Various candidates for the latter date have been advanced, including the Wall Street Crash in October, 1929 (Watson 157); the death of A'Lelia Walker in 1931 (Hughes, *Big Sea* 247); the Harlem riot in 1935 (D. Lewis 306–07); and Joe Louis's defeat of Max Schmeling in 1938 (Early 54–55). Early differentiates between the New Negro Movement and the Harlem Renaissance, conceiving the latter as a distinct phase within the former. For Early, the broader New Negro Movement begins when Jack Johnson, the African-American boxer, wins the heavyweight title in 1908, and it concludes with Louis's defeat of Schmeling in 1938. Johnson, for Early, represents an early, aggressive phase in the development of a New Negro consciousness; whereas, by the time Louis fought Schmeling thirty years later, he was as much the champion of white Americans eager for the defeat of the German Schmeling as an exclusive figure of New Negro pride. "The emergence of Louis," writes Early, "effectively ended the New Negro Movement. . . . Blacks achieved a satisfaction with discharging a certain tense preoccupation they had with having a reshaped or more positive involvement with the national mythology and having a more compelling and powerful image in American popular culture, which is what the New Negro Movement was really all about" (55). Stepto conveniently sketches the implications for various configurations of the Harlem Renaissance.

Chapter 5. Wallace Stevens and the Limits of Imagination

1. Unless otherwise indicated parenthetically, all quotations from Stevens's poetry are from the *Collected Poems*.
2. "Tea at the Palaz of Hoon" seems to exist as some midpoint between the poems collected in *Harmonium* and those in the later *Ideas of Order*. Although its final stanza contains lines that clearly anticipate others in "The Idea of Order at Key West," it is otherwise written in a manner more in keeping with the earlier poetry.
3. *Owl's Clover* (1936) obviously constitutes the single most significant exception to this observation. Stevens seems to have considered the volume as his contribution to the debate in the thirties about how the economic and social crises could be effectively addressed. It appears that Stevens was drawn into this debate by Stanley Burnshaw's review in *New Masses* of *Ideas of Order*, a review that in retrospect seems most remarkable for being so temperate. The old woman in "The Old Woman and the Statue" is certainly seen more closely and drawn with more compassion than is usual in Stevens; but the sequence as a whole is

finally as void of specific social content and as preoccupied with general ideas as Stevens's other work. Recent efforts by Filreis and others to rehabilitate Stevens by demonstrating his engagement with contemporary issues and concern for the disadvantaged will need not only to account for this abstractness but also for his occasional expressions of disregard for the less fortunate, as in this quotation from Jean Schlumberger copied into Stevens's commonplace book with apparent approval: "But because I am enjoying an especially sweet melon, must I take an interest in the gardener and endure his gossip? Be quiet and leave me to contemplate this grand spectacle in peace" (*Sujects* 39). These are hardly the sentiments of a person with a passion for social justice. For more on this episode in Stevens's career, see Bates (*Mythology of Self* 155–94), Burnshaw ("Wallace Stevens"), Filreis (220–47), Riddel (120–35), and Vendler (*Extended Wings* 79–118).

4. Stevens's typical attitude toward the past is perhaps expressed most forcefully by Marie Borroff: "The past as foisted upon the present is suffocating and stultifying; our veneration of it is the object of Stevens' constant and endlessly resourceful attack. It is labeled 'history,' 'doctrine,' 'definitions,' 'the rotted names'; it is a garbage dump, a junk shop, a theater beaten in by a tempest in which the audience continues to sit; it is the second-rate statuary on savings banks, the equestrian statues in public squares, the vested interests of the academies and the museums" (3). Stevens apparently came to this attitude early on; Milton Bates quotes from an oration Stevens made when a high school senior: "There is one triumph of a republic, one attainment of Catholicism, one grand result of Democracy, which feudalism, which caste, and which monarchy can never know—the self-made man. We cannot help but admire the man, who with indomitable and irrepressible energy breasting the wave of conditions, grows to become the concentration of power and worth" (qtd. in Bates, *Mythology of Self* 4). This early composition demonstrates the compatibility between Stevens's later confidence in the imagination and pervasive cultural pieties about the self-reliant individual. It is also worth observing that the phrase "one attainment of Catholicism" seems out of place; one might have expected any allusion to Catholicism to be aligned with feudalism and monarchy, and thus for it to be numbered among the social institutions that do not know the pleasures to be had from fostering the "self-made man."

5. Please observe that for the purposes of this exercise I am asking you to believe that this is the best of all possible worlds, not simply the best yet available to mankind. The latter possibility is considerably more plausible, and on most days I would be tempted to argue for it myself.

6. In a letter to Gilbert Montague, written in March 1943, a few months after his encounter with the doubtful Trinity student, Stevens returned to these issues: "It ['Notes'] is a collection of just what I have called it: Notes. Underlying it is the idea that, in various predicaments of belief, it might be possible to yield, or to try to yield, ourselves to a declared fiction. This is the same thing as saying that it might be possible for us to believe in something we know to be untrue. Of course, we do that every day, but we don't make the most of the fact that we do it out of the need to believe, what in your day, and mine, in Cambridge was called the will to believe" (*Letters* 443). I call attention to this letter for two reasons. First, its assertion about the possibility of belief in fictions is more measured than was Stevens's wont. I find it particularly suggestive that

at this date, almost a year after composing "Notes toward a Supreme Fiction," he can only declare that such beliefs "might be possible," as though he has not at this late date resolved the issue to his satisfaction. Second, Stevens again alludes, as he had earlier when describing his encounter with the Trinity student, to William James's "Will to Believe," as though it provides some warrant for his own position. But James does not claim that one can believe just anything, much less that we can believe what "we know to be untrue." Indeed, early in his essay James observes that we are free to *say* many things (such as that this is the best of all possible worlds) that "we are absolutely impotent to believe" (15–16). In this piece James wants to stress two circumstances in which the volitional aspects of belief are especially important—namely, those in which a belief might make something more likely to happen, such as when my trust that others will treat me kindly increases the probability that they will; and those others in which we have no compelling reason to withhold belief. James puts religious belief in the latter category. Religious beliefs, on this account, are beliefs we hope will be true, even though we cannot now offer compelling arguments for their truth. In short, James offers no support for Stevens's hope that we can come to believe what "we know to be untrue."

7. The important documents in this controversy include Hanley's testimony about the conversion in Brazeau (294–96), the final pages of Bates's *Wallace Stevens: A Mythology of Self* (296–302), Bates's response to Sister Bernetta Quinn, Quinn's own article, and Yuhaus's published letter. Brazeau reports that Holly Stevens "vigorously denies" (310n) that her father converted; see also Helen Vendler's otherwise admiring review of Bates's book. Joan Richardson, Stevens's biographer, does not take a position in this debate (2: 426–27).

8. In both *Poets of Reality* (276–84) and his contribution to the *Columbia Literary History of the United States* (990–92), J. Hillis Miller provides different accounts of Stevens's failure to produce a satisfactory supreme fiction. In both he is obliged to introduce a new term into Stevens's own account of his procedures. In the former, Miller identifies this term as "being"; in the latter, and in keeping with his revised critical assumptions, it is simply an indefinite "it" that finally disrupts the emergence of any supreme fiction. I would argue that Miller is forced to the expedient of introducing these new terms by his prior disinclination to question the adequacy of Stevens's conception of his project. Miller's new terms, in short, are an attempt to rescue Stevens's own self-understanding and thus a way of avoiding the recognition of its inherent inadequacy.

Chapter 6. The Thirties and the Failure of the Future

1. Distributivism was a mainly British movement, its name a reference to its conviction that ownership of property should be distributed as widely as possible among citizens in any society. Jay Corrin provides a useful account of the movement.

2. I am indebted to Thomas DePietro for calling Lewis to my attention. Further information about Lewis and many other marginal figures is now available in Cary Nelson's *Repression and Recovery*.

3. A similar anomaly occurs in Conroy's *The Disinherited*. Although he has

worked in various factories, the novel's protagonist is finally moved to become a labor organizer by witnessing a farm auction.

4. As we shall see, there is some confusion as to when Wright resigned from the Communist Party. Here and elsewhere I am following the chronology proposed by Webb. For accounts of communist racial policies during the war, see Klehr and Naison; Isserman argues with less success that the party's pursuit of racial justice continued unabated throughout this period.

5. This unpublished passage makes it impossible to accept Wright's published claim that he defected in 1936. The terms in which he here characterizes various allegiances to the Communist Party are also noteworthy. People who defected as a result of the Soviet-German pact were only "rebels against capitalism," whereas those who remain in the fold are more militant "rebels against the limits of life." Needless to say, these are not categories that would have set well with Wright's more orthodox comrades, since he is already viewing himself less as a Marxist than as a defiant existential hero.

6. Ellison's commentary on the African-American intellectual tradition is seemingly woven deeply into his novel. Early in *Invisible Man*, for instance, when the young narrator must participate in a battle royal with other African-American youths for the entertainment of white townsmen, he becomes its tenth participant, and thus Ellison's ironic representation of W. E. B. DuBois's "talented tenth," those "leaders of thought and missionaries of culture" (403) who should assume leadership of the race. However, the mutual antipathy between the narrator and the other participants in the battle royal make it difficult to see how and why the former could assume the role DuBois would assign him.

7. The narrator is not given any more specific explanation for these changes. The lack of specificity contributes to the depiction of the Brotherhood as authoritarian and keeps *Invisible Man* from becoming historically specific. Despite this calculated lack of specificity, I believe that this change of policy has a very specific antecedent, namely, what many black Americans, including Richard Wright, took to be the Communist Party's abandonment of racial justice during World War II.

8. The narrator falls into a troubled sleep soon after his escape down the open manhole. He awakes with a new sense of his situation: "And now I realized that I couldn't return to Mary's, or to any part of my old life. I could approach it only from the outside, and I had been as invisible to Mary as I had been to the Brotherhood. No, I couldn't return to Mary's, or to the campus, or to the Brotherhood, or home" (558). I have never understood why he cannot return to Mary's. It seems to me that at best the narrator is guilty of faulty judgment when, in this final sentence, he seemingly equates Mary and the Brotherhood; at worst, his failure here and elsewhere to appreciate the anxiety his unexplained absence might be causing others suggests something deeply unattractive about him.

9. The issue of the "small object" is among the vaguer in the novel. Hollingsworth obviously believes that McLeod took something when he left his post in the government; the apparent theft makes him suspect that McLeod had only feigned defection and had remained all along an active member of the Communist Party. The object is never identified. McLeod initially denies taking it, but prior to his final confrontation with Hollingsworth he contemplates

whether to return it. He doesn't and is shot by the frustrated federal agent. In the brief final chapter, Lovett claims to be in possession of both McLeod's will and the object: "So the heritage passed on to me, poor hope, and the little object as well, and I went out into the world" (311). The reader must wonder how Lovett came by the small object, for we do not see him retrieve it from McLeod's body or his apartment. Perhaps the socialist heritage is the small object, but then one wonders why Lovett and Mailer at times differentiate between them, or how McLeod came by it in a government agency. This confusion is a small example of Mailer's lack of authorial control in *Barbary Shore*.

10. Although it is not explicitly identified, it is clearly implied that the Communist Party is the "revolutionary party" at issue. Given Bellow's own former affiliation with various Trotskyite groups, which had their own quarrel with the party, he was not disposed to think well of it. By the time Bellow wrote *Dangling Man*, Joseph's (and Bellow's) objections to the party do not seem to be distinctively Trotskyite; instead, they seem applicable to all parties with revolutionary pretensions.

11. The story of *Partisan Review*'s evolution has been told many times in recent years. See Alexander Bloom, Cooney, and James Gilbert; its editors, William Phillips and Philip Rahv, offer their own version in "In Retrospect: Ten Years of *Partisan Review*." Homberger provides the rationale and brief history of the John Reed Clubs.

12. The career of Granville Hicks is perhaps illustrative. Hicks joined the Communist Party in 1935, having already signed a manifesto supporting Foster and Ford (the 1932 Communist presidential ticket) and published *The Great Tradition*, a Marxist survey of American literature. He was the literary editor of *New Masses* throughout the late thirties. He resigned from the party in 1939, citing the signing of the Soviet-German nonaggression pact as his reason. Hicks subsequently undertook humbler activities directed toward a comparable end. In *Small Town*, he reports the satisfactions and frustrations of participating in the community life of a small town in upstate New York. A few years earlier he had participated in meetings devoted to the prospects for revolution; now, chastened, he serves as trustee of the local one-room school and attends meetings debating the possible purchase of fire-fighting equipment by the town. Hicks seemingly has few illusions about the people or institutions of his town. He freely acknowledges on the one hand its provincialism and, on the other, its increasing endangerment as an independent entity. His life in "Roxborough" is nonetheless animated by the same concerns about others and desires for community life that earlier led him to join the Communist Party.

Afterword

1. Aldridge is in other ways an interesting transitional figure. On the one hand, his prose suggests that he deliberately modeled himself after Edmund Wilson, Malcolm Cowley, and other literary journalists of the previous generation. On the other hand, he has primarily been an academic, even though he does not possess the advanced degrees that have subsequently become prerequisites for an academic career. Individuals like Aldridge and his near contemporary

Stanley Edgar Hyman might be among the last who could hope to straddle successfully the now distinct spheres of literary journalism and academic criticism. 2. I believe that Thomas Schaub's reluctance to make this concession weakens his otherwise insightful reading of American literary culture in the fifties; see his *American Fiction in the Cold War.*

WORKS CITED

Ackroyd, Peter. *T. S. Eliot: A Life*. New York: Simon, 1984.

Adams, Robert M. "What Was Modernism?" *Hudson Review* 31 (1978): 19-33.

Agar, Herbert, and Allen Tate, eds. *Who Owns America? A New Declaration of Independence*. Boston: Houghton, 1936.

Aldridge, John W. *After the Lost Generation: A Critical Study of the Writers of Two Wars*. New York: McGraw, 1951.

———. *The Devil in the Fire: Retrospective Essays on American Literature and Culture, 1951-1971*. New York: Harper's Magazine P, 1972.

Alexander, Charles C. *Here the Country Lies: Nationalism and the Arts in Twentieth-Century America*. Bloomington: Indiana UP, 1980.

Altieri, Charles. *Painterly Abstraction in Modernist American Poetry: The Contemporaneity of Modernism*. New York: Cambridge UP, 1989.

Alvarez, Alfred. *Beyond All This Fiddle: Essays, 1955-1967*. New York: Random, 1969.

Baker, Houston A., Jr. *Modernism and the Harlem Renaissance*. Chicago: U of Chicago P, 1987.

Bates, Milton J. "To Realize the Past: Wallace Stevens' Genealogical Study." *American Literature* 52 (1981): 607-27.

———. *Wallace Stevens: A Mythology of Self*. Berkeley: U of California P, 1985.

———. "Wallace Stevens' Final Yes: A Response to Sister Bernetta Quinn." *Renascence* 41 (1989): 205-08.

Beebe, Maurice. "What Modernism Was." *Journal of Modern Literature* 3 (1974): 1065-84.

Bellah, Robert. *Beyond Belief: Essays on Religion in a Post-traditional World*. New York: Harper, 1970.

Bellow, Saul. *The Adventures of Augie March*. 1953. New York: Penguin, 1984.

———. *Dangling Man*. New York: Vanguard, 1944.

———. "The Mexican General." *Partisan Review* 9 (1942): 178-94.

Bender, Thomas. *New York Intellect: A History of Intellectual Life in New York City, from 1750 to the Beginnings of Our Own Time*. New York: Knopf, 1987.

Benston, Kimberly W., ed. *Speaking for You: The Vision of Ralph Ellison*. Washington: Howard UP, 1987.

Blake, Casey Nelson. *Beloved Community: The Cultural Criticism of*

Randolph Bourne, Van Wyck Brooks, Waldo Frank, and Lewis Mumford. Chapel Hill: U of North Carolina P, 1990.

———. "The Young Intellectuals and the Culture of Personality." *American Literary History* 1 (1989): 510–34.

Bloom, Alexander. *Prodigal Sons: The New York Intellectuals and Their World*. New York: Oxford UP, 1986.

Bloom, Edward A., and Lillian D. Bloom. "On the Composition of a Novel." *Willa Cather's Gift of Sympathy*. Carbondale: Southern Illinois UP, 1962. 197–236. Rpt. in Schroeter 323–55.

Bloom, Harold. *Wallace Stevens: The Poems of Our Climate*. Ithaca: Cornell UP, 1977.

Bohlke, L. Brent, ed. *Willa Cather in Person: Interviews, Speeches, and Letters*. Lincoln: U of Nebraska P, 1986.

Borroff, Marie. "Wallace Stevens: The World and the Poet." *Wallace Stevens: A Collection of Critical Essays*. Ed. Marie Borroff. Twentieth Century Views. Englewood Cliffs: Prentice, 1963. 1–23.

Bourke, Paul F. "The Status of Politics, 1909–1919: *The New Republic*, Randolph Bourne, and Van Wyck Brooks." *Journal of American Studies* 8 (1974): 171–202.

Bourne, Randolph. *History of a Literary Radical*. Ed. Van Wyck Brooks. New York: Huebsch, 1920.

———. "Our Cultural Humility." *Atlantic Monthly* Oct. 1914: 503–07.

———. "Trans-National America." *Atlantic Monthly* July 1916: 86–97. Rpt. in *The Radical Will: Randolph Bourne, Selected Writings, 1911–1918*. Ed. Olaf Hansen. New York: Urizen, 1977. 248–64.

Bradbury, Malcolm. "The Nonhomemade World: European and American Modernism." *American Quarterly* 39 (1987): 27–36.

Bradbury, Malcolm, and James McFarlane, eds. *Modernism, 1890–1930*. New York: Penguin, 1976.

———. "The Name and Nature of Modernism." *Modernism* 19–55.

Brazeau, Peter. *Parts of a World, Wallace Stevens Remembered: An Oral Biography*. New York: Random, 1983.

Brooks, Cleanth. "T. S. Eliot and the American South." *Southern Review* ns 21 (1985): 899–913. Rpt. in *Community, Religion, and Literature*. Columbia: U of Missouri P, 1995. 214–24.

Brooks, Van Wyck. *America's Coming-of-Age*. New York: Huebsch, 1915. Rpt. in Sprague 81–158.

———. *An Autobiography*. New York: Dutton, 1965.

———. *The Confident Years: 1885–1915*. Vol. 5 of *Makers and Finders*. New York: Dutton, 1952.

———. *The Flowering of New England, 1815–1865*. Vol. 2 of *Makers and Finders*. New York: Dutton, 1936.

———. Introduction. *History of a Literary Radical*. By Randolph Bourne. Ed. Brooks. New York: Huebsch, 1920. ix–xxxv.

——. *Letters and Leadership*. New York: Huebsch, 1918.

——. *Makers and Finders*. 5 vols. New York: Dutton, 1936–52.

——. "On Creating a Usable Past." *The Dial* 11 Apr. 1918: 337–41. Rpt. in Sprague 219–26.

——. *On Literature Today*. New York: Dutton, 1941.

——. *Opinions of Oliver Allston*. New York: Dutton, 1941.

——. *The Ordeal of Mark Twain*. New York: Dutton, 1920.

——. "Personal Statement." *Direction* 2 (1939): 6–9, 40–44.

——. *The Pilgrimage of Henry James*. New York: Dutton, 1925.

——. "Randolph Bourne." *Fenollosa and His Circle*. New York: Dutton, 1962. 259–321.

——. "A Reviewer's Notebook." *The Freeman* 8 Aug. 1923: 527.

——. *The Van Wyck Brooks–Lewis Mumford Letters: The Record of a Literary Friendship, 1921–1963*. Ed. Robert E. Spiller. New York: Dutton, 1970.

——. *The Wine of the Puritans*. London: Sisley's, 1908. Rpt. in Sprague 2–60.

——. *The World of Washington Irving*. Vol. 1 of *Makers and Finders*. New York: Dutton, 1944.

——. *The Writer in America*. New York: Dutton, 1953.

Brown, Sterling A. *The Collected Poems of Sterling A. Brown*. Ed. Michael S. Harper. Chicago: Another Chicago P, 1989.

——. "A Literary Parallel." *Opportunity* May 1932: 152–53.

——. "The New Negro in Literature (1925–1955)." *The New Negro Thirty Years Afterward*. Ed. Rayford W. Logan et al. Washington: Howard UP, 1955. 57–72.

——. "A Romantic Defense." *Opportunity* Apr. 1931: 118.

Bruccoli, Matthew J. " 'An Instance of Apparent Plagiarism': F. Scott Fitzgerald, Willa Cather, and the First *Gatsby* Manuscript." *Princeton University Library Chronicle* 39 (1978): 171–78.

Burnshaw, Stanley. "Turmoil in the Middle Ground." Rev. of *Pittsburgh Memorandum* by Haniel Long and *Ideas of Order* by Wallace Stevens. *New Masses* 1 Oct. 1935: 41–42. Rpt. in Burnshaw, "Wallace Stevens" 363–66.

——. "Wallace Stevens and the Statue." *Sewanee Review* 69 (1961): 355–66.

Carpenter, Lynette. "The Battle Within: The Beleaguered Consciousness in Allen Tate's *The Fathers*." *Southern Literary Journal* 8 (1976): 3–23.

Carroll, Latrobe. "Willa Sibert Cather." *Bookman* 3 May 1921. Rpt. in Bohlke 19–24.

Cather, Willa. *April Twilights*. 1903. Ed. Bernice Slote. Lincoln: U of Nebraska P, 1962.

——. "The Best Stories of Sarah Orne Jewett." *On Writing* 47–59.

———. *Death Comes for the Archbishop*. 1927. Boston: Houghton, 1938. Vol. 9 of Library Edition. 13 vols. 1937–41.

———. "Escapism." *On Writing* 18–30.

———. *A Lost Lady*. 1923. Vol. 7 of Library Edition.

———. *Lucy Gayheart*. 1935. Vol. 11 of Library Edition.

———. *My Ántonia*. 1918. Vol. 4 of Library Edition.

———. "My First Novels (There Were Two)." *On Writing* 89–97.

———. *Obscure Destinies*. 1932. Vol. 12 of Library Edition.

———. "On *Death Comes for the Archbishop*." *On Writing* 3–13.

———. *On Writing: Critical Studies on Writing as an Art*. New York: Knopf, 1949.

———. *O Pioneers!* 1913. Vol. 1 of Library Edition.

———. *The Professor's House*. 1925. Vol. 8 of Library Edition.

———. *Sapphira and the Slave Girl*. 1940. Vol. 13 of Library Edition.

———. *Shadows on the Rock*. 1931. Vol. 10 of Library Edition.

———. *Song of the Lark*. 1915. Vol. 2 of Library Edition.

Chabot, C. Barry. "Faulkner's Rescued Patrimony." *Review of Existential Psychology and Psychiatry* 13 (1974): 274–86.

———. "Fiction, Truth, and the Character of Beliefs." *Georgia Review* 37 (1983): 835–46.

Chambers, Clarke A. *Paul U. Kellogg and the "Survey": Voices for Social Welfare and Social Justice*. Minneapolis: U of Minnesota P, 1971.

Chefdor, Monique, Ricardo Quinones, and Albert Wachtel, eds. *Modernism: Challenges and Perspectives*. Urbana: U of Illinois P, 1986.

Coady, Robert J. "American Art." *The Soil* Dec. 1916: 3–4; Jan. 1917: 54–56.

Conroy, Jack. *The Disinherited*. 1933. Westport: Lawrence Hill, 1982.

Cooney, Terry A. *The Rise of the New York Intellectuals: "Partisan Review" and Its Circle, 1934–1945*. Madison: U Wisconsin P, 1986.

Corrin, Jay P. *G. K. Chesterton and Hilaire Belloc: The Battle against Modernity*. Athens: Ohio UP, 1981.

Costello, Bonnie. "Effects of an Analogy: Wallace Stevens and Painting." *Wallace Stevens: The Poetics of Modernism*. Ed. Albert Gelpi. New York: Cambridge UP, 1985. 65–85.

Cowley, Malcolm. —*And I Worked at the Writer's Trade*. New York: Viking, 1978.

Croly, Herbert. *The Promise of American Life*. Ed. Arthur M. Schlesinger, Jr. Cambridge: Belknap–Harvard UP, 1965.

Crossman, Richard H. S., ed. *The God That Failed*. New York: Harper, 1950.

Crowell, Chester T. "The World's Largest Negro City." *Saturday Evening Post* 8 Aug. 1925: 8–9, 93–94, 97.

Cunard, Nancy. "Harlem Reviewed." *Negro*. Ed. Nancy Cunard. 1934. Rpt. Ed. Hugh Ford. New York: Ungar, 1970. 47–55.

Cunningham, J. V. "The Styles and Procedures of Wallace Stevens." *Collected Essays of J. V. Cunningham.* Chicago: Swallow, 1976. 379–98.

———. "Tradition and Modernity: Wallace Stevens." *Collected Essays* 225–43.

DePietro, Thomas. "Tradition and the Adversarial Talent." *Poetry East* 9–10 (1983): 87–104.

Djikstra, Bram. *The Hieroglyphics of a New Speech: Cubism, Steiglitz, and the Early Poetry of William Carlos Williams.* Princeton: Princeton UP, 1969.

Dos Passos, John. "Whither the American Writer." *Modern Quarterly* 6.2 (1932): 11–12.

Douglas, Ann. *Terrible Honesty: Mongrel Manhattan in the 1920s.* New York: Farrar, 1995.

DuBois, W. E. B. Rev. of *Home to Harlem,* by Claude McKay. *Crisis* Sept. 1928: 202.

———. "The Talented Tenth." *The Seventh Son: The Thought and Writings of W. E. B. DuBois.* Ed. Julius Lester. 2 vols. New York: Random, 1971. 1: 385–403.

Early, Gerald. Introduction. *My Soul's High Song: The Collected Writings of Countee Cullen, Voice of the Harlem Renaissance.* Ed. Gerald Early. New York: Doubleday, 1991.

"Editorial." *Seven Arts* Nov. 1916: 52–56.

Eliot, T. S. *After Strange Gods: A Primer of Modern Heresy.* New York: Harcourt, 1934.

———. "Christianity and Communism." *The Listener* 16 Mar. 1932: 382–83.

———. *The Cocktail Party.* New York: Harcourt, 1950.

———. *Collected Poems, 1909–1962.* New York: Harcourt, 1970.

———. *For Lancelot Andrewes: Essays on Style and Order.* New York: Doubleday, 1929.

———. "The Function of Criticism." *Selected Essays* 12–22.

———. "The Humanism of Irving Babbitt." *Selected Essays* 383–92.

———. "John Bramhall." *Selected Essays* 301–09.

———. *The Letters of T. S. Eliot.* Ed. Valerie Eliot. Vol. 1. New York: Harcourt, 1988.

———. "The Metaphysical Poets." *Selected Essays* 241–50.

———. "Preface to the 1928 Edition." *The Sacred Wood: Essays on Poetry and Criticism.* New York: Knopf, 1930. vii–x.

———. Rev. of *The Wine of the Puritans,* by Van Wyck Brooks. *Harvard Advocate* 7 May 1909: 80.

———. "Second Thoughts about Humanism." *Selected Essays* 393–402.

———. *Selected Essays, 1917–1932.* New York: Harcourt, 1932.

———. "Thoughts after Lambeth." *Selected Essays* 310–32.

———. "Tradition and the Individual Talent." *Selected Essays* 3–11.

———. "*Ulysses,* Order and Myth." *The Dial* Nov. 1923: 480–83. Rpt. in *The Selected Prose of T. S. Eliot.* Ed. Frank Kermode. New York: Harcourt, 1975. 175–78.

Ellison, Ralph. *Going to the Territory.* New York: Random, 1986.

———. *Invisible Man.* 1952. Introd. by Ellison. New York: Vintage, 1982.

———. "Invisible Man: Prologue to a Novel." *Partisan Review* 19 (1952): 31–40.

———. *Shadow and Act.* New York: Random, 1964.

Fabre, Michel. "From *Native Son* to *Invisible Man:* Some Notes on Ralph Ellison's Evolution in the 1950s." Benston 199–216.

Fain, John Tyree, and Thomas Daniel Young, eds. *The Literary Correspondence of Donald Davidson and Allen Tate.* Athens: U of Georgia P, 1974.

Faulkner, Peter. *Modernism.* The Critical Idiom 35. London: Methuen, 1977.

Faulkner, William. *Absalom, Absalom!* 1936. New York: Random, 1964.

———. *Faulkner in the University: Class Conferences at the University of Virginia, 1957–1958.* Ed. Frederick L. Gwynn and Joseph L. Blotner. Charlottesville: U of Virginia P, 1959.

———. *Intruder in the Dust.* New York: Random, 1948.

———. *The Reivers.* New York: Random, 1962.

Fauset, Arthur Huff. "Educational Procedure for an Emergency." *Opportunity* Jan. 1933: 20–22.

Fauset, Jessie Redmon. *The Chinaberry Tree and Selected Writings.* 1931. The Northeastern Library of Black Literature. Boston: Northeastern UP, 1995.

———. *Comedy: American Style.* 1933. College Park, MD: McGrath, 1969.

———. *Plum Bun: A Novel without a Moral.* 1928. Boston: Beacon P, 1990.

———. Rev. of *The Weary Blues,* by Langston Hughes. *Crisis* Mar. 1926: 239. Rpt. in Mullen 39–41.

———. *There Is Confusion.* 1924. The Northeastern Library of Black Literature. Boston: Northeastern UP, 1989.

Filreis, Alan. *Modernism from Right to Left: Wallace Stevens, the Thirties, and Literary Radicalism.* New York: Cambridge UP, 1994.

Fischer, Russell G. "*Invisible Man* as History." *CLA Journal* 17 (1974): 338–67.

Fishbein, Leslie. *Rebels in Bohemia: The Radicals of* The Masses, *1911–1917.* Chapel Hill: U of North Carolina P, 1982.

Fisher, Rudolph. *The City of Refuge: The Collected Stories of Rudolph Fisher.* Ed. John McCluskey, Jr. Columbia: U of Missouri P, 1987.

———. *The Conjure-Man Dies.* 1932. Ann Arbor: U of Michigan P, 1992.

———. *The Walls of Jericho.* New York: Knopf, 1928.

Fitzgerald, F. Scott. *The Great Gatsby.* New York: Scribner's, 1925.

Foley, Barbara. *Radical Representations: Politics and Form in U.S. Proletarian Fiction, 1929–1941.* Durham: Duke UP, 1993.

Frank, Joseph. "Ralph Ellison and a Literary 'Ancestor': Dostoevski." *New Criterion* Sept. 1983: 11–21. Rpt. in Benston 231–44.

Frank, Waldo. "Emerging Greatness." *Seven Arts* Nov. 1916: 73–78.

———. *Memoirs.* Ed. Alan Trachtenberg. Amherst: U of Massachusetts P, 1973.

———. "Seriousness and Dada." *1924* (1924): 70–73. Rpt. in *In the American Jungle: 1925–1936.* New York: Farrar & Rinehart, 1937. 128–34.

Fryer, Judith. *Felicitous Space: The Imaginative Structures of Edith Wharton and Willa Cather.* Chapel Hill: U of North Carolina P, 1986. 289–318.

Fuller, Henry B. *The Cliff-Dwellers.* New York: Harper, 1893.

Fullinwider, S. P. *The Mind and Mood of Black America: Twentieth-Century Thought.* Homewood: Dorsey, 1969.

Geismar, Maxwell. *The Last of the Provincials: The American Novel, 1915–1925.* Cambridge: Riverside-Houghton, 1947.

Gilbert, James Burkhart. *Writers and Partisans: A History of Literary Radicalism in America.* New York: Wiley, 1968.

Gilbert, Sandra M., and Susan Gubar. *Sexchanges.* New Haven: Yale UP, 1989. Vol. 2 of *No Man's Land: The Place of the Woman Writer in the Twentieth Century.* 3 vols. to date. 1988–.

Godine, Amy. "Notes toward a Reappraisal of Depression Literature." *Prospects* 5 (1980): 197–239.

Gold, Michael. *Jews without Money.* 1930. New York: Carroll & Graf, 1984.

Gordon, Lyndall. *Eliot's Early Years.* New York: Oxford UP, 1977.

Hamner, Eugenie Lambert. "The Unknown, Well-Known Child in Cather's Last Novel." *Women's Studies* 11 (1984): 347–57.

Harrison, John R. *The Reactionaries: A Study of the Anti-Democratic Intelligentsia.* New York: Schocken, 1967.

Heale, M. J. *American Anticommunism: Combating the Enemy Within, 1830–1970.* Baltimore: Johns Hopkins UP, 1990.

Hicks, Granville. "The Case against Willa Cather." *English Journal* Nov. 1933: 703–10. Rpt. in Schroeter 139–47.

———. "On Leaving the Communist Party." *New Republic* 4 Oct. 1939: 244–45.

———. *Small Town.* New York: Macmillan, 1946.

———. "Steinbeck's Powerful New Novel." *New Masses* 2 May 1939: 22–24. Rpt. in *Granville Hicks in* The New Masses. Ed. Jack Alan Robbins. Port Washington: Kennikat, 1974. 138–43.

Hilfer, Anthony Channell. *The Revolt from the Village, 1915–1930.* Chapel Hill: U of North Carolina P, 1969.

Hogue, W. Lawrence. *Discourse and the Other: The Production of the Afro-American Text*. Durham: Duke UP, 1986.

Hollinger, David A. "Ethnic Diversity, Cosmopolitanism, and the Emergence of the American Liberal Intelligentsia." *American Quarterly* 27 (1975): 133–51. Rpt. in *In the American Province: Studies in the History and Historiography of Ideas*. Bloomington: Indiana UP, 1985. 55–73.

Holman, C. Hugh. "*The Fathers* and the Historical Imagination." *Literary Romanticism in America*. Ed. William L. Andrews. Baton Rouge: Louisiana State UP, 1981. 80–93.

Homberger, Eric. "Proletarian Literature and the John Reed Clubs, 1929–1935." *Journal of American Studies* 13 (1979): 221–44.

Hoopes, James. *Van Wyck Brooks: In Search of American Culture*. Amherst: U of Massachusetts P, 1977.

Horowitz, Howard. "*O Pioneers!* and the Paradox of Property: Cather's Aesthetics of Divestment." *Prospects: An Annual of American Cultural Studies*. Vol. 14. New York: Cambridge UP, 1988. 61–93. Rpt. in *By the Law of Nature: Form and Value in Nineteenth-Century America*. New York: Oxford UP, 1991. 218–45.

Howe, Irving. "Black Boys and Native Sons." *Decline of the New*. New York: Horizon, 1970. 167–89.

Huggins, Nathan Irvin. *Harlem Renaissance*. New York: Oxford UP, 1971.

Hughes, Langston. *The Big Sea*. 1940. New York: Hill & Wang, 1993.

———. *The Collected Poems*. Ed. Arnold Rampersad and David Roessel. New York: Knopf, 1994.

———. "My Early Days in Harlem." *Freedomways* 3 (1993): 312–14.

Isserman, Maurice. *Which Side Were You On? The American Communist Party during the Second World War*. Middletown: Wesleyan UP, 1982.

James, William. "The Will to Believe." *"The Will to Believe" and Other Essays in Popular Philosophy*. The Works of William James. Cambridge: Harvard UP, 1979. 13–33.

Jameson, Fredric. "Wallace Stevens." *New Orleans Review* 11 (1984): 10–19.

Johnson, James Weldon. *Black Manhattan*. New York: Knopf, 1930.

———, ed. *The Book of American Negro Poetry*. 2nd ed. New York: Harcourt, 1931.

Josephson, Matthew. "The Great American Billposter." *Broom* 3 (1922): 304–12.

Kates, George N. "Willa Cather's Unfinished Avignon Story." *Five Stories*. By Willa Cather. New York: Vintage-Random, 1956. 177–214.

Keeler, Clinton. "Narrative without Accent: Willa Cather and Puvis de Chavannes." *American Quarterly* 17 (1965): 119–26.

Kenner, Hugh. *A Homemade World: The American Modernist Writers.*
New York: Knopf, 1975.
———. *The Pound Era.* Berkeley: U of California P, 1971.
Kermode, Frank. "Modernisms." *Continuities.* New York: Random,
1968. 1–32.
Kessler, Edward. *Images of Wallace Stevens.* New Brunswick: Rutgers
UP, 1972.
Kiely, Robert, ed. *Modernism Reconsidered.* Harvard English Studies 2.
Cambridge: Harvard UP, 1983.
Kingsley, Lawrence. "The Texts of Allen Tate's 'Ode to the Confederate
Dead.'" *Papers of the Bibliographical Society of America* 71 (1977):
171–89.
Klein, Marcus. *After Alienation: American Novels at Mid-Century.*
Cleveland: World, 1964.
Klehr, Harvey. *The Heyday of American Communism: The Depression De-
cade.* New York: Basic, 1984.
Knapp, James F. *Literary Modernism and the Transformation of Work.*
Evanston: Northwestern UP, 1988.
Kostelanetz, Richard. "The Politics of Ellison's Booker: *Invisible Man*
as Symbolic History." *The Black Novelist.* Ed. Robert Hemenway.
Columbus: Merrill, 1970. 88–110.
———. "Ralph Ellison: Novelist as Brown-Skinned Aristocrat." *Master
Minds: Portraits of Contemporary American Artists and Intellectu-
als.* New York: Macmillan, 1967. 36–59.
Kronenberger, Louis. "In Dubious Battle." Rev. of *Not Under Forty,*
by Willa Cather. *Nation* 19 Dec. 1936: 738–39.
Krupnick, Mark. *Lionel Trilling and the Fate of Cultural Criticism.*
Evanston: Northwestern UP, 1986.
Law, Richard. "'Active Faith' and Ritual in *The Fathers.*" *American
Literature* 55 (1983): 345–66.
Lentricchia, Frank. *Ariel and the Police: Michel Foucault, William James,
Wallace Stevens.* Madison: U of Wisconsin P, 1988.
———. *Modernist Quartet.* New York: Cambridge UP, 1994.
Levenson, Michael. *A Genealogy of Modernism: A Study of English Lit-
erary Doctrine, 1908–1922.* New York: Cambridge UP, 1984.
Levin, Harry. "What Was Modernism?" *Massachusetts Review* 1 (1960):
609–30. Rpt. in *Refractions: Essays in Comparative Literature.* New
York: Oxford UP, 1966. 271–95.
Levine, Lawrence W. *Highbrow/Lowbrow: The Emergence of Cultural Hier-
archy in America.* Cambridge: Harvard UP, 1988.
Levy, David W. *Herbert Croly of The New Republic: The Life and
Thought of an American Progressive.* Princeton: Princeton UP, 1985.
Lewis, David Levering. *When Harlem Was in Vogue.* New York: Knopf,
1981.

Lewis, Edith. *Willa Cather Living: A Personal Record.* New York: Knopf, 1953.

Lewis, H. H. "The Sweeter Our Fruits . . . " *Social Poetry of the 1930s: A Selection.* Ed. Jack Salzman and Leo Zanderer. N.p.: Franklin, 1978. 143–44.

Locke, Alain. *The Critical Temper of Alain Locke: A Selection of His Essays on Art and Culture.* Ed. Jeffrey C. Stewart. New York: Garland, 1983.

———. "Harlem: Dark Weather-Vane." *Survey Graphic* Aug. 1936: 457–62, 493–95.

———, ed. *The New Negro.* 1925. New York: Atheneum, 1992.

———. Rev. of *The Weary Blues,* by Langston Hughes. *Palms* 1 (1926–27): 25–27. Rpt. in Mullen 44–46.

———. "Spiritual Truancy." *The Critical Temper* 63–66.

———. "Sterling Brown: The New Negro Folk-Poet." *The Critical Temper* 49–53.

Longenbach, James. *Modernist Poetics of History: Pound, Eliot, and a Sense of the Past.* Princeton: Princeton UP, 1987.

Macdonald, Dwight. "Kulturbolschewismus Is Here." *Partisan Review* 8 (1941): 442–51.

Mailer, Norman. *Advertisements for Myself.* New York: Putnam's, 1959.

———. *Barbary Shore.* New York: Rinehart, 1951.

———. "Interview." *Paris Review* 31 (1964): 28–58. Rpt. in *Conversations with Norman Mailer.* Ed. J. Michael Lennon. Jackson: UP of Mississippi, 1988. 77–99.

Martin, Terence. "The Drama of Memory in *My Ántonia.*" *PMLA* 84 (1969): 304–11.

May, Henry F. *The End of American Innocence: A Study of the First Years of Our Own Time, 1912–1917.* New York: Knopf, 1959.

McKay, Claude. *Home to Harlem.* 1928. The Northeastern Library of Black Literature. Boston: Northeastern UP, 1987.

McLendon, Jacquelyn. *The Politics of Color in the Fiction of Jessie Fauset and Nella Larsen.* Charlottesville: UP of Virginia, 1995.

Merrill, Flora. "A Short Story Course Can Only Delay, It Cannot Kill an Artist, Says Willa Cather." *New York World* 19 Apr. 1925, sec. 3: 1+. Rpt. in Bohlke 73–80.

Michaels, Walter Benn. *Our America: Nativism, Modernism, and Pluralism.* Durham: Duke UP, 1995.

Miller, J. Hillis. "Wallace Stevens." *Poets of Reality: Six Twentieth-Century Writers.* Cambridge: Belknap–Harvard UP, 1965. 217–84.

———. "William Carlos Williams and Wallace Stevens." *Columbia Literary History of the United States.* Gen. ed. Emory Elliott. New York: Columbia UP, 1988. 972–92.

Mills, Hilary. *Mailer: A Biography.* New York: Empire, 1982.

Modern and Postmodern. Spec. issue of *New Literary History* 3.1 (1971): 5–223.

"Mr. Eliot's New Essays." Rev. of *For Lancelot Andrewes,* by T. S. Eliot. *Times Literary Supplement* 6 Dec. 1928: 953.

Mullen, Edward J., ed. *Critical Essays on Langston Hughes.* Boston: Hall, 1986.

Mumford, Lewis. *The Culture of Cities.* New York: Harcourt, 1938.

Murry, John Middleton. "The 'Classical' Revival." *Adelphi* 3 (1926): 585–95, 648–53.

Naison, Mark. *Communists in Harlem during the Depression.* Urbana: U of Illinois P, 1983.

Nelson, Cary. *Repression and Recovery: Modern American Poetry and the Politics of Cultural Memory, 1910–1945.* Madison: U of Wisconsin P, 1989.

Nelson, Raymond. *Van Wyck Brooks: A Writer's Life.* New York: Dutton, 1981.

Nicholls, Peter. *Modernisms: A Literary Guide.* Berkeley: U of California P, 1995.

O'Brien, Michael. *The Idea of the American South, 1920–1941.* Baltimore: Johns Hopkins UP, 1979.

O'Brien, Sharon. *Willa Cather: The Emerging Voice.* New York: Oxford UP, 1987.

Odets, Clifford. *Three Plays.* New York: Covici, 1935.

"On the 'Brooks-MacLeish Thesis.' " *Partisan Review* 9 (1942): 38–47.

Oppenheim, James. "The Story of *The Seven Arts.*" *American Mercury* June 1930: 156–64.

Osofsky, Gilbert. *Harlem: The Making of a Ghetto, Negro New York, 1890–1930.* New York: Harper, 1966.

"Our Country and Our Culture." *Partisan Review* 19 (1952): 282–326, 420–50, 562–97.

Perloff, Marjorie. *The Futurist Moment: Avant-Garde, Avant Guerre, and the Language of Rupture.* Chicago: U of Chicago P, 1986.

———. "Pound/Stevens: Whose Era?" *New Literary History* 13 (1982): 485–514. Rpt. in *The Dance of the Intellect: Studies of the Pound Tradition.* New York: Cambridge UP, 1985. 1–32.

Phillips, William, and Philip Rahv. "In Retrospect: Ten Years of *Partisan Review.*" *The Partisan Reader: Ten Years of "Partisan Review," 1934–1944: An Anthology.* Ed. William Phillips and Philip Rahv. New York: Dial, 1946. 679–88.

Pound, Ezra. *Gaudier-Brzeska, a Memoir.* 1916. New York: New Directions, 1970.

———. "Mr. Eliot's Quandaries." *New English Weekly* 29 Mar. 1934: 558–59.

———. "Patria Mia." *Selected Prose, 1909–1965.* Ed. William Cookson. New York: New Directions, 1973. 101–41.

Pritchard, William H. "Wallace Stevens: Poet of the Academy." *Lives of the Modern Poets.* New York: Oxford UP, 1980. 203–33.

Quinn, Sister Bernetta. "Wallace Stevens: 'The Peace of the Last Intelligence.' " *Renascence* 41 (1989): 191–204.

Quirk, Tom. "Fitzgerald and Cather: *The Great Gatsby.*" *American Literature* 54 (1982): 576–91.

Rabinowitz, Paula. *Labor and Desire: Women's Revolutionary Fiction in Depression America.* Chapel Hill: U of North Carolina P, 1991.

Rampersad, Arnold. *The Life of Langston Hughes.* 2 vols. New York: Oxford UP, 1986–88.

Richardson, Joan. *Wallace Stevens.* 2 vols. New York: Beech Tree–Morrow, 1986–88.

Riddel, Joseph N. *The Clairvoyant Eye: The Poetry and Poetics of Wallace Stevens.* Baton Rouge: Louisiana State UP, 1965.

Rolland, Romain. "America and the Arts." *Seven Arts* Nov. 1916: 47–51.

Rose, Phyllis. "The Case of Willa Cather." *Writing of Women: Essays in a Renaissance.* Middletown: Wesleyan UP, 1985. 136–51.

Rosowski, Susan J. *The Voyage Perilous: Willa Cather's Romanticism.* Lincoln: U of Nebraska P, 1986.

Rubin, Louis D. *The Wary Fugitives: Four Poets and the South.* Baton Rouge: Louisiana State UP, 1978.

Sanborn, Robert Alden. "A Champion in the Wilderness." *Broom* Oct. 1922: 174–79.

Schaub, Thomas Hill. *American Fiction in the Cold War.* Madison: U of Wisconsin P, 1991.

Schroeter, James, ed. *Willa Cather and Her Critics.* Ithaca: Cornell UP, 1967.

Schuchard, Ronald. "T. S. Eliot as an Extension Lecturer, 1916–1919." *Review of English Studies* ns 35 (1974): 163–73, 292–304.

Schwartz, Nina. "History and the Invention of Innocence in *A Lost Lady.*" *Arizona Quarterly* 46.2 (1990): 33–54.

Sencourt, Robert. *T. S. Eliot: A Memoir.* New York: Dodd, 1971.

Shechner, Mark. *After the Revolution: Studies in the Contemporary Jewish-American Imagination.* Bloomington: Indiana UP, 1987.

Shusterman, Richard. *T. S. Eliot and the Philosophy of Criticism.* New York: Columbia UP, 1988.

Sigg, Eric. *The American T. S. Eliot: A Study of the Early Writings.* New York: Cambridge UP, 1989.

Singal, Daniel Joseph, ed. *Modernist Culture in America.* Spec. issue of *American Quarterly* 39 (1987): 5–173.

———. "Towards a Definition of American Modernism." *American Quarterly* 39 (1987): 7–26.

Spears, Monroe K. *Dionysus and the City: Modernism in Twentieth-Century Poetry.* New York: Oxford UP, 1970.

Sprague, Claire, ed. *Van Wyck Brooks: The Early Years*. New York: Harper, 1968.

Squires, Radcliffe. *Allen Tate: A Literary Biography*. New York: Pegasus, 1971.

Steinbeck, John. *In Dubious Battle*. New York: Collier, 1936.

———. *The Grapes of Wrath*. New York: Viking, 1939.

———. *Of Mice and Men*. New York: Covici-Friede, 1937.

———. "To Elizabeth Otis." 13 May 1935. *Steinbeck: A Life in Letters*. Ed. Elaine Steinbeck and Robert Wallsten. New York: Viking, 1975. 109–10.

Steinman, Lisa. *Made in America: Science, Technology, and American Modernist Poetry*. New Haven: Yale UP, 1987.

Stepto, Robert. "Sterling A. Brown: Outsider in the Harlem Renaissance." *The Harlem Renaissance: Revaluations*. Ed. Amritjit Singh, William S. Shiver, and Stanley Brodwin. New York: Garland, 1989. 73–81.

Stevens, Wallace. *The Collected Poems of Wallace Stevens*. New York: Knopf, 1954.

———. *Letters of Wallace Stevens*. Ed. Holly Stevens. New York: Knopf, 1966.

———. *The Necessary Angel: Essays on Reality and the Imagination*. New York: Knopf, 1951.

———. *Opus Posthumous: Poems, Plays, Prose*. Rev. ed. Ed. Milton J. Bates. New York: Knopf, 1989.

———. *Sur Plusieurs Beaux Sujects: Wallace Stevens' Commonplace Book*. Ed. Milton J. Bates. Stanford: Stanford UP–Huntington Library, 1989.

Stewart, Jeffrey Conrad. "A Biography of Alain Locke: Philosopher of the Harlem Renaissance, 1886–1930." Diss. Yale U, 1979.

Stewart, John L. *The Burden of Time: The Fugitives and Agrarians*. Princeton: Princeton UP, 1965.

Stouck, David. *Willa Cather's Imagination*. Lincoln: U of Nebraska P, 1975.

Sultan, Stanley. " 'Our Modern Experiment.' " *Eliot, Joyce, and Company*. New York: Oxford UP, 1987. 91–133.

Taggard, Genevieve. " 'May Days.' " *Nation* 30 Sept. 1925: 353–56.

Tashjian, Dickran. *Skyscraper Primitives: Dada and the American Avant-Garde, 1910–1925*. Middletown: Wesleyan UP, 1975.

———. *William Carlos Williams and the American Scene*. Berkeley: U of California P, 1978.

Tate, Allen. *Collected Poems, 1919–1976*. New York: Farrar, 1977.

———. *Essays of Four Decades*. Chicago: Swallow, 1968.

———. "The Fallacy of Humanism." *The Criterion* July 1929: 661–81. Rpt. as "Humanism and Naturalism," *Memoirs* 170–94.

——. The Fathers *and Other Fiction*. 1938. Baton Rouge: Louisiana State UP, 1977.

——. *Jefferson Davis: His Rise and Fall*. New York: Minton, 1929.

——. "Last Days of the Charming Lady." *Nation* 28 Oct. 1925: 485–86.

——. "Liberalism and Tradition." *Reason in Madness: Critical Essays*. New York: Putnam's, 1941. 196–216.

——. "A Lost Traveller's Dream." *Memoirs* 3–23.

——. "The Man of Letters in the Modern World." *Essays of Four Decades* 3–16.

——. *Memoirs and Opinions, 1926–1974*. Chicago: Swallow, 1975.

——. "Narcissus as Narcissus." *Essays of Four Decades* 593–607.

——. "Notes on Liberty and Property." *American Review* 6 (1936): 596–611.

——. "The Profession of Letters in the South." *Essays of Four Decades* 517–34.

——. "Regionalism and Sectionalism." *New Republic* 23 Dec. 1931: 158–61.

——. "Remarks on the Southern Religion." *I'll Take My Stand*. New York: Harper, 1930. 155–75.

——. *Stonewall Jackson, the Good Soldier: A Narrative*. New York: Minton, 1928.

——. "A View of the Whole South." *American Review* 2 (1934): 411–32.

——. "What Is a Traditional Society?" *Essays of Four Decades* 547–57.

Tichi, Cecelia. *Shifting Gears: Technology, Literature, Culture in Modernist America*. Chapel Hill: U of North Carolina P, 1987.

Toomer, Jean. *Cane*. 1923. Ed. Darwin T. Turner. New York: Norton, 1988.

"To the Friends of *The Seven Arts*." *Seven Arts* Oct. 1917: n. pag.

Trilling, Lionel. Afterword. *The Unpossessed*. By Tess Slesinger. New York: Avon, 1966. Rpt. as "A Novel of the Thirties." *The Last Decade: Essays and Reviews, 1965–1975*. Ed. Diana Trilling. New York: Harcourt, 1979. 3–24.

——. *The Middle of the Journey*. 1947. New York: Scribner's, 1975.

——. "Our Country and Our Culture." *Partisan Review* 19 (1952): 318–26.

Tuma, Keith. "Ezra Pound, Progressive." *Paideuma* 19.1–2 (1990): 77–92.

Twelve Southerners. *I'll Take My Stand*. New York: Harper, 1930.

Van Ghent, Dorothy. *Willa Cather*. Pamphlets on American Writers 36. Minneapolis: U of Minnesota, 1964.

Vendler, Helen. *On Extended Wings: Wallace Stevens' Longer Poems*. Cambridge: Harvard UP, 1969.

——. Rev. of *Wallace Stevens: A Mythology of Self*, by Milton Bates. *New York Review of Books* 20 Nov. 1986: 42–47.

Wald, Alan M. *The New York Intellectuals: The Rise and Decline of the Anti-Stalinist Left from the 1930s to the 1980s.* Chapel Hill: U of North Carolina P, 1987.

Wall, Cheryl A. *Women of the Harlem Renaissance.* Bloomington: Indiana UP, 1995.

Warren, Robert Penn. "Literature as a Symptom." Agar and Tate 264–79.

Watson, Steven. *The Harlem Renaissance: Hub of African-American Culture, 1920–1930.* New York: Pantheon, 1995.

Webb, Constance. *Richard Wright: A Biography.* New York: Putnam's, 1968.

Wertheim, Arthur Frank. *The New York Little Renaissance: Iconoclasm, Modernism, and Nationalism in American Culture, 1908–1917.* New York: New York UP, 1976.

Whitfield, Stephen J. *The Culture of the Cold War.* Baltimore: Johns Hopkins UP, 1991.

Williams, William Carlos. *The Autobiography.* 1951. New York: New Directions, 1967.

Wilson, Edmund. "The Aesthetic Upheaval in France." *Vanity Fair* Feb. 1922: 49, 100.

———. *Axel's Castle: A Study in the Imaginative Literature of 1870–1930.* New York: Scribner's, 1931.

———. "An Imaginary Conversation: Mr. Paul Rosenfeld and Mr. Matthew Josephson." *New Republic* 9 Apr. 1924: 179–82.

———. "T. S. Eliot and the Church of England." *New Republic* 2 Apr. 1929: 283–84. Rpt. in *The Shores of Light: A Literary Chronicle of the Twenties and Thirties.* New York: Farrar, 1952. 436–41.

Winters, Yvor. "Wallace Stevens, or the Hedonist's Progress." *In Defense of Reason.* Denver: Swallow, 1947. 431–59.

Wintz, Cary D. *Black Culture and the Harlem Renaissance.* Houston: Rice UP, 1988.

Woodress, James. *Willa Cather: A Literary Life.* Lincoln: U of Nebraska P, 1987.

Wright, Richard. *American Hunger.* New York: Harper, 1977.

Yuhaus, Fr. Cassian J. "A Personal Letter to the Editor: Wallace Stevens and Catholicism." *Renascence* 41 (1989): 209–10.

Zilczer, Judith D. "Robert J. Coady, Forgotten Spokesman for Avant-Garde Culture in America." *American Art Review* Nov.–Dec. 1975: 77–89.

———. "Robert J. Coady, Man of *The Soil.*" *Dada/Surrealism* 14 (1985): 31–43.

INDEX

Aldridge, John, 247–55, 271 (n. 1)
American literary modernism, 2–14; and internationalism, 10–13, 257–58

Baker, Houston A., Jr., 170
Bellow, Saul, 220, 239–43, 246, 252, 255
Bourne, Randolph, 26–27, 28, 40, 253
Brooks, Van Wyck, 1–2, 6, 9, 12, 15–47, 132, 138–41, 143, 157, 207, 255, 259 (n. 1), 260 (nn. 2, 3, 14), 266 (n. 3); *America's Coming of Age*, 5, 19, 20–23, 25, 29, 32, 34, 43, 45, 132, 138–39, 143, 207, 255
Brown, Sterling A., 10, 145–46, 156, 162–68, 171, 172, 208, 265 (n. 14), 267 (n. 7)

Cather, Willa, 1, 2, 4, 6, 39, 41–42, 48–87, 120, 124, 127, 142, 144, 176, 183, 193–95, 217, 249, 253; *Death Comes for the Archbishop*, 41–42, 75, 76–79, 80, 83–86, 194; *The Lost Lady*, 6, 41–42, 51–65, 66–67, 68, 69–71, 74, 78, 79, 81, 82, 84, 120, 124, 142, 144, 194, 262 (n. 1); *My Antonia*, 41–42, 51–53, 54, 55, 57, 61–62, 66, 67, 70, 71, 72, 74, 78, 79; *O Pioneers!*, 39, 41–42, 51–53, 54, 55, 57, 61, 62, 68, 75, 78, 79; *Shadows on the Rock*, 41–42, 65–66, 75, 79–86, 194
Coady, Robert J., 27–30
Conroy, Jack, 207, 215, 269–70 (n. 3)
Cowley, Malcolm, 11, 219, 247, 248, 271 (n. 1)
Croly, Herbert, 2, 22–24, 260 (n. 5)

The Dial, 16, 30, 36
Dos Passos, John, 25, 225, 248
DuBois, W. E. B., 135, 136, 144, 145, 146, 154, 270 (n. 6)

Eliot, T. S., 1, 3, 4, 5, 10, 15–16, 35–39, 42, 45, 47, 48, 88–108, 121, 126–28, 129, 142, 170, 175, 177, 182, 183, 191–93, 204, 207, 217, 254, 260 (n. 2), 264 (n. 6); "The Love Song of J. Alfred Prufrock," 92–96, 102, 103, 110; "Tradition and the Individual Talent," 100–102, 104–6, 109, 111, 121
Ellison, Ralph, 130–31, 154–55, 171, 220, 229–35, 243–45, 246, 252

Faulkner, William, 8, 48, 69, 72–75
Fauset, Jessie Redmon, 130, 132, 133, 141, 144, 146–54, 156, 158, 170, 171, 208
Fisher, Rudolph, 130–31, 141
Fitzgerald, F. Scott, 8, 39, 69–72, 247, 248
Frank, Waldo, 11–12, 24, 205, 218, 259 (n. 1)
Frost, Robert, 8, 10, 25, 49–50
Fuller, Henry B., 262 (n. 3)

Gold, Michael, 47, 215

Hicks, Granville, 210, 227, 262 (n. 5), 271 (n. 12)
Hughes, Langston, 130, 132, 138, 145, 146, 155, 156–62, 163–64, 171–73, 208, 229, 266 (n. 1)

James, William, 197, 269–70 (n. 6)
Johnson, James Weldon, 131–32, 138–41, 156, 266 (n. 1)
Josephson, Matthew, 11